GENDERING W

Identity and mental ' through the lifecourse

Suzanne Clisby and Julia Holdsworth

First published in Great Britain in 2014 by

Policy Press
University of Bristol
6th Floor
Howard House
Queen's Avenue
Clifton
Bristol BS8 1SD
UK
t: +44 (0)117 331 5020
pp-info@bristol.ac.uk
www.policypress.co.uk

North America office:
Policy Press
c/o The University of Chicago Press
1427 East 60th Street
Chicago, IL 60637, USA
t: +1 773 702 7700
f: +1 773-702-9756
sales@press.uchicago.edu
www.press.uchicago.edu

© Policy Press 2014

British Library Cataloguing in Publication Data
A catalogue record for this book is available from the British Library

Library of Congress Cataloging-in-Publication Data
A catalog record for this book has been requested

ISBN 978 1 84742 677 2 hardcover

Cover design by Policy Press
Front cover illustration: Fairy Tales of London 1, 1992 (oil on canvas) by John Keane, c/o Bridgeman Images
Printed and bound in Great Britain by CPI Group (UK) Ltd, Croydon, CR0 4YY
Policy Press uses environmentally responsible print partners

Contents

About the authors

Suzanne Clisby is the director of postgraduate studies in the School of Social Sciences at the University of Hull, UK, and an editor of the international *Journal of Gender Studies*. Her research focuses on gender, social policy and development both in British and international contexts and she has published across a range of areas, including gender mainstreaming in Bolivia, environmental relations in Costa Rica, and youth, desire and the carnivalesque at the English seaside. Suzanne is the coordinator of the Joint European Master's Degree in Women's and Gender Studies (GEMMA) at the University of Hull in a European-wide consortium managed through the University of Granada, and is developing a joint European doctorate in women's and gender studies as a pathway beyond the GEMMA programme. As co-coordinator of the Centre for Gender Studies, Suzanne organises the biennial international and interdisciplinary gender research conference held at the Wilberforce Institute for the Study of Slavery and Emancipation around November 25th – the international day to mark the elimination of violence against women. For many years she has worked in a voluntary capacity with women's services in the city of Hull.

Julia Holdsworth has a background in social anthropology and sociology and holds a lectureship in social science in the School of Social Sciences at the University of Hull. She has worked in both academic and applied contexts with particular focus on social change, development, migration and gender. She has experience working in the field as a practitioner in community development, especially in Central and Eastern Europe which complements her academic interests in social change in Ukraine. In recent years her academic work has explored issues of gender in adult and higher education, gender and mentoring in professional contexts and barriers to women's aspirations and achievements. Julia has for many years been an active member of a women's community group working to address disadvantage and social inequality in Hull.

Acknowledgements

This book would not have been possible without the support of Hull Women's Network, the European Social Fund, the Learning and Skills Council, the University of Hull and the hundreds of women and men who participated in the research. We would like to thank everybody involved, especially those who shared their life stories and contributed their knowledge and experiences to facilitate the creation of such a rich dataset. We are grateful to all the staff and users at Willow and Hull Women's Centre for their friendship and support throughout this research. We also thank the original project team: Hannah Miles, Anne Fairbank, Andrea Broadbent and Clare Kerridge. Finally, thanks to Mark Johnson and Glyn Green for all their support in the completion of this book.

We would also like to thank John Keane who kindly gave us permission to use his artwork for the cover of this book. John Keane achieved success and notoriety in 1990 when he was chosen as the official artist to document the Gulf War. Keane's work, which often deals with social and political issues, gains much of its impact through his use of ironic humour. We chose this painting in part because she has become something of an old friend, as she hangs in the Ferens Art Gallery in Hull, and mainly because it seemed an appropriate choice. In this powerful image from a series John painted called Fairy Tales of London (1992) a young woman battles her way through a threatening urban landscape, burdened by the weight of the shopping and her children. In the distance her husband holds her on a lead in a comment on the constraints and controls many women feel they deal with through their lives in our society. Thus it seemed an appropriate choice both for the subject matter and because it is a popular and familiar painting for many of the women who participated in this study. Dating from 1992, it also has something of a retro feel to it, and as our research encountered many similar themes to those raised by women during the feminist Second Wave and since, for us it reflects the commonality of threads of experience across time.

ONE

Gendering, inequalities, and the limits of policy

Introduction

We begin this book with a statement that should come as no surprise to the reader, but which remains no less significant for its lack of novelty: despite several decades of equality legislation and positive and affirmative action, it remains the case that women in the UK, as a group, continue to experience greater inequality when compared to men, as a group. We also know that deeply rooted socio-cultural factors in contemporary British society continue to act to create significantly different life chances and experiences for men and women. So if we know this already what is the point of this book? The answer lies in the key word in the statements above: *continue*. Gender-based inequalities continue and while they do so, it remains imperative that we also continue to analyse, debate and challenge these realities.

In doing so we tend to focus throughout this book more on commonality than difference. This is not to dismiss the critical importance of difference, a concern that has been key within feminist theory and epistemology for many decades and has more recently come to be referred to as intersectionality. Understanding the impacts of diverse identities for people's lived experiences is of course extremely important, and much work has been done in this field to explore how intersections of identities such as class, ethnicity, sexuality, ability and age intertwine and affect women's experiences (see, for example, Stanley, 1990; Lennon and Whitford, 1994a; Franken et al, 2009; McCann and Seung-Kyung, 2013 to cite but a few of many). Nevertheless our concern here is to recover some of the possible commonalities of experience for many women *qua* women. We do this because we recognise there can be a danger within academic debates about gender of leaving real women and men behind which risks losing sight of the materiality of women's and men's embodied realities. The real risk of this is that we fail to acknowledge the actual *lack* of transformation at many levels for many women, and in the rush to recognise diversity, a danger that the continued commonalities in the material conditions of many women's lives both locally and globally are overlooked.

Thus we argue that 'woman' and 'man', while not being the only gendered spaces available to us, continue to be necessary and valid categories not least because they continue to be significant material and perceptual categories in our highly gendered worlds. Threads of common gendered experiences continue to link and weave together 'women' as they do 'men'. To see commonality, however, does not render difference invisible: commonality and diversity are not necessarily dichotomous and 'differentiation does not depend on opposition' (Whitbeck, 1989, 51). Moreover, as Stanley and Wise (1990) argue, to talk about commonalities of experience does not infer the *same* experiences. Our individual ways of experiencing our genders are nuanced, infinitely diverse and ever shifting over time and space. As Lennon and Whitford state:

> Women as a group are not homogeneous. They have very different experiences, perspectives and problematics, depending on variables such as class, country, age, colour or sexuality. Their positions in power relationships also vary considerably. In addition to this lack of unity within the category of the female subject, there is…a lack of unity *within* each individual female subject. (1994b, 4, emphasis in original)

Nevertheless, at the same time as our gendered experiences are diverse we also experience commonalities, but these shared gendered experiences

> derive, not causally from supposed 'biological facts'… 'woman' is a socially and politically constructed category, the ontological basis of which lies in a set of experiences rooted in the material world. [Moreover] the experience of 'women' is ontologically fractured and complex because we do not all share one single and unseamed material reality. (Stanley and Wise, 1990, 21–2)

Iris Young has provided a similar understanding of femaleness, stating that,

> I take 'femininity' to designate not a mysterious quality or essence that all women have by virtue of their being biologically female. It is, rather, a set of structures and conditions that delimit the typical *situation* of being a

woman in a particular society, as well as the typical way
which this situation is lived by the women themselves.
(1990, 143–4)

The same can of course be said about the category 'male' and
masculinities. We begin this book, then, with an understanding
that gender is socially, culturally and politically as well as materially
constituted; that we are complex gendered beings who continue to
share many experiences through our gendered identities; and that
these shared experiences are simultaneously nuanced and uniquely
understood and experienced at the individual level.

The first aim of this book is to facilitate, through gender analysis, a
greater understanding of underlying factors which contribute to the
continued existence of gender-based inequality in the UK. We explain
more fully what we mean by gender analysis later in this chapter but
suffice to say at this point that to talk about gender analysis can be
seen as another way of talking about feminist praxis: a concern both
with the underlying causes of gender-based inequities and a desire
to achieve positive change for women. As Liz Stanley has eloquently
explained, feminist praxis is 'a political position in which "knowledge"
is not simply defined as "knowledge *what*" but as "knowledge *for*"
(Stanley, 1990, 12, emphases in original). We also start from a feminist
standpoint that understands that 'feminism' is not merely a 'perspective',
a way of seeing; nor even this plus an epistemology, a way of knowing;
it is also 'an ontology, or a way of being in the world' (Stanley, 1990,
14). We are, however, neither suggesting that there is some essentialist
way of being or knowing for women *qua* women nor for feminists *qua*
feminists. As Stanley points out,

> an ontological state comes into existence, not in relation
> to something essentially female, but rather the facts of
> the present social construction of 'women' as this is seen,
> understood and acted upon (however imperfectly, and with
> whatever backsliding) by those who call themselves feminist;
> *and* who name this present social construction of women
> as *oppressive*. (1990, 14, emphasis in original)

A key component of both gender analysis and feminist praxis is that
we continue to talk to women, that their voices are heard and listened
to, and that our research is 'not only located in' but proceeds from 'the
grounded analysis of women's material realities' (Stanley and Wise,
1990, 25). This book is based on long-term empirical research in the

Yorkshire and Humber region of England and driven by women's voices. Through listening to women we can see that women are reflexive and situated knowers who are able to coherently articulate how processes of gendering can and do have an impact on their sense of self, and on the lived realities of their everyday lives.

This concept of situated knowledge is important to feminist epistemology. Feminist epistemology understands gendered beings as knowers situated in relation to what is known and experienced by both themselves and in relation to other knowers. What is known, and the way that it is known, thereby reflects the situation or perspective of the knower. This itself is legitimate knowledge. As Hawkesworth has explained, 'feminist standpoint theories reject the notion of an "unmediated truth", arguing that knowledge is always mediated by a host of factors related to an individual's particular position in a determinate socio-political formation at a specific point in history' (1989, 536). For feminist analysis and feminist epistemology this means that while malestream understandings and knowledge constructions may well be hegemonic, all knowledge is partial and subjective and other ways of knowing and understanding based on different class, ethnic, or gendered positions are of equal validity (Smith, 1979; Fricker, 1994). It is, therefore, important to recognise that in this book we are not claiming that all women (or indeed men) occupy the same position, instead we are exploring points where women are able to offer both alternative accounts of their social and material conditions and where these accounts share some common ground.

Haraway (1988), in her renowned article argues that '[f]eminist objectivity means quite simply *situated knowledges*' (1988, 581, emphasis in original). Indeed, when we talk about women as situated knowers in this volume, we are drawing on Haraway's work in which she states that we,

> seek not the knowledges ruled by phallogocentrism (nostalgia for the presence of the one true Word) and disembodied vision. We seek those ruled by partial sight and limited voice – not partiality for its own sake but, rather, for the sake of the connections and unexpected openings situated knowledges make possible. Situated knowledges are about communities, not isolated individuals...Situated knowledges require that the object of knowledge be pictured as an actor and agent, not as a screen or a ground or a resource, never as slave to the master that closes off

the dialectic in his unique agency and his authorship of 'objective' knowledge (1988, 590–2).

The second fundamental point of this book is to make the critical links between continued gender-based inequalities, normative processes of gendering and the consequences of these processes for women through the lifecourse. In particular, we consider one significant negative consequence of normative processes of gendering for women in the UK: their experiences of mental wellbeing, self-esteem and confidence. Here we are taking a different and explicitly feminist approach to the gendering of mental wellbeing to much of the literature on mental health. Focusing on feminist theories and debates that have emerged over the past four decades we explore the relationships between ill health, constructions of femininities and the socio-cultural conditions of women's lives. As we demonstrate, there continues to be a strong connection between contemporary cultural constructions of femininity and negative experiences of mental wellbeing. The term *mental wellbeing* is used here to include a broad range of mental health issues, such as low self-esteem, lack of confidence, feelings of low self-worth, anxiety and depression. These symptoms and experiences may not be medicalised or identified as *mental health* problems by women themselves, and medical treatment may not have been sought, nevertheless such feelings have a significant impact on women's health and wellbeing as well as upon more material aspects of their lives such as their aspirations, achievements and professional lives.

We frame this argument through the concept of violence which takes three key forms: 'symbolic', 'structural' and 'visceral' and much of this book shows how these forms of violence are played out across different arenas of women's lives. In our use of the concept of symbolic violence we draw on Bourdieu (2001) where he refers to the ways in which:

> the established order, its rights and prerogatives, privileges and injustices, ultimately perpetuates itself so easily, apart from a few historical accidents, [to the extent that] the most intolerable conditions of existence can so often be perceived as acceptable and even natural. And I have also seen masculine domination, and the way it is imposed and suffered, as the prime example of this paradoxical submission, an effect of what I call symbolic violence, a gentle violence, imperceptible and invisible even to its victims, exerted for the most part through the purely symbolic channels of communication and cognition (more

precisely misrecognition), recognition, or even feeling. (Bourdieu, 2001, 1–2)

Further, we frame these processes of gendering by thinking about structural violence, as Farmer (2004) does, to refer to violence exerted systematically yet indirectly against people within a given social order. Like Bourdieu, and as we argue here, he is not talking simply about visceral violence, rather about the violence of

> 'sinful' structures characterized by poverty and steep grades of social inequality, including racism and gender inequality…In short, the concept of structural violence is intended to inform the study of the social machinery of oppression. Oppression is a result of many conditions, not least of which reside in the consciousness. (Farmer, 2004, 307)

These, combined with the impacts of physical harm through visceral gender-based violence, create a powerful triad – the symbolic, the structural and the visceral – that has profound impacts on people's gendered identities. We are not arguing that *all* aspects of our gendered beings are negative or that *all* processes of gendering do violence unto us, but we are arguing that more processes of gendering than we perhaps realise can in fact be understood in this way. Moreover, it is worth emphasising that while this volume focuses deliberately and specifically on women's lives as gendered beings, we would argue that processes of gendering as experienced by men can also be framed in this way, as potential forms of symbolic, structural and visceral violence.

Here we are using the term 'violence' as a broad concept played out along a very long continuum. Through this framework of gendering as forms of violence, from the gentle to the visceral, we can understand how women's experiences of becoming and being a woman can be damaging to mental wellbeing. Poor wellbeing in turn has a major impact on women's opportunities and aspirations and is itself a driver of inequality. Because, however, these issues are deeply embedded within everyday gendered practices and experiences, and as such are complex, amorphous and difficult to quantify, they often remain under-acknowledged in mainstream policy making. Drawing on women's narratives, we explore the links between processes of gendering and women's self-esteem, and the profound impacts these can have on their experiences and opportunities through the lifecourse. The lifecourse approach has informed the structure of the book, leading us through women's lives and focusing on pivotal points and significant gendered experiences including: women's childhood experiences and early identity formation; impacts of gender-based violence; experiences of education and training; motherhood; employment and career development.

Conceptualising the embodiment of infrastructure

Finally, and what is equally important, in this book we demonstrate how women themselves are able to reflect on their normative conditioning and are working through women's services and spaces to effect change in their own and others' lives. Here we argue that women and women's services act as forms of *embodied infrastructure*. By this we refer to the ways that women's bodies and material actions themselves become the vehicles, the catalysts, the embodied infrastructure, facilitating access to services and enabling change and support through women's networks. This infrastructure is created through a range of encounters, from those women who act as mentors to other women within their working lives, to the services and formal and informal networks women have established that serve to provide a framework, an infrastructure of support for women. As Luce Irigaray has said: 'Women's bodies through their use, consumption, and circulation provide for the condition making social life and culture possible, although they remain an unknown infrastructure of the elaboration of that social life and culture' (Irigaray, 1977, 171).

When we think about infrastructure we usually think of the physical buildings and highways, of concrete and steel rather than of flesh and blood, if we give it any thought at all. However the significance and nature of infrastructure has been developed and understood in different ways by several authors in recent years. Leigh Star (1999) has called for an ethnography of infrastructure, noting the importance of what is so often taken for granted. She talks of infrastructure as both relational and ecological by which she means that infrastructure is context dependent and how one relates to it depends on one's situatedness. For example 'within a given cultural context, the cook considers the water system as working infrastructure integral to making dinner. For the city planner or the plumber, it is a variable in a complex planning process or as a target of repair' (Leigh Star, 1999, 380). While she does not extend her concept of infrastructure to people themselves *being* a form of infrastructure, she does talk about infrastructure as 'part of human organisation, and as problematic as any other' (1999, 380) with a range of properties including: embeddedness, 'sunk into and inside of other structures' (1999, 381); transparency, 'it is transparent to use, in the sense that it does not have to be reinvented each time or assembled for each task' (1999, 381); learned as part of the membership of a community of practice; and something that both shapes and is shaped by the conventions of that community of practice. Similarly, Graham and Thrift have produced an 'urban phenomenology' (2007, 2) through looking closely at the significance of infrastructures, specifically the importance of the mundane maintenance and repair of our urban infrastructures:

> Think only of some of the familiar sounds of the city as an instance: from the sirens denoting accidents, to the noises of pneumatic drills denoting constant upkeep of roads, through the echoing clanks and hisses of the tyre and clutch replacement workshop, denoting the constant work needed just to keep cars going. (Graham and Thrift, 2007, 2)

Again, while Graham and Thrift (2007) do not extend the concept to include embodied infrastructure, they do highlight the importance of the maintenance of our mundane and embedded infrastructures for our social and interpersonal relations and understandings of our habitus. More recently the journal *Ethnography* published a special issue on 'infrastructural violence' in which infrastructure is considered as an 'ethnographically graspable manifestation' through which 'broader processes of marginalization, abjection and disconnection often become operational and sustainable in contemporary cities' (Rodgers and O'Neill, 2012, 401). In their introduction to the journal, Rodgers and O'Neill argue that:

> infrastructure emerges as an ideal ethnographic site for theorizing how broad and abstract social orderings such as the state, citizenship, criminality, ethnicity and class play out concretely at the level of everyday practices, revealing how such relationships of power and hierarchy translate into palpable forms of physical and emotional harm. (2012, 402)

Here various authors consider the ways in which uses and abuses of infrastructure, lacking or decaying infrastructures can affect the people who inhabit them. They argue that infrastructure 'is not just a material embodiment of violence (structural or otherwise), but often its instrumental medium, insofar as the material organisation and form of a landscape not only reflect but also reinforce social orders, thereby becoming a contributing factor to reoccurring forms of harm' (Rodgers and O'Neill, 2012, 404). So here we see that the concept of infrastructure is being developed and extended beyond the material and technological to consider its moral, political and socio-cultural relations. Indeed, the notion of infrastructures of violence adds a further important dimension to the forms of violence we have set out earlier in this chapter: the structural, symbolic and visceral. While the violence of infrastructures is not something we specifically develop further in this volume we feel that it is something worthy of further consideration elsewhere. What is important here is that these are all useful and interesting ways of extending our understandings of infrastructures – as moving beyond the purely logistical and as having both positive and negative impacts for people who live in and around these landscapes. This leads us to a critical conceptualisation for our purposes, the work of AbdouMaliq Simone (2004) which explores far more positive infrastructural engagements. Most significantly Simone (2004) makes the leap from the infrastructures of steel and concrete to those of flesh and blood. He developed the idea of *people as infrastructure* in the context of the urban landscapes of Johannesburg, emphasising the economic collaboration among marginalised urban residents, stating that;

> I wish to extend the notion of infrastructure directly to people's activities in the city. African cities are characterized by incessantly flexible, mobile, and provisional intersections of residents that operate without clearly delineated notions of how the city is to be inhabited and used. These intersections, particularly in the last two decades, have depended on the ability of residents to engage complex combinations of objects, spaces, persons, and practices. These conjunctions become an infrastructure – a platform for providing for and reproducing life in the city. (2004, 407)

This leap from people *and* infrastructure to people *as* infrastructure is highly significant for our analysis. More significant for the development of our analysis, however, has been the work of Mark Johnson (2013). Taking Simone's (2004) concept of *people as infrastructure*, his work on 'migration infrastructures' and 'in particular the way that forms of lateral surveillance features in migrant practices of care, an overlooked but vital part of the way that migrants create 'platforms for living', as well as enact social control and normative conformity, in sometimes precarious situations' (Johnson, 2013, 1) has been key to our own theoretical development here. Indeed it was through personal conversations with Mark Johnson at the University of Hull that we first came to make the link between people and infrastructure. This dialogue led us to think about women's roles as mentors, women's networks and services as forms of embodied infrastructure and this dialogue in turn contributed to Johnson's own analysis. The importance of his analysis for the development of ours and *vice versa* becomes clearer in the extract below:

> adopting a people as infrastructure approach that is, I suggest, a corollary of the infrastructural violence people in majority worlds live with daily, discloses the ways that migrants themselves fill in the gaps and missing links, recycle, repair or reengineer social and material technologies that are broken, obsolete or, just as often, designed by and for others and quite literally through their bodies, as well as their creative labours, become their own 'platforms for living'. Infrastructure, so we are told, is invisible normally. That may be partially true for a privileged minority. For many others, perhaps the majority, the backstage is more often than not the condition of existence. If, as feminist observers contend, many women face not just a double but triple burden of paid, domestic and care work, the latter two, as we know, increasingly contracted out and fulfilled partially in minority worlds by migrant women and men from the majority world, we might say that some, perhaps many, women and men, face a fourth and even less visible burden, that of filling in the cracks of and becoming the infrastructure of their own lives. That is the situation for many migrants who not only wo/man the backstage infrastructural operations of the minority world's front stage, but who also must create the offstage infrastructures that enables them to travel to, live in and work in those backstage operations. (Johnson, 2013, 18–19)

From this extract then, we can see how closely our analysis of infrastructures links to that of Johnson (2013). We are both concerned with the often hidden work of non-hegemonic social groups – women, migrants, migrant women – that forms what Johnson describes as a 'platform for living' and what we suggest becomes an 'embodied infrastructure'. Thus, drawing on Simone's idea of *people as infrastructure* and Johnson's work on *migration infrastructures* we argue that we can see forms of infrastructure that are *embodied*, and that these embodied infrastructures are highly gendered constructs. Here, as previously discussed, we are thinking about the roles women often play in acting as role models and mentors to other women, and women's work in women's services and networks. Thus women's bodies play a critically important role in 'making social life and culture possible' (Irigaray, 1977, 171), although as Irigaray highlighted over three decades ago, it is still too often the case that these infrastructures and networks that comprise the fabric of social life remain under-acknowledged as 'an unknown infrastructure of the elaboration of that social life and culture' (Irigaray, 1977, 171).

The idea of women as embodied infrastructure also links to the understanding of the gendered terrain of community management work, a concept usefully highlighted within gendered analyses of development but again one often overlooked or taken for granted (see, for example, Clisby, 2005; Momsen, 2010). As we discuss further towards the end of this chapter, community management work forms the third element of the triad of gendered labour, the other two spokes being work conceptualised as reproductive and/or productive (see Momsen, 2010 for a fuller discussion of these forms of labour). Community management work is the usually informal, unpaid and often invisible but nonetheless critically important labour that is performed at the community level that also acts as a form of embodied infrastructure to facilitate and support families and communities. As with reproductive labour (referring both to the nurturing of kin and maintenance of households), this is a highly gendered form of labour inasmuch as it tends to be performed overwhelmingly by women and is often perceived as an extension of women's biologically essentialised but socially constructed caring and nurturing roles. As such it confers the concomitant low status and undervaluation of this labour one associates with much of these gendered social roles.

Some examples of community management work can include visits made and support offered to elderly or otherwise vulnerable neighbours, developing voluntary community-based groups to provide services for young or elderly people in the area, establishing and maintaining friendship networks with neighbours, maintaining family networks with both biological and non-biological kin through social care networks, for example, sending gifts and cards at birthdays and religious festivals or hosting friends and family in one's home to celebrate significant events. All this work that goes into the creation and maintenance of these embodied infrastructures, is expensive in terms of time and emotional labour as well as more directly financial costs. It demands persistence and long-term commitment and it is of critical but often unacknowledged importance in the knitting together of and maintenance of social networks. Indeed one could argue that it is these embodied infrastructures and this community management labour that form the (highly gendered) bedrock of society.[1]

Framing the study: which women's voices? Why women's voices?

Through a gender analysis of women's lived experiences, and led by their narratives, this volume encourages further debate about the significance of connections between constructions of femininity, women's wellbeing and continued gender inequalities. We explore the impacts of gendering on women's lives and, within this, the existence, causes and consequences of problems women articulate in terms of their mental wellbeing and how these have an impact on women's choices, opportunities and constraints. While our focus is deliberately on women, we are not of course suggesting that men are not gendered beings, nor that it is not important to talk to men and explore their life histories and gendered identities. Indeed we intend to explore men's life histories and gendered identities in relation to their wellbeing in an upcoming study. This book is, however, the culmination of two research phases spanning a period of several years which specifically aimed at exploring women's lives. During the first phase, between 2005 and 2008, we conducted the initial empirical research focusing particularly on women's experiences of education, training, employment and career development in the Yorkshire and Humber region of the UK.[2] Data arising from this phase has subsequently helped to inform planning for future delivery of accessible, gender-aware and socially inclusive learning opportunities.

It was during this initial research period that it soon became clear that mental wellbeing, self-esteem and confidence were important and recurrent issues for most of the women with whom we spoke. We are not suggesting that indices of difference such as socio-economic background, age, ethnicity, educational attainment and occupation do not have important impacts on women's experiences of mental wellbeing through the lifecourse. Of course they do in multifarious and complex ways, but we nevertheless found that wellbeing issues simultaneously *cut across* difference and seemed to be a common thread emerging from diverse narratives.

We felt this was such a significant recurrent theme – one that emerged strongly even though we were not at that point explicitly asking about mental wellbeing – that it merited further investigation.

We thus developed the study into a second phase with a more specific exploration in the region of the connections between wellbeing and processes of gendering. Between 2008 and 2013, we continued a process of qualitative research and reflection through ethnographically informed methods including participant observation, informal interviews, focus groups, extended conversations and discussions with women, key professionals and within two women's centres. This time we focused particularly on Hull and East Yorkshire.

Over this period we generated a rich and unique dataset that draws on the knowledge, experience and histories of over 500 women from across generational, social, cultural and economic backgrounds. We did not originally intend to spend so long collecting data and that we did so is partly a product of our own lives as women. We are, as similarly gendered beings, also fully implicated in this study and during the course of the research have worked alongside and around many common multiple roles and lifecourse experiences. While completing this book, we have juggled competing demands of full-time careers, voluntary community work, caring responsibilities for older and younger family members, new motherhood, change of jobs, moving house and working around chronic illness. Life has a habit of getting in the way, but this has also allowed us to develop more extensive, in-depth and reflexive research as similarly situated knowers.

The women's voices reflected in this research can be categorised as largely, but by no means exclusively, white, working class and heterosexual which broadly reflects the dominant social composition of the region. We deliberately avoided purposive sampling of categories of women in terms of indices of difference such as ethnicity, class, sexuality, ability and so on. We are not making claims to represent the views of specific identity categories other than that of a self-identification with a female gender within a geographical region. We did, however, focus on collecting experiences of women involved in different areas of employment, training and education to reflect women's experiences within traditionally feminised arenas such as care work and traditionally masculinised areas such as construction. We also ensured that we spoke to women from a wide age range, ultimately reaching women between the ages of 16 and 93. Thus, while we believe this is the largest study of its kind in the region, we make no claims to representation of identities beyond that of gender as a common link. Neither are we suggesting that there is a specific link between the regional context in which this research is located – which is itself diverse – and women's wellbeing. Rather, we would suggest that these findings have a far wider resonance for women in both national and international contexts.

In sum, placing particular emphasis on the fields of family life, education, employment and mothering, we apply social science understandings, through a gender analysis, to the relations between gendered socio–cultural expectations and experiences and how women feel about themselves, and their roles, aspirations and achievements. Simply put: our key argument is that processes of gendering have an impact on mental wellbeing and this in turn has an impact on girls' and women's abilities to imagine and create certain life choices for themselves.

Finally, we explore the contribution of the embodied infrastructure of women's spaces within voluntary sector organisations in meeting women's everyday needs, raising aspirations and providing the necessary support to enable women to achieve their ambitions. Through this we highlight that women themselves possess a reflexive and sophisticated gender awareness as situated knowers. Thus, working closely with women's groups and the voluntary and statutory sectors across the region, we have explored what women themselves think *would* help and what *has* helped them get to where they want to be.

Methods and methodologies

In this section we briefly outline the methods and methodologies underpinning our research and reflect on how our findings actually emerged. Our research combined both qualitative and quantitative methods, underpinned by a methodological approach grounded in feminist research and praxis as well as ethnographic understandings. The adoption of a mixed-methods approach, led by qualitative data gathering, was chosen to best facilitate the collection and analysis of individual understandings and commonalities of women's lived experiences. In line with this feminist approach we have been concerned to address power imbalances between researchers and participants, beginning with the experiences and standpoint of women and aim to promote social change (Maynard, 1994; Hammersley, 1995; Edwards and Ribbens, 1998; Letherby, 2003).

In some ways this study could have been framed as an example of a phenomenological approach, although this is not the methodological or theoretical standpoint we explicitly set out to adopt. Nevertheless in as much as we have been concerned with the study of experience from the perspective of the individual, based on women's knowledges and narratives and with the aim of understanding subjective experience and gaining insights into women's life experiences, motivations, actions and understandings of their worlds, all of which would fit into a phenomenological approach, then this frame would not be altogether unfitting (Marshall and Rossman, 1995; Heinämaa, 2003). We did not, however, set out to simply describe rather than explain our field of enquiry, nor do we believe it is ever possible to set out with no preconceptions or hypotheses as some more traditional phenomenological approaches might attempt to do (Patton, 1990; Marshall and Rossman, 1995). Rather, we see the importance of making clear how interpretations and meanings have been placed on findings, as well as locating the researcher in the frame of the research as an interested and subjective actor rather than a detached and impartial observer (Stanley and Wise, 1993). For us this is implicit in the ethnographically informed approach we have taken.

Given the nature of the study the main data collection strategy was in-depth, semi-structured and life history interviews, in addition to numerous extended conversations, informal discussions and observations. A total of 120 life history interviews were conducted with women and key professionals across the Yorkshire and Humber region. Life histories were collected over the course of several hours in single or repeated sessions. Life history interviews have long been a favoured method for many social scientists and feminist researchers, noted for their humanising and empowering capacities in which participants are better able to determine the focus and direction of the research (Anderson and Jack, 1991; Peacock and Holland, 1993; DeVault, 1999, cited in Bradshaw, 2014). We found that a life history approach also helps to capture the complex interrelations which exist between different parts of women's experience and to elucidate the ways in which gendered identity constructions have an impact on women's lives. For those participants who were also key service providers (including two men), in addition to collecting their life histories, we also conducted semi-structured interviews specifically exploring their professional roles. We focused on service providers working in the arenas of education, vocational training, community and voluntary services, employment, business, social and emotional support provision, local government and statutory services.

A series of discussion groups were held involving a further 96 people from a broad range of backgrounds. Groups of participants included young people in further education, women returners to education, women in 'traditional' gendered occupations, women making decisions around work/care after having a first child, young parents, female users of community and voluntary services and service providers. We found the focus groups useful both because they can encourage participation from people who may feel nervous about a one-to-one interview, and also because they facilitate observation of group dynamics by promoting open discussion, questioning and interaction between group members. This means that the parameters were not set entirely by the researcher, but instead came to reflect the issues that members of the group felt were important and relevant to the topic introduced.

The final aspect of the qualitative research we employed was more ethnographically informed. We have both been involved with two women's centres in Hull for several years, and this ethnographic and situated approach has in no small way contributed to the depth of this research. Indeed for the first two years of the research part of the original research team were based in a working women's centre in Hull. Participant observation has provided insight into the issues which women face on a daily basis as well as those experienced by people working in the voluntary and community sector.

The quantitative aspect of the study was developed because we felt that we would benefit from a wider overview of people's understandings and perspectives than could immediately be gained through one-to-one interviews. To this end a questionnaire was designed to cover themes that emerged from initial interviews and secondary analysis and was delivered through both electronic and paper media. This resulted in a total of 323 responses collected from across the Yorkshire and Humber region. Of these 273 identified as women, 41 identified as male and eight as transgender or other. We believe that the lower response rate from men is a reflection of a combination of the kinds of networks it was circulated among and the subject matter.

Although we circulated it as widely as possible across both virtual and physical spaces (as electronic and hard copies) throughout the region and expressly indicated that we would like men to participate, the fact that it was entitled 'Exploring gendered experiences of education, employment and leisure in the Yorkshire and Humber regions', meant that it was probably more likely to be perceived as relevant to women rather than men. We also feel that the lower response rate from men may have been because the questionnaire was detailed, took about 20 minutes or more to complete, and included questions about household earning – who earned more – and gender divisions of labour within the household. One man, for example, who took a hard copy of the questionnaire, returned it uncompleted in person, pointedly saying 'there was no way' he would answer those kinds of questions even though the questionnaire was wholly anonymous. Women seemed to be more willing to spend time completing the questionnaire and responding to the quite personal questions. One could argue that this is in itself an interesting gender issue, and one not merely arising from the fact that 'gender' is often seen as a woman's concern. The willingness of more women to complete the questionnaire could also be connected to some of the themes developed in this book such as, for example, how women may learn to be more 'docile bodies' (Foucault, 1979), with a desire to help others.

Our feminist methodological approach fed through the process of research itself in a range of ways. The original research project was developed in collaboration with Hull Women's Network (HWN), a strategic partnership of women's service providers in the city of Hull on the North Sea coast of England. The research activities were designed with the needs of participants in mind (in terms of context, location, timing and so on) and we adopted a reflexive and engaged approach. Early findings, for example, were fed back to participants and they were encouraged to comment on the appropriateness of the emerging themes and our depictions of women's lives.

Being involved in research of this nature, and re-telling life histories can call up all manner of emotional experiences for women. For many this is, ultimately, a positive experience and most women commented after the interviews on the fact that having someone to just sit and listen to them was itself a rewarding experience. Some women raised aspirations during interviews, such as wanting to get back into education, and, where appropriate, we were able to signpost them to relevant services. While this is not the primary role of researchers, in a research project exploring gender inequalities, we felt that not to do so would have been failing the participants and undermining our feminist praxis. Strategically, taking part in a research project such as this can enable women to reflect on their lives and on the ways in which individual, socio-cultural and structural factors have an impact on their situation and the choices available to them. This facilitates both women's understandings of their lives as situated knowers and promotes a greater appreciation of their gendered opportunities and constraints.

Finally, the dissemination of the first phase of the research is also an example of feminist praxis: a diverse range of people were invited to the events, including the research participants, service providers, policy makers, academics and members of the public. Dissemination events were participatory, held in accessible locations, were free of charge, and bursaries were made available to pay for travel and child-care costs. Copies of the executive summaries and the initial reports were made freely available.

Box 1.1: Portrait of the Yorkshire and Humber region

The following snapshot of facts and statistics has been collated from a range of the latest available government figures. The data presented here is not intended to be exhaustive, but it should provide the reader with at least some sense of place.

Introduction

The Yorkshire and Humber region is located in the lower north east of England and covers 15,408 square kilometres. It is the fifth largest region in England with an estimated population of 5.2 million living within 2.8 million households. Over 80 per cent of the population live in urban areas with populations of more than 10,000. It is comprised of four sub-regions: North, West and South Yorkshire, and East Yorkshire and North Lincolnshire (combined together as the fourth region).

The region has a beautiful eastern coastline facing the North Sea and to the west the Pennine Hills separate it from Lancashire and the North West. It has more National Parks than any other English region. It also contains several significant cities, including Sheffield, Bradford, Leeds, Kingston upon Hull (commonly referred to as Hull) and York. Over a third of the population of the region live in Leeds, Sheffield or Bradford.

The four sub-regions

North Yorkshire, with a population of 0.6 million, has the lowest population but is the largest of the four sub-regions and arguably the most beautiful, being largely rural. Almost half of the region's agricultural produce comes from North Yorkshire and it contains the two National Parks – the North York Moors and Yorkshire Dales. The fishing port and town of Whitby is an important tourist destination, famous for its links to Captain Cook and Dracula. The city of York stands at the heart of Yorkshire and as a gateway to North Yorkshire. Famed for its spectacular Minster and Viking and Roman heritage, York is another key tourist destination in the region. The University of York is a highly respected HE institution with a student population of around 16,000.

East Yorkshire and North Lincolnshire has 0.9 million residents and is significant for its manufacturing industry (approximately a quarter of its output compared with around 15 per cent in other sub-regions). It contains the ports of Grimsby and Immingham, the UK's largest, and the Humber Bridge, formerly the longest single suspension bridge in the world (until it was overtaken in 1996) which connects East Yorkshire and North Lincolnshire over the Humber Estuary. Hull, a port city, is a major urban hub for the sub-region, and is famous for its fishing industry, although this declined in the mid-twentieth century. Due to its key strategic position as a major port and industrial centre, Hull was heavily targeted by German bombers and suffered from the most severe bomb damage of any UK city during the Second World War, with 95 per cent of houses damaged or destroyed – a fact that was not widely acknowledged for many years.

The legacy of the war, the decline of fishing, and more recently the loss of several key manufacturing industries in the economic recession of the 2000s, as well as the devastating floods of 2007, have all contributed to Hull's socio-economic profile. As a city it is often perceived negatively by outsiders and has been much maligned, for example being labelled the worst place to live in the UK by a pocket guide book in 2003 (Jordison and Kieran, 2003). People who are more familiar with, or live in Hull are often better informed and thus less critical. It has a highly respected campus university with a population of approximately 20,000 students.

South Yorkshire boasts the dramatic hills and countryside of the Peak District but is also highly urbanised, being the second most densely populated sub-region with 1.3 million residents. Sheffield is famous for its coal and steel industries, which declined with serious socio-economic and cultural consequences in the late twentieth century, as portrayed in the 1990s' films *Brassed Off* and *The Full Monty*. Sheffield has a large student population of around 55,000 across two esteemed universities.

West Yorkshire is the most densely populated sub-region with 2.2 million residents (over 40 per cent of the total population of the region). The main cities in this sub-region are Leeds, Bradford and Huddersfield. Leeds is locally famed for having a 'Harvey Nichols' department store – seen as a sign of gentrification, and linked to the relocation from London of the major central government office of Social Security. Bradford is known in particular for having an ethnically diverse population because it is home to the largest Pakistani community in England who comprise 20 per cent of the city's population, although 64 per cent of people identify as white British. Leeds–Bradford is the highest airport in England and serves approximately 3 million passengers. The sub-region has a significant student population with a combined population of over 90,000 students studying at the respected universities in Leeds, Bradford and Huddersfield.

Population

There are a higher proportion of 20–24 years olds in the region than in the UK as a whole. The number of people of state pension age is higher than the number of children under 16, which is also the case in the UK more generally. Estimates of population by ethnic breakdown suggest that people who identify as white British make up about 90 per cent of the population. Black or black British identified people constitute just 1 per cent of the population and Asian or Asian British comprise 5 per cent. Around 90 per cent of the region's residents were born in the UK. In line with national figures, the mean household size is 2.3 but expected to fall to 2.1 by 2026. Married couples account for 44 per cent of households but this is falling and expected to stand at around 36 per cent by 2026. Single person households are increasing and make up around one third of all households in the region. Based on 2009–2010 figures teenage pregnancy rates in the region are relatively high, standing at 47 conceptions per 1000 women aged 15–17 as compared with just under 36 for the UK as a whole. Within this the city of Hull had a higher than average teenage pregnancy rate of 64 conceptions per 1000 women aged 15–17 although rates have dropped in the last few years in line with an overall decline for the UK as a whole.

Wealth, education and employment

The region is clearly diverse and contains many areas of relative wealth and low levels of deprivation, but this is balanced against twice as many areas of high deprivation. Of course, as Kay (2009) points out, not all deprived people live in deprived areas and not everyone living in deprived areas is deprived. The region has the lowest proportion of pupils (62 per cent) of the English regions achieving five or more A*–C grades at GCSE – but the highest in England was 66 per cent so the figures are not so dissimilar. It has the lowest proportion of 16 year olds in post-compulsory education (80 per cent), but again this figure is not a long way behind the UK average of 84 per cent. It is also the English region with the second highest proportion of residents aged between 19 and 65 with no qualifications (34 per cent). The average percentage of working age people in employment is 72 per cent for the region as a whole (ranging from Hull with 64 per cent to Harrogate with 84 per cent). The percentage mean of economically inactive residents of working age is 22 per cent, which is only slightly higher than the UK average of 21 per cent. Median weekly earnings for full-time employees in the region in 2008 was £444 (£485 for men and £373 for women), which is lower than all but one other English region. Approximately 16 per cent of children live in workless households dependent on benefits, which is close to average for England, but this proportion rises in areas of deprivation.

Health

Female life expectancy stands at just over 81 years which is only slightly lower than the national average of just under 82 years. Male life expectancy is just under 77 years which is again slightly lower than the English average for men of just below 78 years. Hull has the lowest life expectancy for men and women (76 and 80 years respectively), which is a more significant difference: people in Hull appear to be losing, on average, two years of their lives. The region has one of the highest levels of male and female alcohol consumption and smoking and more than a fifth of adults (23 per cent of men and 22 per cent of women) smoked in 2009, one of the highest rates in Britain. Age standardised mortality rates for the region show 866 deaths per 100,000 residents in 2007, compared with 809 for England. The infant mortality rate (deaths under one year) was 5.6 per 1000 in 2007, the second highest after the West Midlands.

Sources: Kay, 2009; DH, 2010, ONS 2012a, 2012b

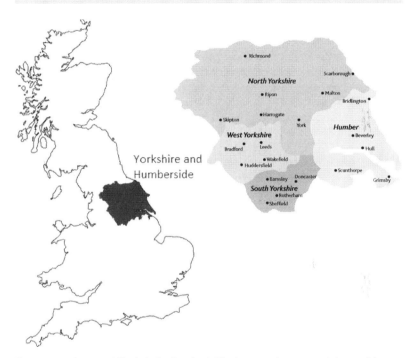

Sources: www.hse.gov.uk/Statistics/regions/yorkshire.jpg, www.focus-on-training.co.uk/ funding/yorkshire_humberside_enhancement_fund/

Gender analysis and the persistence of patriarchy in contemporary British society

To return to a question we raised at the beginning of this introduction: why is an analysis of women's lives in twenty-first century Britain important? Gender analyses of women's lived experiences are important quite simply because we have yet to see a genuine transformation of equalities legislation and policies into practice as a fundamental basis of both men's and women's lives. In this context there is a continued imperative to examine people's lived experiences critically in order to understand why and how policy has failed to eradicate identity-based inequities in our society. Through a gender analysis we have sought to understand and articulate women's perspectives and experiences as they are framed within the patriarchal context of contemporary British society.

When we refer to patriarchy we are doing so consciously in the context of the ongoing and lengthy debates within feminist academic and political circles as to its meanings, usefulness and shortcomings as a concept, perhaps most notably through the work of Sylvia Walby (see for example, Walby, 1986; 1990; 1994; 1997; 2009; 2011). Thus when we talk about patriarchy we are referring to an inequitable system of male dominated power that works through interlocking structures operating through both public and private spheres (Walby, 1990). Patriarchal relations and power dynamics are fluid and can be played out simultaneously in multiple arenas including through family life, state institutions, through cultural transmission, and embedded in constructions of femininities, masculinities and sexualities.

In her more recent work Walby prefers to talk about 'gender regimes' rather than, but meaning the same as, 'patriarchy' precisely because the term patriarchy is so often 'incorrectly presumed to entail an ahistoric, essentialist, unchanging, reductionist approach to the analysis of gender relations' (Walby, 2011, 104). In part Walby is, by her own admission,[3] being pragmatic when she avoids using the term 'patriarchy' in recognition of it being a tainted concept. To talk about 'gender regimes' seems somehow less challenging and controversial within political and policy circles. While adopting Walby's concept of gender regimes, here we also continue to refer to patriarchy, although, we accept, not unproblematically, precisely because we do not want to render the unacceptable even slightly more acceptable. 'Patriarchy', despite its baggage, still lends a critical and political edge that we feel is important to retain in this analysis.

Gender analyses are essential in facilitating our understandings of the ways in which women's and men's lives are conditioned by socio-cultural, heteronormative patriarchal structural frameworks, or gender regimes (Walby, 2011). When using these concepts, we also need to understand the variability of patriarchies and how these gender regimes are contextually specific and differently articulated through time and space, but without losing sight of threads of commonality that enable us to see and understand both local difference as well as global connections. To understand what we mean by gender analyses we paraphrase Nayak and Kehily (2008, 5) who have summarised this so clearly. As they explain, it is through examining gender practices, and particularly the ways in which they are 'produced, regulated, consumed and performed, that we can gain a fuller insight into broader gender patterns and arrangements'. This in turn allows us to understand and articulate the relationships between gender and power and 'to see how gender is institutionally organized, discursively constituted, embodied and transfigured in social life'. Thus 'gender analyses can explain how gender relations are embedded within the social fabric of human societies and serve to shape the choices and possibilities open to us as gendered subjects' (Nayak and Kehily, 2008, 5).

Women have come a long way since our grandmothers and great grandmothers fought for the right to vote. We have made major advances in the kinds of work we are permitted to do, the institutions of which we are allowed to be members, and the levels of political, educational, cultural and sporting attainment we have reached. From being excluded from many areas of education, over the course of the past hundred years women have entered educational institutions at every level to the extent that they are now out-performing boys and men in most, if not all, subjects at primary, secondary and higher educational levels (Department for Education and Skills, 2007; Higher Education Policy Institute, 2009; Batho, 2009; Department for Education, 2012b).

Women are now allowed to become doctors, lawyers, judges and 'captains' of industry. We see high profile women succeed in all walks of life and enter previously male-only domains. Indeed, the extent to which women have pushed at the glass ceilings, jumped off the sticky floors, and knocked down barriers to equality of opportunity can lead many younger women in Britain today to feel as if they have it all, to believe that they do not face discrimination on a daily basis. Despite the real advances we have made as a result of women's continued and extensive struggles throughout history, however, the goal of gender equality has not yet been reached. Gender discrimination and segregation across public and private spheres continues to be a pervasive and pernicious aspect of many women's lives in twenty-first century Britain. Indeed, as the Centre for Women and Democracy conclude in their wide-ranging analysis of power in the UK, 'Britain is [still] a country run largely by men' (2013, 13). As even the most cursory glance at a few equalities facts and statistics reveals, women's lives, both in the Yorkshire and Humber region and in the UK as a whole, continue to be conditioned by socio-cultural, heteronormative patriarchal structural frameworks, despite equalities legislation which might suggest otherwise.

Politics is still a man's world

Formal politics is still largely a man's world, and this in itself inhibits women's entry and participation. Politics continues to be seen as a male space (Clisby, 2005, 27; Centre for Women and Democracy, 2013). The House of Commons, for example, has historically been likened to a gentlemen's club, famous for having a shooting range but no crèche, a barber's but no hairdressers, and far too few women's toilets. While some facilities may have become more inclusive in the past few decades, as the authors of the 2012 Democratic Audit state, '[u]nsurprisingly, our conclusion in 2002 that both Houses of Parliament "are essentially white, male, middle-aged, well-educated and comparatively wealthy assemblies" holds true almost a decade later' (Wilks-Heeg et al, 2012, np).

Thus, after almost a century of women's suffrage just under 23 per cent of MPs and 17 per cent of the Cabinet in the UK parliament are women (Fawcett, 2012; Centre for Women and Democracy, 2013). To look at this another way, just over 77 per cent of MPs, 78 per cent of peers and 83 per cent of the Cabinet are male (Centre for Women and Democracy, 2013, 5). This places the UK 60th (out of 190) in global gender equity league tables, and within Western Europe 'only Italy, Ireland and Monaco had a lower percentage of women legislators than the UK in 2012' (Centre for Women and Democracy, 2013, 5). At this rate 'a child born today will be drawing her pension before she sees equal numbers of [white] men and women in the House of Commons' (Fawcett, 2012, 1; Centre for Women and Democracy, 2013, 5). In 2007 Fawcett reported that there were only two black female MPs and there had never been an Asian woman MP (Fawcett, 2007). The alarmingly low representation of black minority ethnic (BME) women in politics continues to date. These facts speak volumes about the status of women in positions of power and decision-making. According to the findings of a survey by Kantar in 2012, such low levels of representation cause many women to feel that politicians do not represent them or their needs and, consequently, to lack active interest in politics. At the same time 44 per cent of women asked said that if there were more women in politics 'Britain would be a better place to live' (Harrison, 2012, np).[4]

Gender segregation in education is improving but continues

Despite girls outperforming boys at every level of education, they continue to be faced with complex socio-cultural pressures that lead to persistent segregation in education along traditional gender lines. This is significant because we know that subject choice during early schooling and onwards through educational levels leads to a narrowing of subsequent career choice. This contributes to inequalities in gendered pay levels which are in turn linked to feminised arenas attracting lower pay. What we can note, however, is that despite extremes of segregation persisting in many areas, we have seen some positive shifts in recent years in gendered subject selection.

There is some evidence, for example, that at further and higher education levels the gender gap is narrowing and even reversing in some subject areas previously dominated by men. According to 2012 figures women now make up most students enrolled in medicine, business, veterinary sciences and law at higher education institutions across the UK, all historically male-dominated subjects (Ratcliffe, 2013). Even in vocational arenas that continue to be heavily male dominated, such as engineering and construction, girls are beginning to outperform (but not outnumber) boys. According to a 2012 study conducted by Pearson, the organisation which runs the Edexcel exam board, although far fewer girls take such subjects, those who do are now gaining higher grades in many 'male' arenas. To provide a couple of the examples they cite in their report: 18 per cent of girls gained the highest mark in a construction and built environment course as opposed to 7 per cent of boys and 38 per cent of girls were awarded a distinction in engineering compared with 16 per cent of boys taking that qualification (Paton, 2012, np).

Nevertheless, in subjects that remain particularly 'gendered' the gap persists with, for example, the majority of students studying literature and languages being female, while the majority of those studying sciences, engineering and computing are male (Joint Council for Qualifications, 2012; Higher Education Statistics Agency, 2013). Vocational training is even more highly segregated: over 90 per cent of early years care and education and hairdressing apprentices are women, while men constitute almost 100 per cent of apprentices in construction, engineering manufacture and in the motor industry (Fuller et al, 2005a; Kirkup, 2011). We talk more about gender, education and mental wellbeing in Chapter Five.

This in turn contributes to gender segregation in paid employment

Women continue to be concentrated in low-paid, gender stereotyped (and often part-time) jobs, a fact which is linked backwards to subject choices in education and forwards to lower paid and less secure employment. As Johnson and Kossykh (2008, 39) conclude in their review, female dominated subjects (humanities and languages) 'are associated with a higher risk of unemployment and lower average pay in general [and] [w]omen tend to work in a limited number of occupations associated with lower wages'. When the now disbanded Equal Opportunities Commission (EOC) conducted a survey of gender and occupational segregation in 2006, they found that women represented 79 per cent of workers in the health and social care sector, 98 per cent of childcare workers, 95 per cent of receptionists, and 76 per cent of cleaners. At the other end of the scale, only 10 per cent of senior police officers and 9 per cent of the judiciary were female, while 83 per cent of directors and chief executives and over 70 per cent of private sector managers were male (EOC, 2006). These trends persist, and continue to have serious impacts on women's life choices, status, pay levels and career opportunities (Johnson and Kossykh, 2008).

Nevertheless, there has been some slight improvement in some sectors since the EOC report in 2006, with women constituting just over 13 per cent of the senior judiciary (a rise of 4 per cent) and 17 per cent of senior police officers (a rise of 7 per cent) in 2013, although, with 83 per cent still being male, there has been no discernible change in the representation of women in the directorships of FTSE100 companies (Centre for Women and Democracy, 2013). The Centre for Women and Democracy similarly reported that in 2013 women in the UK made up just 12 per cent of local authority council leaders, 14 per cent of university vice-chancellors, only 5 per cent of editors of national newspapers, and less than 2 per cent of the senior ranks in the armed forces. All of these are important roles not only in terms of national leadership, governance and decision making, but they also play an important part in wider socio-cultural and gendered perceptions and perspectives. As the *Sex and power 2013* report we are citing here states, providing a telling illustration:

> Women are absent not just from policy and decision-making; they are also often invisible in discussion and debate, even where the issues being considered relate directly to them. In October 2012 the presenter John Humphries, chairing an all-male discussion on breast cancer screening, had to ask the participants to imagine they were women in order to answer the question. This is an extreme example, but by no means an isolated one. (Centre for Women and Democracy, 2013, 31)

There continues to be an invisibility of women generally in certain areas of the media, and according to a website set up to address the issues of gender balance in the media, it remains the case that 'three quarters of the media's "experts" are men. The media says that this is because there just aren't that many female experts around, and the media just reflects the reality of the world' (The Women's Room, 2013, np). It was this incident on BBC's *Today* programme, combined with another in which an all-male panel discussed the issue of teenage girls and contraception that led to the establishment of 'The Women's Room' (http://thewomensroom.org.uk/index.php). This is an online space for women who are willing to be contacted by the media to register themselves as experts in particular fields and attempt to address the gender imbalance in popular media, especially television.

Equally persistent, and unsurprising, is the continued gender pay gap[5] in the UK. Women still earn less than men for work of equal value despite legislation introduced in 1970 which made this practice illegal. In recent years the gap has tended to hover around the 15–18 per cent mark for full-time work rising to a gender pay gap of between 37 per cent and 40 per cent for part-time employees (EOC, 2007a; Johnson and Kossykh, 2008, 39; Fawcett, 2010 and 2013a). Based on an analysis of the latest official statistics available in 2013, women in full-time work currently earn an average of 15 per cent less per hour than men across public and private employment sectors combined (Fawcett, 2013a, 4). To put this in real terms, '[t]he gap between women and men for full-time work is equivalent to men being paid all year round, while women work for free after 2nd November' (Fawcett, 2010, 2).

According to the Office for National Statistics (ONS), when combining both full and part-time work, the gender pay gap for all employees based on hourly average earnings stands at just below 20 per cent (ONS, 2013a). There is a wider gap in the private sector: 20 per cent for full-time work, rising to 24 per cent when part-time work is included. This pattern persists across sectors, with the hourly wage gap between full- and part-time work standing at 37 per cent in 2012 (ONS, 2013b, cited in Fawcett, 2013a,14). This significant discrepancy is in part explained by the fact that, despite being illegal, those in part-time work are more than twice as likely as their full-time counterparts to be paid less than the minimum wage (ONS, 2013a; Fawcett, 2013a, 14). When we consider that women make up the vast majority (74 per cent) of part-time workers and over two thirds (62 per cent) of those on low pay (paid at or below minimum wage), we can see how this pay gap is both stark and, so, starkly gendered (ONS, 2013b; Fawcett, 2013a, 14).

Within individual employment sectors the gender pay gap can be even wider, for example, as the EOC reported in 2006, women earned 41 per cent less per hour than men in the banking and insurance sector. Even taking into account key indices of difference for all men and women, '[t]here is persistent gender disadvantage across equalities areas' (Longhi and Platt, 2008, viii). All of these factors combine to have a significant impact on economic wellbeing not only through the lifecourse, but into later life, with women's average personal pensions being just 62 per cent of the average value of men's. It comes as no surprise then that women make up the majority of pensioners living below the breadline (Fawcett, 2013a, 4). These are themes developed further in Chapter Seven.

Gender discrimination at home

> The irony behind the idyllic happy family as a place of repose is the consumption of female labour power.
> (Rowbotham, 1973, 67)

Women clearly continue to experience gender discrimination in the public sphere, and despite women's place supposedly being 'in the home', discrimination also permeates the private sphere. Sheila Rowbotham's comment made over 40 years ago rings as true today, women continue to perform, and take responsibility for, most of the reproductive and community management work in the household (Momsen, 2010). Women also take most responsibility for emotional labour and caring work: for children, for disabled or sick relatives, for elderly family members, and even for work colleagues (Richardson and Robinson, 2008; Connell, 2009).

As mentioned briefly earlier in this chapter, reproductive labour is a broad term that encompasses childbearing and early nurturing of infants (which is biologically linked to the female body) but also social reproduction such as housework and the management of household resources and provisions. This includes cleaning, cooking, washing and ironing, as well as assuming responsibility for the health, education and socialisation of children, caring for sick, elderly or disabled family members, and being generally responsible for the reproduction and care of the current and next generation of the labour force.

Community management work is also of critical importance but is often overlooked. As explained earlier, this chapter forms a critical element of the embodied infrastructure of society and refers to the work that is done building and maintaining both kin and non-kin networks, which can be of particular importance in times of economic and social difficulty. This includes the maintenance of good relations among family, friendship and community circles, such as sending birthday cards, gifts, making phone calls, checking in on elderly neighbours and so on. It can also include working towards community development, improvements in local services, sitting on neighbourhood committees, engaging in community voluntary work, supporting each other at times of need through emotional labour, and through provision of skills, economic and social resources. World-over, women tend to do most of this labour in addition to both their reproductive roles and paid work, and it not only forms much of the glue of human society, but investing in this labour can make the difference between survival or not for many families in times of crisis (Stein, 1997, 1; Clisby, 2005, 26; Momsen, 2010).

The feminist movement has been calling for greater recognition of this work for decades, including demanding wages for housework on the basis of its direct value to the national economy. Rowbotham argued in the 1970s that,

> [b]ecause housework does not fit into the prevailing notions of work it mysteriously becomes not work at all. It is not counted. The woman at home is described as the woman who doesn't work…If it were admitted that the family is maintained at the expense of women, capitalism would have to devise some other way of getting the work done…the political and social consequences as well as the economic cost would be considerable. At present it would seem to be more profitable for the capitalist system to continue to 'preserve the family'. (Rowbotham, 1973, 67–8)

Much of Rowbotham's argument is equally pertinent today, but what has perhaps changed is that we have increasingly admitted that women maintain the family and underpin the capitalist economy as unpaid labour. A 2002 UK government report, through the Office for National Statistics, made an attempt to put a value on housework. They calculated that if the time spent on unpaid work was valued at the average rate for paid employment it would be worth over £700 billion a year more than three quarters of the value of the paid economy (BBC News Online, 2002), which is just as Rowbotham predicted. What she perhaps overestimated, however, was the extent to which capitalist society would be moved to act, for as we have seen, after this fact has been 'admitted', society has not felt the need to 'devise some other way of getting the work done' as she optimistically predicted (Rowbotham, 1973, 67).

Depending on which data you look at, women spend an average of between 2.6 and just over 3.5 hours per day on unpaid domestic and childcare tasks in addition to their regular paid work. While the time spent on household labour has seen a significant reduction with the advent of labour saving household devices over the past few decades (around 18–24 hours per week in the 2010s compared to approximately 44 hours per week in the 1960s), that is still almost twice as much time as the average man spends on similar tasks (Gershuny et al, 2006; Fine, 2010, 80; Peacock, 2012). What is clear, then, is that not only do women continue to do the bulk of all reproductive and community management labour, without which contemporary human society could not function, but that if women were actually paid for this labour it would bankrupt the nation. To put it another way, we are worth it, but they cannot afford us. We consider the impacts of processes of gendering in family life for women's and girl's identities in Chapter Three.

The home as a site of domestic violence

Despite, and because of, all their hard work within it, women can and should find their homes a source of comfort and security, but all too often the home is a site of fear, abuse and violence. Looking at a few of the available statistics over the past few years clearly illustrates the pernicious and pertinacious nature of domestic and sexual violence against women and girls. A frequently cited headline statistic is that in the UK one incidence of domestic violence is reported to the police every minute and one in four women experience domestic violence during their lifetime (Women's Aid, 2013). According to Women's Aid (2013), citing Home Office statistics, national figures repeatedly indicate that on average two women are killed every week by a male partner or former partner (Women's Aid, 2013). Indeed, over half of all homicides against women are committed by a partner or ex-partner (ONS, 2013c).

More recently, the British Crime Survey (England and Wales) (ONS, 2013c) reported that in line with previous years, 1.2 million women were victims of domestic and sexual abuse during 2011–12, around one third (31 per cent) of women reported experiencing domestic abuse since the age of 16, equivalent to 5 million women, and almost one fifth (19 per cent) of women had experienced sexual assault and attempted sexual assault since the age of 16 (Smith et al, 2012, 83; ONS, 2013c). While sexual and domestic violence is taken more seriously by the police and general public than has historically been the case, it still remains one of the more serious and most common causes of death and injury for women and girls both in the UK and worldwide. In Chapter Four we focus in more detail on gender-based violence and the impacts structural, symbolic and visceral forms of such violence can have on women's mental wellbeing.

Conclusion: from the Equal Pay Act to the Equality Act: why policy-led approaches alone cannot work

From this brief overview it is clear that gender inequalities continue to exist at both national and regional levels across public and private spheres. To point out, however, that gender inequalities continue is not to suggest that positive advances in policy and equalities legislation have not taken place or that these have not made a real difference to women's lives. Since the 1970s in particular, and thanks in no small part to the women's movement, second wave feminism and to continued feminist and gay/lesbian/trans lobbying and campaigning, we have seen a plethora of policies introduced that have attempted to eradicate inequalities based on gender and sexuality. To highlight a few of the relevant changes we have produced a timeline of in/equalities at the end of this chapter (see Box 1.2). This is not an exhaustive account, rather a selective 'snapshot' of some key political and policy events within a demarcated period spanning 30 years.

What we are arguing here is not that equalities policy and legislation is a failure *per se*. On the contrary, such legislation is crucial and we must remain ever vigilant that it is effectively progressed, updated and enforced. Indeed in the UK we should be proud of the advances we have made in terms of legislation and policy that attempts to protect people from discrimination and unfair treatment in both public and private spheres.[6] The problem we highlight in this book is that policy-led approaches alone are bound to be inadequate in and of themselves not only because policy can be changed or weakened, but because policy does not, and many would argue cannot, effectively address underlying issues of gendering. Pernicious and persistent gender inequalities such as those highlighted in the statistics and examples summarised in this chapter continue due to insidious, amorphous and deeply embedded patriarchal gender constructs, or gender regimes. Policy can and should attempt to address and protect us from the worst manifestations of these processes, but policy alone has as yet failed to stamp out inequalities.

One could, perhaps more controversially, suggest that to expect policy legislation to overcome gender inequality and discrimination is a project doomed to fail from the inception. The expectation that equality law can be a tool that acts as a catalyst for the realisation of feminist goals may be trying to put a square peg in a round hole. As Standing (2007, 104–5) argues, the problem is in the 'relocation of the possibility of political transformation to an inherently non-transformatory context' because, as she goes on to say, '[b]ureaucracies are not engines of social and political transformation. Indeed as Orwell and Kafka remind us, we need to be ever vigilant that they are not.'

Standing wisely warns us against placing too much ideological power or faith in the hands of bureaucracies, not least because we do not necessarily know whose hands these may be and with which political agendas they are aligned. Nevertheless, the need for caution notwithstanding, in the context of equalities legislation in the UK, it is critically important that we have protection and a commitment to equality of opportunities enshrined in the law. While the law may not have the power to eradicate gender-based inequity from our gender regime, it does send out powerful messages about cultural norms and social expectations of a nation. That homosexuality is still punishable by death in eight countries worldwide, that women are not permitted to drive in Saudi Arabia, that abortion is still illegal in Ireland for all but life-threatening cases, that female genital mutilation is condoned in many parts of Africa, all say something about dominant attitudes, beliefs and cultural norms in these contexts.

Thus, if bureaucracy cannot, and perhaps should not, itself be an *engine* of social and political change, it can serve to support and underpin such change, although this leaves us with a continued problem and returns us to the beginning of this introduction. Normative processes of gendering continue to have a negative impact on women's wellbeing. How this plays out for women at various stages of their lifecourse is what we will be exploring in the following chapters.

Box 1.2: Timeline of in/equality in the UK: 1970–2010
The 1970s

1970 Working women are refused mortgages in their own right as few women work continuously. They are only granted mortgages if they can secure the signature of a male guarantor.

1970 Britain's first national Women's Liberation Conference is held at Ruskin College. This is the first time that women's groups from across Britain have met in a single place. The Women's Liberation Movement (WLM), influential throughout the 1970s, develops from the conference.

1970 The Equal Pay Act makes it illegal to pay women lower rates than men for the same work. The act covers indirect as well as direct sex discrimination. It is a direct result of women's strike action over equal pay at a Ford car plant in Dagenham in 1968 and continued pressure from the women's movement.

1970 The Miss World competition is interrupted by feminist protestors claiming that the contest is a cattle market. They throw flour and smoke bombs, inaugurating the first protest event organised by the women's movement.

1971 Over 4,000 women take part in the first women's liberation march in London.

1972 Erin Pizzey sets up the first women's refuge in Chiswick, London.

1974 The National Women's Aid Federation is set up to bring together nearly 40 refuge services across the country.

1974 Contraception becomes available through the NHS.

1975 The Sex Discrimination Act makes it illegal to discriminate against women in work, education and training.

1975 The Equal Opportunities Commission (EOC) is set up under the Sex Discrimination Act and has statutory powers to enforce this Act.

1975 The Employment Protection Act introduces statutory maternity provision and makes it illegal to sack a woman because she is pregnant.

1976 The EOC comes into effect to oversee the Equal Pay Act and Sex Discrimination Act.

1976 Lobbying by women's organisations ushers in the Domestic Violence and Matrimonial Proceedings Act to protect women and children from domestic violence. The Act gives new rights to those at risk of violence through civil protection orders.

1977 Mainly Asian women workers mount a year-long strike at Grunwick's in London for equal pay and conditions.

1977 International Women's Day is formalised as an annual event by the UN General Assembly.

1977 The first Rape Crisis Centre opens in London.

1978 The Women's Aid Federation of Northern Ireland is established.

1978 The Organisation of Women of African and Asian Descent is set up. It is the first black women's organisation in Britain to organise at a national level, drawing black women from across the country to form an umbrella group for black women's organisations.

1979 The feminist journal *Feminist Review* is founded. It goes on to play a crucial role in promoting contemporary feminist debate in the UK.

1979 Margaret Thatcher becomes Britain's first female prime minister.

The 1980s

1980 Lesley Abdela forms the 300 Group to push for equal representation of women in the House of Commons.

1980 Women working at Hoover, Merthyr Tydfil, take strike action against 'women out first' redundancy plans.

1980 Women can apply for a loan or credit in their own names.

1981 Baroness Young becomes the first woman leader of the House of Lords.

1982 30,000 women gather at Greenham Common Peace Camp. The camp remained open for 19 years during which time thousands of female protesters visited and lived in the camp.

1982 The Court of Appeal decides that bars and pubs are no longer able to refuse to serve women at the bar as this constitutes sex discrimination.

1983 Lady Mary Donaldson becomes the first woman Lord Mayor of London.

1984 During the miners' strike, wives of picketing miners organise themselves into a powerful women's group. The movement eventually becomes national and leaves a legacy of a common class struggle against sexism, women's oppression and against capitalism itself.

1985 The Equal Pay (Amendment) Act allows women to be paid the same as men for work of equal value.

1985 Campaigning against female genital mutilation by the Foundation for Women's Health, Research and Development leads to the Prohibition of Female Circumcision Act. The Act is further strengthened with the introduction of the Female Genital Mutilation Act in 2003.

1986 The Sex Discrimination (Amendment) Act enables women to retire at the same age as men. It also lifts the legal restrictions which prevent women from working night shifts in factories.

1987 Diane Abbot becomes the first black woman member of the Westminster Parliament.

1988 Julie Hayward, a canteen cook at a shipyard in Liverpool, is the first woman to win a case under the amended Equal Pay Act.

1988 Section 28 of the Local Government Act was introduced, making it illegal for any council or government body to 'intentionally promote homosexuality, or publish material with the intention of promoting homosexuality'.

1988 Elizabeth Butler-Sloss becomes the first woman Law Lord when she is appointed an Appeal Court Judge.

The 1990s

1990 Independent taxation for women is introduced. For the first time, married women are taxed separately from their husbands.

1992 Betty Boothroyd becomes the first female Speaker of the House of Commons.

1993 United Nations Declaration on the Elimination of Violence against Women affirms that violence against women violates their human rights.

1994 Rape in marriage is made a crime after 15 years of serious campaigning by women's organisations.

1994 Equal rights of part-time workers is granted in a ruling by the House of Lords.

1997 Increase in women MPs: the general election sees 101 Labour women MPs elected as a result of the controversial (and subsequently declared illegal) introduction of all-women shortlists in 1993.

1998 The Human Rights Act is passed by the European Union.

1999 Refugee law is extended to gender persecution: the House of Lords delivers a historic judgement in the Shah and Islam case that women who fear gender persecution should be recognised as refugees.

1999 Maternity and Parental Leave Regulations are extended to enable both men and women to take up to 13 weeks off to care for children under the age of five years.

1999 Sex Discrimination (Gender Reassignment) Regulations is introduced, this makes it illegal for employers to discriminate against trans people.

The 2000s

2000 Asylum Gender Guidelines are introduced by the UK's Immigration Appellate Authority (the immigration and asylum tribunal) for use in the determination of asylum appeals. The guidelines note that the dominant view of what constitutes a 'real refugee' has been of a man and this has meant that women asylum seekers in the UK may not benefit equitably from the protection offered by the Refugee Convention.

2001 London Partnerships Register is launched by Mayor of London, Ken Livingstone, allowing lesbians, gay men and unmarried heterosexual couples to register their partnerships.

2002 Adoption law changes. Parliament passes measures allowing lesbian and unmarried couples to adopt children.

2003 Employment Equality (Sexual Orientation) Regulations are introduced to protect people against discrimination based on their sexual orientation.

2003 Section 28 is repealed following a prolonged campaign and lobbying by voluntary and community organisations, particularly lesbian, gay, bisexual and transgender organisations.

2004 Civil Partnerships Act comes into force giving same sex couples the same rights and responsibilities as married heterosexual couples. In the same year the historical crimes of 'buggery' and 'gross indecency' are abolished.

2004 Gender Recognition Act is introduced which allows trans people who have taken decisive steps to live fully and permanently in their acquired gender to gain legal recognition in that gender.

2007 Equality and Human Rights Commission (EHRC) is established. This involves the closure and merger of the EOC, Commission for Racial Equality (CRE) and the Disability Rights Commission (DRC) into a single Commission. There have been criticisms of the loss of focus on and resources concerning women's and gender equality/inequality as a result of the closure of the EOC.

2007 Gender Equality Duty (GED) comes into force which requires all public bodies in the UK to consider gender equality in all areas of policy making. The duty requires more than simply equal treatment for men and women. Public bodies should promote and take action to bring about gender equality, which involves looking at issues for men and women; understanding why inequalities exist and how to overcome them; creating effective service provision for all, so that everyone can access services that meet their needs. All local authorities, public institutions and private and voluntary organisations carrying out public functions are required to produce a Gender Equality Scheme (GES) which details how their institution effectively implements gender equality measures and takes action to bring about gender equality in their organisation.

2010 Equality Act is introduced which replaces previous anti-discrimination laws with a single Act covering nine protected characteristics: age; disability; gender reassignment; marriage and civil partnership; pregnancy and maternity; race; sex; religion or belief; sexual orientation. The Act established the range of unlawful treatment on grounds of protected characteristics, including direct and indirect discrimination, harassment, victimisation and failing to make a reasonable adjustment for a disabled person. The Act applies to 'unfair treatment in the workplace, when providing goods, facilities and services, when exercising public functions, in the disposal and management of premises, in education and by associations (such as private clubs)' (Home Office, 2012).

TWO

Gendering women's minds: identity, confidence and mental wellbeing

Gender and mental wellbeing

In this chapter we explore the links between processes of gendering and mental wellbeing and discuss some of the impacts poorer mental wellbeing can have on women's lives. Outlining some headline policy and statistical data pertaining to gender and mental health we provide a contextual map of some key issues within regional, national and global contexts. Focusing on feminist theories and debates that have emerged over the past four decades we explore the relationships between ill health, constructions of femininities and the socio-cultural conditions of women's lives. While recognising that women are both more likely than men to self-identify as having mental wellbeing issues and be identified by health professionals as experiencing problems with their mental health, we argue that the cultural construction of the mental health sector as *feminised* should be resisted. The feminisation of mental health is problematic for woman as a whole, and also for men. As we discuss at the end of this chapter, the construction of mental health as a 'woman's problem' creates a cultural barrier for men who would benefit from accessing support within the sector and perpetuates the myth of the physically and mentally 'strong male' which can be damaging for both men and women.

Our focus on the links between gender and mental wellbeing emerged from our research with women. While exploring women's life histories and experiences, initially specifically in relation to educational and employment trajectories, it soon became clear that mental wellbeing was a recurrent issue for women from all backgrounds. Women's self-confidence, self-esteem and mental wellbeing emerged as a significant theme in almost all of the qualitative interviews and focus group discussions. In addition to clinically significant experiences of depression, self-harming and other mental health issues, women repeatedly raised – both explicitly and implicitly – a range of broader wellbeing issues, such as low self-confidence and low self-esteem, as obstacles to their personal and professional development. The questionnaire survey data yielded on the whole more positive responses to questions of wellbeing than the more in-depth qualitative research, and 73 per cent of women agreed or strongly agreed that they were 'usually a confident person', although this was somewhat undermined by the simultaneous finding that 75 per cent of women agreed or strongly agreed that they 'often underestimated their abilities' in the same survey. Could both be the case? Perhaps so, after all, we are complex and contradictory beings. Moreover, surveys are notoriously limited tools, lacking the depth and nuance that the interviews in this study yielded. While not without complexity and contradiction, the qualitative voices of women were more consistent and unambiguous in their articulation of pernicious under-confidence.

What many participants seemed to be articulating was an inner voice that whispers in the ears of women of all ages, from all backgrounds and in all areas of life; the voice that tells them that they are 'not really very good', they 'could do better', that they 'do not really deserve that job, that salary, that promotion', that they are 'inadequate mothers, poor wives or partners and failing daughters'. While many of the women we spoke with did feel confident and happy with whom they were, even in the most confident and successful life histories lack of esteem was raised in some way. Danielle, for example, talked about her professional insecurities, which she still feels despite her successful career in catering:

> 'I still now have that little doubt even when I hire staff, which just sounds really silly but, "They're going to take my job"…and I think "Why am I frightened of someone that's been here a week?" But that's a confidence thing.' (Danielle, early 40s, manager, catering sector, North Yorkshire)

As is discussed in greater depth in later chapters, low confidence and undervaluing oneself can have tangible and long-term implications for a woman's career. This can include women not permitting themselves to recognise and value their skills, which in turn can have an impact on their willingness to apply for promotion. As Alice said:

> 'I think women aren't necessarily encouraged to be proud of their achievements in quite the same way [as men]. Um, I know that personally for a very long time, I felt quite embarrassed telling people how well I've done [educationally and professionally].' (Alice, late 30s, manager, education sector, volunteer, mother, West Yorkshire)

Underselling oneself can also have direct monetary impacts. May is a highly qualified professional, but felt undervalued when she discovered that she was being paid less than a male colleague. She explained that when she was appointed to a new post she was offered the lowest salary on that pay scale. A male colleague who was appointed to a similar post at the same time was also offered the lowest scale point but he queried this and his salary was increased. When asked if she felt that this was in some way a gendered issue she said:

> 'I think that, in a way, it could be a gendered issue because it was just like, oh someone's offered me a job so, you know, someone wants me and, yes, of course I'll take the money. I was just kind of, you know, happy to be offered a job, really. I didn't think about challenging the amount of money, really.' (May, late 30s, part time, education sector, North Yorkshire).

For May, the issue was not that her colleague was being paid more *per se*, although this in itself is poor employment practice, rather, the issue was that she had lacked the confidence to ask for a salary which she really did feel was more commensurate with the level of responsibility she was taking on. Fundamentally, May undervalued herself, she was simply grateful that she had been offered the job rather than recognising her worth and this came to be reflected in longer-term economic disadvantage, which over the years amounted to tens of thousands of pounds in differential earnings.

So prevalent were underlying feelings of inadequacy and lack of self-confidence throughout the interviews that it might even be seen as a common thread that tenuously connects women, a negative undercurrent of femininity that sits at the very core of women's sense of self. Rita, for example, has ongoing health problems but she continues to work in a voluntary capacity. She feels, however, that the biggest barrier to progressing in her life is:

> 'Self-confidence: I just wish somebody would just say "Rita, just do it, just do it!"…I just need a big push to do something…I wish I had the confidence to say "Right, I want to do this."' (Rita, early 40s, volunteer, Humberside)

Carla, who runs self-confidence courses for a group of women, recognises that the causes of low self-esteem among women, while diverse, are deeply embedded in gendered issues of power and women's identity formation from an early age:

'I'm working with, you know, some people who have issues with husbands and things like that, and boyfriends, like domestic abuse etc, so that knocks confidence anyway; so it could come from things like that, but it could be just the simple fact that they've got no self-esteem, it comes back from childhood and you know they've never been told that they're good at anything, you know they even go to work but you've never been given any praise whatsoever.' (Carla, mid–40s, manager, community sector, mother, North Yorkshire)

This is not to suggest that all women lack confidence and have low self-esteem. Nor are we suggesting that men do not experience low self-esteem and a lack of confidence at times in their lives. Both men and women are inevitably affected by the multifarious obstacles life throws in our paths, and we are particularly vulnerable to lack of confidence and mental wellbeing issues at higher stress points, such as losing or changing jobs, moving house, becoming a parent, experiencing relationship breakdown or suffering a death in the family. Throughout this book, however, we are focusing on the ways *women* in particular feel that lowered confidence and self-esteem have had an impact on their aspirations and achievements through their lifecourse.

The global and local contexts of gender and mental health

The prevalence of mental health problems which people experience is not an issue confined to specific geographic contexts or particular human societies. Globally, mental health and wellbeing continue to pose major challenges for the public health agenda. It has been estimated that mental health disorders affect approximately 450 million people worldwide, accounting for over 12 per cent of the global burden of disease (World Bank, 2004; Diaz–Granados and Stewart, 2007) and in England alone the annual cost of mental health problems is estimated at over £100 billion (Centre for Mental Health, 2010).

While the terms 'mental health' or 'mental wellbeing' incorporate an enormous range of experiences, symptoms, illnesses and diseases, one of the most common manifestations of mental health problems is in the form of depression. The World Health Organisation (WHO) states that depression, predicted to be the second leading cause of global disability by 2020, is twice as common in women (WHO, 2012). Similarly, in the UK 'mixed anxiety and depression' is the most common mental health disorder 'with almost 9 per cent of people meeting criteria for diagnosis' (Mental Health Foundation, 2007, 9; see also ONS, 2010, 37). Nevertheless, for many years the impacts of chronic depression and mental health problems have been neither fully understood nor taken as seriously as they could be within health services both in the UK and globally.

In an attempt to address this issue, in 2007 the WHO conducted the largest worldwide study of the impacts of depression. They found that in comparison with other prevalent chronic diseases such as angina, arthritis and diabetes, depression impairs health 'to a substantially greater degree' (Moussavi et al, 2007, 861–2). Moreover, they found that women experienced higher levels of depression and subsequent health problems. Contributing factors to incidences of depression include: lower educational attainment and income levels; being unemployed; being separated, divorced or widowed.

The combination or comorbidity of depression and other chronic diseases was found to be an especially lethal cocktail, and in recognition of this, the WHO report concluded by urging primary care providers 'not to ignore the presence of depression when patients present with a chronic physical condition, in view of the marked effect that it has on an individual's health' (Moussavi et al, 2007, 861). In addition to academic research, in recent years there has been a more general growing global recognition of the significance, prevalence and, often, gendered nature of mental health problems. Global institutions such as the WHO and the United Nations as well as national governments are increasingly acknowledging – at least at the level of policy rhetoric – the links between mental health problems on the one hand and gendered socio-cultural and environmental factors such as alienation, powerlessness, poverty and discrimination on the other (Joseph, 2001, 370). In more extreme cases, we can understand that being criminalised can undoubtedly have negative impacts on mental ill health, but one could argue that mental ill health may contribute to criminalisation. It seems too much of a coincidence that 'three-quarters of the female prison population in Britain suffer from mental health problems' (Appignanesi, 2008, 3). While it is beyond the scope of this volume to fully engage with this debate here, it poses a key question for analysis elsewhere: did they all become mentally unwell after being incarcerated or was their poor mental health a contributing factor in their criminalisation?

Mental health disorders, treatment and outcomes are gendered issues with evidence of significant differences in levels of diagnosis, patterns and symptoms (Busfield, 1996). Indeed, as Ussher states, '[f]or centuries women have occupied a unique place in the annals of insanity. Women outnumber men in diagnoses of madness, from the 'hysteria' of the eighteenth and nineteenth centuries, to 'neurotic' and mood disorders of the twentieth and twenty-first' (Ussher, 2011, 1). Throughout the world women are, for example, more likely than men to experience depression, anxiety, seasonal affective disorders, eating disorders, panic disorders, have a higher incidence of attempted suicide and are more likely than men to suffer from more than one mental illness or disability (Appignanesi, 2008). Women are also more likely to be subject to psychiatric treatment and the range of 'therapies' experienced within this realm such as electro-convulsive therapy (ECT) (Ussher, 2011, 1).

Men, as a group, on the other hand, experience more overt problems with anger, engage in high risk behaviours, have higher rates of completed suicide and higher prevalence of alcohol and substance misuse (WHO, 2002; Diaz–Granados and Stewart, 2007, 197; Mental Health Foundation, 2007, 27). Gender differences in patterns of mental health service access are also evident with women making greater use of services, receiving more medication and having higher rates of hospitalisation than men. As Malatesta (2007, 1) points out, however, it is 'ironic' that despite women being the primary consumers of mental health services, 'research addressing their unique needs lags behind that of men's issues'.

Recognising the need for a greater global focus on, and strategies towards, tackling the gendered impacts of mental health disorders, in 2007 the World Health Assembly (WHA) issued a resolution urging member states (the UK included) to mainstream a gender analysis across all levels of policy formulation, planning, delivery and training throughout the health sector. Similarly, for Diaz–Granados and Stewart, a gender analysis of health provision at national and regional levels is essential in order to tackle gender disparities in mental wellbeing. Specifically:

> a gender–sensitive national mental health surveillance program that includes health system indicators as well as community indicators would not only ensure that appropriate care reaches those at higher risk (ie refugees, immigrants, single-parent mothers, women who experience intimate partner violence), but it would also promote the use and planning of community programs aimed at increasing mental well-being. (2007, 198)

Gendered experiences of mental health and wellbeing both in the UK as a whole and within the Yorkshire and Humber region itself tend to reflect global trends identified above. It is recognised, for example, that in Yorkshire and Humber, as across the UK more generally, mental health problems affect more women than men (Palmer et al, 2003; Mental Health Foundation, 2007). Similarly, risks of developing mental health problems can be exacerbated by the material conditions of people's lives including socio-economic class and income levels, the kinds of employment people are engaged in, periods of unemployment, and the social contexts of one's cultural or ethnic background. Adults in the poorest fifth of the population, for example, are twice as likely to develop mental illness as those on average incomes and people from manual backgrounds are at higher risk than those from non-manual backgrounds (Mental Health Foundation, 2007).

Mental health problems can in turn have a disproportionate impact on an individual's socio-economic context, leading to a vicious circle of significant social isolation. People with mental health problems are, for example, more likely to live alone, have little contact with their families, have fewer friends, be divorced or separated and are more than twice as likely to be lone parents than those without a mental health problem – a situation that again affects more women than men (Mental Health Foundation, 2007).

Thus, to provide a few illustrative examples, the incidence and prevalence of depression and anxiety is higher among women than men and the same gendered pattern is consistent across ethnic groups (Melzer et al, 2001, cited in Myers et al, 2005). Rates of suicide, schizophrenia and of alcohol and drug use are higher for men but there are rising levels of alcohol-related harm among women, especially among younger women (Myers et al, 2005). Interestingly, Soni-Raleigh reported in 1996 that Asian women aged between 15–35 years are two to three times more likely to be vulnerable to suicide and self-harm than their non-Asian counterparts (Soni-Raleigh, 1996). These rates have continued and a report published 15 years later by the Southall Black Sisters (2011) states that British Asian women continue to commit suicide at a rate that is twice the national average, being three times more likely to kill themselves than other ethnic groups.

In the UK, the highest rates of mental illness are found in the North East, affecting approximately 18 per cent of the population. The Yorkshire and Humber region itself is in line with national averages with approximately 12 per cent of the adult population deemed at high risk of mental illness (ONS, 2011d). As outlined in Box 1.1, however, indices of social deprivation and health problems tend to be relatively high in many areas of the Yorkshire and Humber region which has an impact on and is in turn affected by ill health and poorer mental wellbeing.

In summary, despite being so prevalent and having such serious socio-economic impacts, and despite the chronic effects poor mental health has on both the individual and society as a whole, there continues to be a global lack of attention to provision of mental health services. This is a problem which is similarly reflected in both regional and national UK contexts with mental health and wellbeing continuing to be perceived as the 'Cinderella' of the health service. In recent years, however, successive governments have made some encouraging policy statements and developed some positive initiatives. In the mid-2000s, pre-empting the World Health Assembly's 2007 resolution mentioned earlier, the former Labour government recognised the need to mainstream gender into mental health in local planning and social care services and called for a 'cultural change' within mental health services in order to understand the needs of women and develop more gender-aware training and provision. Within this, one of the policy initiatives highlighted in the women's mental health strategy is the need for women-only community day services and support in every health authority. As the Department of Health (DH) stated:

> The needs of women are central to the government's programme of reform and investment in public services and to our commitment to addressing discrimination and inequality. Modernising mental health services is one of our core national priorities [There is also a recognition that] understanding the needs of women – both as service users and in the workforce – requires cultural change. (DH, 2004, np)

That the government made a public commitment to gender mainstreaming in mental health sectors was a welcome advance. Nevertheless there is a long way to go in order to achieve the 'cultural change' required across health services and greater resources need to be allocated to more targeted and gender-aware service provision and training. In the climate of recession following the 2009 global banking crisis and financial mismanagement, and the subsequent service cuts witnessed across the UK and internationally, the resourcing and modernising of the mental health sector has not, however, been a political priority.

Gendering and engendering selves: how being a 'man' and being a 'woman' can make you sick

That so many women experience problems with their mental wellbeing, ranging from a lack of confidence in their abilities or low self-esteem to serious mental health issues such as chronic depression, could lead one to believe that there is something about the formation of women's gendered identity, their sense of self, that is seriously flawed. Recognition of the 'problem' of gender identity formation can, however, lead to quite different responses and perceived solutions. As Prior (1999) explains, and as will be explored in more detail below, some of these reasons include 'arguments about the intolerable constraints involved in traditional female roles, the acceptability of illness as a mode of protest and attention-seeking for women, and the inability of a male-dominated society to accept creative but different female behaviour' (Prior, 1999, 78). Prior, however, warns against making overly simplistic connections between gender and mental health, emphasising that to gain a better understanding of 'the relations between gender and psychiatric disorder requires a very careful unravelling of the complex character of psychiatric ideas and practice as well as of gender relations' (Prior, 2002, 160).

While the feminisation of mental health has tended to characterise the contemporary health arena over the course of the twentieth and twenty-first centuries, it is interesting to note that until the late nineteenth century, men were more likely than women to be labelled and committed to asylums as 'mad'. The feminisation of mental health gathered pace rapidly during the late Victorian period, however, so that 'by the 1890s the predominance of women had spread to include all classes of patients in all kinds of institutions except for asylums for the criminally insane, a dominance that has continued ever since' (Holmshaw and Hillier, 2000, 41). There are several reasons suggested for this gender shift, linked, for example, to gender differences in poverty, power and a popular view held among the (male) psychiatric and medical profession that 'women were more vulnerable to insanity than men because the instability of their reproductive systems interfered with their sexual, emotional and rational control' (Holmshaw and Hillier, 2000, 41; see also Bernheimer and Kahane, 1985; Levine-Clark, 2004).

In Showalter's (1987) classic work *The Female Malady*, she explores the image of the feminine as synonymous with 'madness', arguing that this link goes beyond women's statistical overrepresentations in mental health circles. She highlights the ways in which representations of the 'mad' as feminine, and vice versa, leach into cultural representations such as in art and literature and are underpinned by the gendered dualisms famously outlined by Ortner (1974) of female/male–nature/culture–irrational/rational: 'While the name of the symbolic female disorder may change from one historical period to the next, the gender asymmetry of the representational tradition remains constant. Thus madness, even when experienced by men, is metaphorically and symbolically represented as feminine: a female malady' (Showalter, 1987, 4, cited in Prior, 1999, 79).

Philip Martin also alludes to classic feminist analysis of the masculine 'One' and the feminine 'Other' when he argues that, '[w]oman and madness share the same territory…they may be said to enter a concentric relationship around a central point occupied by fundamental male normality' (Martin, 1987, 42, cited in Ussher, 2011, 1). Considering the framework of the triad of violence played out along a long continuum we set out in Chapter One, we can see how both Showalter (1987) and Martin (1987) are talking here about forms of symbolic violence (Bourdieu, 2001) being done unto women's gendered identities.

Historically, however, and particularly outside of the realms of feminist understandings, the lack of self-confidence many women feel has often tended to be individualised – seen as the woman's personal problem – rather than understood as resulting from structural and ideological factors, integral to the social construction of women's gendered identities in society. From this perspective, then, the woman herself is the root cause of her illness. Unfortunately, this process of individuation is all too apparent to this day within key social institutions such as the medical profession, the media and within the family.

We accept that there are aspects of self-esteem and mental wellbeing that can be especially gendered experiences for women *qua* women. In line with several other feminist analyses, however, the required 'cultural change' referred to by the Department of Health (DH, 2004) involves a reconfiguration of the individuation of these issues and a recognition of the fundamental implication of socio-cultural structures in the creation of mental illness as a 'woman's problem'. We suggest that a focus on women's wellbeing requires an examination of what it is about women's lives that makes them vulnerable to illness. We need to examine the ways in which '[i]ncreased responsibilities place tremendous physical and psychological demands on women, putting them at risk of developing an array of mental health problems' (Antai-Otong, 1997, 330). We also need to understand the ways in which in both local and global contexts women's lives are so often characterised by a range of complex conditions including hard labour, gender-based discrimination, poorer nutrition, exposure to violence and that all these 'difficult circumstances faced by many women negatively affect their health and well-being and produce some common needs' (Stein, 1997, 1–2). What is important, however, is that there is a need to critically explore 'how social institutions, such as medicine, frame women's experience of health and illness and help to maintain their social subordination' (Hockey, 1993, 250).

A similar point is made by Goudsmit (1994), although her analysis forms a useful and significant counterpoint to the problem of individuation of poor wellbeing, that of the 'psychologisation' of women's illness (Goudsmit, 1994, 7). As Goudsmit (1994) illustrates, gender stereotyping by (often male) medical professionals can lead to the diagnosis of women presenting with physical symptoms as mentally or psychologically unwell. Goudsmit cites several illuminating examples dating from the late 1980s and early 1990s, including that of a woman who presented to her doctor with fatigue and abdominal pains and was given a diagnosis of irritable bowel syndrome brought on by the stress of recently starting a new job. After returning to her GP on several occasions as her symptoms worsened, but not receiving further treatment or diagnosis, she eventually went to a hospital casualty department where a (female) doctor conducted a physical examination which revealed a tumour that turned out to be cancer of the colon. In another example, Goudsmit cites the cases of three women who were all diagnosed with 'hysterical hyperventilation' which turned out, only after requiring hospitalisation, to be diabetes.

In each of these cases, the assumption that the problem was psychological led to a failure to conduct a physical examination which put their lives at risk. Goudmsit also conducted an analysis of medical texts and found that women were 'often portrayed as weak, suggestible, emotionally unbalanced, irrational, manipulative and unable to cope with even relatively minor stress' (1994, 8). As she goes on to point out, in the literature she examined, there was no recognition that chronic physical symptoms can in turn 'undermine a woman's self-confidence and self-esteem and that this could also account for the raised scores in psychometric tests [conducted on women]. The literature simply didn't, and still doesn't, acknowledge the fact that emotional problems may often be the result, rather than the cause of certain [physical] conditions' (Goudsmit, 1994, 8).

It can, then, clearly be harmful, indeed life-threatening, to assume that women's health problems are mentally rather than physically based. It is equally problematic to assume that mental wellbeing problems which women may experience are the result of her individual personality traits – perhaps because she is a 'weak' woman (Goudsmit, 1994, 8), rather than resulting from her socio-economically and culturally located gendered positionality, or indeed resulting from the effects of a physical illness. In all of these possible scenarios, the underlying problem lies with particular perceptions of and constructions of women as gendered beings within wider gender regimes.

The perspective that constructions of women's gendered identities and the circumstances of women's lives can lead to mental ill health and that, moreover, psychiatric responses to such disorders can serve to reinforce and reproduce women's subordination finds support from a range of theorists (see, for example, Busfield, 1989; 1996; 2002; Women in Mind, 1986; Ehrenreich and English, 1979; Doyal and Elston, 1986). More recently, and possibly most notable within this field, is the work of Jane Ussher (see for example Ussher, 1991; 1997; 1999; 2000a; 2000b; 2000c; 2011). Ussher articulates, synthesises and extends the body of feminist work that has explored and critiqued the links between gender and mental health over the past few decades. As she states, while we must not 'deny the reality of women's experience of prolonged misery or distress, which undoubtedly exists…if we examine the roots of this distress in the context of women's lives, it can be conceptualised as *a reasonable response not a reflection of pathology within*' (Ussher, 2011, 1–2, emphasis added). Along similar lines, American psychologist Paula Caplan asks, '[do] we live in such a crazy-making, sick, impersonal society that it does serious psychological damage to half of us?… Should we be calling [women] the mentally ill…or society's wounded?' (Caplan, 1995, 6).

Much contemporary academic work in this field began to emerge in the early 1970s, an emergence that can be directly linked to the impacts of second wave feminism (Busfield, 1996, 1). Gove and Tudor (1973), for example, explored the relationship between women's mental health and marital status in the United States and found that married women experienced more mental health problems than their male counterparts. Along similar lines to Ann Oakley's arguments in her now famous mid-1970s 'Housework' research in the UK context, they argued that these problems were 'grounded in the lack of alternative gratification available to housewives; the low status of housework; the unstructured and invisible nature of housework; the poor conditions experienced by women in paid employment; and the conflicting role expectations faced by women' (Gove and Tudor, 1973, cited in Hockey, 1993, 251).

Over the past four decades a significant body of work has developed exploring the relationships between ill health, constructions of femininity and the socio-economic and cultural conditions of women's lives.[1] An obvious but important point to emerge from many of these writings and debates is that distinctions between illness, and behaviours associated with illness, are difficult to disentangle, but frequently gendered. Are new mothers, for example, who are diagnosed as suffering from post-natal depression, depressed because they are clinically ill or because they have undergone a major physical, emotional and social upheaval, feel overwhelmed, under-supported, and feel social and familial pressure to be the 'perfect mother'? As Hockey states, '[v]isiting the doctors may not necessarily reflect disease but rather the medicalisation of stresses women experience as a result of [social, cultural or material conditions]' (1993, 252). Conversely, as Goudsmit (1994) warns, it is equally problematic to assume that a woman visiting her GP with feelings of sadness, low self-esteem, fatigue and so on, are *not* physically ill, and to fail to consider that the physical illness and the bodily ill-health she is experiencing could have led to poorer mental wellbeing as a secondary illness.

What is clear is that the extent to which individual incidences of ill health are more or less physiologically or socially constructed is complex and this debate, to some extent, can serve to obscure the fundamental issues at play. The fact that women are more likely to experience poorer mental wellbeing than their male counterparts is not a random phenomenon or a coincidental correlation. Women's wellbeing is inextricably interrelated to the ways in which they experience their lives as gendered beings within specifically spatially and temporally located structural, symbolic and cultural frameworks – frameworks which, we suggest, can themselves be considered to be, at least to some extent, forms of violence (Bourdieu, 2001; Farmer, 2004). Thus, there is something fundamentally flawed about the ways in which women's gendered identity is constructed that means that they are more prone to mental illness, but that flaw lies not within women themselves but in the normative patriarchal constructions of their gendered beings: of femininity, women's roles, divisions of labour and their relative status in society.

Our research supports the conclusions of other authors, such as those cited above, that women's gendered roles and socio-cultural constructions of femininity can have a particularly negative impact on their mental wellbeing at points in their lives. This in turn is in line with the evidence that indicates that mental health issues appear to affect more women than men throughout the world. Nevertheless, an important factor to consider is that the differences in the extent of men's and women's mental health experiences may not be as marked as they at first appear. Statistics that tell us that women experience greater levels of mental health issues are largely based on the numbers of people *reporting* problems with mental wellbeing (which can be quantified), not the *actual* incidence of such issues (which cannot). In other words, those who do not report mental health issues or access formal sources of support or medical treatment are thus largely rendered statistically invisible. One could critique the nature of statistics themselves in that rather than providing 'objective' numerical data as many may surmise, statistics are socially constructed in as much as we often find what we set out to seek. The data we end up with depends on how that data has been collected and on the questions that were asked. As Reinharz explains:

> [d]espite the power and ubiquity of surveys and other forms of statistical research, feminists have also been critical of their use. One root of this criticism is hostility to statistics that are seen as part of patriarchal culture's monolithic definition of 'hard facts'…many factors, including gender, affect the respondents' answers [and] results of a survey hinge on the exact form a question takes. (Reinharz, 1992, 86–7)

Notwithstanding the need for a critical eye to be cast over statistical 'facts', we would concur that women tend to feel more able to access support and seek treatment than their male counterparts. This tendency is underpinned by socio-cultural factors fundamentally connected to constructions of our gendered identities. On the one hand, there continues to exist an underlying cultural belief that women *should* be both mentally and physically weaker than men, while on the other, women tend to be encouraged to form stronger social networks, and to talk more openly about their feelings. This can mean that women are better able to provide support networks to others, as described by Paula, whose friends and colleagues working in the voluntary and community sector recognised her symptoms of depression and assisted her in seeking help:

> 'Erm, but I think for…because…well, certainly in the women's services it's the case that people talk about things all the time, therefore there's always someone who's experienced it who can say to you, "Sounds to me like you're depressed" and understand and be sympathetic.' (Paula, early 50s, financial/community sector, Humberside)

The reasons men do not report or seek help for mental health issues to the same extent as women are also related to socio-cultural constructions of their gendered identities, and more specifically to cultural constructions of hegemonic masculinity.[2] Men are less likely to feel able to be open about their mental health problems – admitting to physiological problems may be difficult enough, unless they were incurred in an acceptably masculine arena such as in the workplace or on the sports field, but admitting to poor mental wellbeing might be perceived by some as demonstrating a level of weakness that no 'real man' would experience. This in turn perpetuates the feminisation of mental illness, both statistically and perceptually: it becomes a woman's problem, another illustration of why women are 'the weaker sex'. It also has a negative impact on men themselves, perpetuating the myth of the hegemonic male to which all men should aspire. It creates a cultural barrier for men who would benefit from social, emotional and medical support at times when they are experiencing poor mental wellbeing.

In sum, it is crucial to recognise that mental health issues have an impact on both women and men, but that women are more likely than men to seek support and medical treatment, and, significantly, are more likely to be offered medical treatment and to be labelled as having mental health problems. While calling for greater support and resources for women and men with mental wellbeing issues, the cultural construction of mental health as a feminised arena *per se* should be resisted. Rather, there is a need to have a wider understanding and acknowledgement, beyond the mental health profession, of the ways in which mental ill health is a condition of human society which is in turn fundamentally conditioned by the constructions of both men's and women's gendered identities into falsely immutable categories.

THREE

Gendering girls, gendering boys: identitics in process

Introduction

In this chapter we explore the ways in which our identities as gendered beings are forged during the early years of our lives. Working with data from the Yorkshire and Humber and drawing on the issue of son preference as an illustrative example, we consider the effect that growing up as a girl in particular gender regimes can have on women's sense of self. We touch on the classic nature–nurture debates to consider how perceived gender differences in our identities are constructed as products of biology or culture and the implications of these binaries for people's lives. We then return to themes developed in Chapter Two to make connections between constructions of femininities, women's identities and mental wellbeing. Drawing on a range of feminist theorists and at the same time keeping in mind the frame of symbolic and structural violence discussed in earlier chapters, we analyse the ways in which women internalise hegemonic codes of normative female embodiment and the impacts of doing so for women's sense of self.

Through these analyses we can see that women's gendered identities continue to be constructed, acquired and performed in ways that can render them more prone to mental ill-health in the broadest sense and that confidence and mental wellbeing are in themselves gendered issues rooted in processes of gendering in British society. The ways in which girls are gendered into being girls, and into becoming women, can have a significant impact on how they feel about themselves, their abilities and their rights to independent success in modern industrial society. One professional woman described being a woman as being:

> 'Never good enough [laughs], you're never a good enough mother, you're never a good enough cook or cleaner, you're never good enough at doing your job. I think being a woman is all about not being good enough, or maybe I'm just having a bad day, I don't know [laughs].' (Alice, late 30s, manager, education sector, volunteer, mother, West Yorkshire)

What is interesting to note here is the last sentence. Alice is an intelligent and highly accomplished woman who knows what she wants to say, and her message is powerful. But she ends by both trivialising and individualising her statement: 'maybe I'm just having a bad day, I don't know'. She then laughs at herself and in doing so she could be seen to undermine her assertion, almost deliberately casting doubt over her competency to make such a claim. Is this an example of lack of self-confidence, ultimately a lack of belief, however subconsciously, in her right to make such claims, even though these are claims she believes to be true? Or is it an example of a woman softening her message to render it less potentially objectionable in a society that, as she is aware, can be hostile to feminist analyses of women's lives? When Alice was asked how she might interpret the tag at the end of her statement, she said she had not realised what she had done, but upon reflection she felt both explanations held some truth. We found numerous examples of women undermining their own worth when we analysed the interviews. As Avril noted, commenting on how she thought women often underestimated their capabilities:

> 'A lot of women are very good at seeing the best in other people, but don't look in the mirror and see the best in themselves.' (Avril, early 40s, self-employed, mother, North Yorkshire)

Belinda, a successful executive, commenting on how she does not feel that she merits her success as represented by her earnings, said:

> 'I mean, I'm embarrassed by it sometimes. I sometimes think, "God, do they really pay me this much? I can't possibly be worth it".' (Belinda, mid-40s, manager, health sector, mother, South Yorkshire)

Processes of gendering are amorphous and manifest themselves in a variety of ways that are often difficult to fully define. Nevertheless, cultural messages about gendered expectations and norms of behaviour are ubiquitous, pervasive and deeply embedded into everyday imagery and imaginations. Helen O'Grady's (2005) work has significant resonance with our research and many of the women with whom we spoke when she talks about the links between women's association as carers, their secondary status and feelings of self-worth. She states that '[u]nsurprisingly, the lack of value and affirmation associated with the legacy of secondary status is likely to generate varying levels of self-doubt or a diminished sense of worth' (O'Grady, 2005, 2). Moreover, for O'Grady, a lack of balance between caring for others and caring for oneself can generate a need within feminised gendered beings to please and accommodate others which

> can render one vulnerable to feeling never quite good enough. These (and other) factors can contribute to women experiencing uneasy or conflictual relationships with themselves that often are characterized by feelings of inadequacy, guilt, shame or dislike. While the degree and intensity of such feelings is likely to vary both for individuals (according to personal experience) and among different groups of women (according to positions of privilege or disadvantage in terms of social relations of race, class, sexuality, health and so on), anecdotally the notion of uneasy self-relations resonates for women from a diverse range of backgrounds and experience. This suggests that even those in relatively advantageous positions are not immune to social processes which devalue and discount women's experience. In this light, the issue of women's self-relationship can be examined as an effect, albeit variable, of gender oppression. (O'Grady, 2005, 2)

To explore the processes of gender identity formation and specifically constructions of femininities, we also draw particularly on the work of American feminist philosopher, Diana Tietjens Meyers (2002) who articulates very well the position we take here. As she explains:

> What are generally taken to be facts about gender within a given culture are encoded in captivating figurations that condense complex behavioural and psychological imperatives into memorable, emotionally compelling forms. The culturally entrenched tropes, mythic tales, and pictorial images that depict women serve as a kind of shorthand in which group norms are crystallized and through which these norms become embedded…Indeed, it would not be inaccurate to say that these figurations *fossilize* gender norms in the geology of culture, for they integrate these norms into the corpus of common sense where they are protected from criticism…Mere social convention – normalized gender – is thus naturalized. (Meyers, 2002, 25, emphasis in original)

To consider the theoretical threads running through this book, we can see that Meyers' analysis here links well to Bourdieu's concept of symbolic violence as well as to the connections Showalter (1987) and Martin (1987) made in Chapter Two between representations of madness and constructions of femininity.

De Beauvoir famously said, 'one is not born, but, rather becomes, a woman. No biological, psychological, or economic fate determines the figure that the human female presents in society; it is civilization as a whole that produces this creature' (1997, 295 [1949]). Socio-cultural discourses around gender identity still have a tendency towards essentialism, however, and that which is 'natural' is proposed to be and can be perceived as immutable, unchanging (for further analysis see, for example, Wittig, 1981; Alsop et al, 2002; Fine, 2010). While most of us probably understand, at some level at least, that this is not true – we can see how what it means to be masculine and feminine varies, shifts and changes through both time and space – these are nevertheless powerful discourses that become deeply embedded in our psyches (Billington et al, 1998). We are of course not suggesting that our gender identities are merely imposed upon us, that we are agentless receptacles of identity. Nor are we entirely 'docile bodies' (Foucault, 1979, 138). As Shilling states, 'bodies are highly malleable phenomena which can be invested with various and changing forms of power' (1993, 79). We are constantly and actively doing and performing, creating and recreating our gender identities (Bradley, 2013, 23; see also, for example, Butler, 1990; Moi, 1991; 1999; Alsop et al, 2002; Wharton, 2005; Connell, 2009).

That we have degrees of agency does not mean, however, that we can choose our identities at will, we are all simultaneously subject to powerful processes of gendering, and girls and boys begin to learn what is expected of them as gendered beings from the moment they arrive in the world. This 'learning' takes place in a variety of socio-cultural settings and institutions throughout their lives, including within educational settings, in the workplace, through the media and through governmental policy and legislation (Charles, 2002; Richardson, 2008). Initially, however, the family and early years care environment is the primary site of gendering. The ways in which young children develop into gendered beings is all too apparent for those who care for them, as these nursery officers explained:

> 'They learn gendered behaviour, the way they're dressed. We put some pink clothes on a boy and a colleague said they looked girly. Some parents don't like them dressing in girly clothes.'

'There's a difference in behaviour, boys like Spiderman, Batman and cars and get rough with each other, fighting like the baddies. Girls like the role play area and read books but a few do play with boys.'

'The TV and media is the main influence, and what parents choose to let them watch.'

'They learn it from each other, the toddlers copy the pre-schoolers, you see their personalities develop just before two years.'

(Nursery Officers' Focus Group, East Yorkshire)

While these nursery officers are talking here about gender differences they see as learned, differences that we perceive between girls and boys from an early age are often ascribed to biology – naturalised – by parents, professionals and society at large. When considering the age-old nature–nurture debate, however, a critical point to make is that we cannot know to what extent nature or nurture play their parts. We are not born into a vacuum, we are born into a culture and so the biological and the cultural can never be wholly separated. We become gendered beings even prior to the point of birth. As soon as a woman becomes pregnant, in the context of a wanted pregnancy at least, a common early question posed is if they know if it is a boy or a girl. This knowledge then tends to structure the ways in which the pre-birth environment becomes a gendered space – affecting the choice of nursery colours, comments about the size and shape of the bump, gifts bought prior to the birth and so on. For many people it can be quite disturbing if they do not know the sex of the child, especially once the baby is born. We look for gendered cues, codes that we can read to assume the gender of the baby, and if we find these are unclear or misleading, this can be a particularly problematic and destabilising experience for many people.

Consider the international furore, anger and outrage that appears to meet any public decision *not* to reveal a child's gender identity. Take, for example, the Canadian couple who in 2011 refused to say whether their baby was a boy or a girl. They were not the first to do so, but the responses they encountered were fairly typical. The first point of note is that their decision was deemed to be newsworthy not merely in their home town, not merely within their own country, but it made international headlines and sparked numerous debates and discussions the world over. This in itself can be a good thing of course, and part of the point no doubt was to raise awareness of taken-for-granted gender stereotypes. The global reactions they faced, however, were often vitriolic, with accusations that their behaviour was almost akin to abuse simply for expressing a desire to attempt to counter gender stereotyping for their own child.

The *Daily Mail*, for example, expressed concern for the child's wellbeing and safety, reporting the story under the headline, 'The baby who is neither boy nor girl: as gender experiment provokes outrage, what about the poor child's future?' (Leonard, 2011). Their response was fairly typical of the tabloid reaction, as was the case they made against the parents. Treating us to the wisdom of not one but two 'leading' American male child psychiatrists, they cited Dr Eugene Bernstein who warned of the grave dangers of such an irresponsible experiment: 'To raise a child not as a boy or a girl is creating, in some sense, a freak. It sets them up for not knowing who they are'. The second expert, Dr Harold Koplewicz, 'said he was "disturbed" that well-meaning parents could be so misguided' (Leonard, 2011).

The online public comments following the *Mail*'s article variously described the parents in question as 'obnoxious', 'beyond stupid', 'crazy', and 'weird', only one (Nina from Australia) said that they initially thought that they were 'crackers' but then thought that something about it made sense because, '[i]t is interesting how freaked people are about not knowing the baby's gender' (Leonard, 2011). Nina makes the point we also want to make. What this story illustrates is how disruptive and disturbing so many people find any challenge to their normative gender order. It is apparently so challenging that it provokes frightening levels of anger and vitriol. One might think the parents had proposed that they wanted to dangle their baby from the top of a skyscraper rather than try and raise a child in a loving home without enforcing normative gender roles.

What the above case also highlights is that in many families traditional gender norms are largely assumed, accepted and underpinned by culture. Many of us are raised within some form of family, and although the composition of that family may be diverse, this combination of familial and cultural messages inculcates children, not always consciously, into the dominant modes of femininity and masculinity. Even those families who consciously attempt to reject the dominant gender stereotypes for their children are faced with powerful forces embedded deeply both within themselves, as similarly gendered beings, and within the society in which they are located to the extent that girls and boys 'are often inducted into cultural expectations – their attitudes and behaviour shaped – despite explicit instruction and parental role models to the contrary. Many parents who try to raise children in non-sexist ways are defeated by cultural influences that they are not conscious of and that consequently they cannot counteract' (Meyers, 2002, 26).

To return to our earlier statement: we cannot fully understand what is 'nature' and what is 'culture' because the 'biological' body is so completely subsumed into culture even before we have taken our first breath. The first critical point to make here is that what is really significant is not so much to what extent something is a product of the biological one or the cultural other but rather to understand that even the one can change. In other words, the biological is not in fact essential or immutable as we are so often led to believe. As human beings, we are no longer, if we ever were, confined by our 'biology'. We have developed the capacity to change and manipulate a great deal of that which we perceive as biological: our bodies are malleable, even processes of reproduction can be decoupled from the body. As that is the case, then arguments for the immutability of nature as justification for gender divisions, differences and discrimination collapse like a house of cards.

The second key point we want to make is that what actually matters are the values placed on gender differences – whether they are perceived as products of nature or nurture. To put it crudely, let us say for the sake of argument that men are perceived to be *naturally* good at housework, attributed to the dexterous and strong hands they are all born with which are perfect for manoeuvring those vacuums around tight corners. Apart from being simply untrue (which is beside the point we are making here), this biological 'fact' is meaningless in and of itself until it is placed into a cultural context: how this skill is perceived and the status attributed to it are *social* constructs. We would suggest that if the above scenario were the case in our gender regime, housework would have a rather higher status than it currently commands. We choose – in particular socio-cultural contexts, variable through time and space – to elevate or demean a skill, an attribute, a behaviour, regardless of its perceived origin, just as we choose to place certain status on some people, roles, behaviours over others.

'Boys are better than girls': the costs of son preference

One illustration of the above discussion is the phenomenon of son preference. While the valorisation of boys may have declined, at least explicitly, in the UK in recent years, that is not the case in many contexts. In some families there may still be a belief that a boy child is more culturally and economically valuable to a family than a girl child. We would suggest that son preference continues to exist in all countries to greater or lesser degrees, although it is certainly more easily identifiable in some parts of the world than others. We should take care, however, to note that the very visibility of more extreme cases of gender discrimination globally serves to conceal and obfuscate the more insidious but persistent inequalities in the UK.

At the most extreme end of the spectrum, the valorisation of boys has a literally deadly impact on the life chances of girl children across the world. In countries where there is a marked cultural preference for boys, sex selection of unborn foetuses means that girl babies are being aborted in their thousands every year. Combined with female infanticide and other deaths as a result of neglect of girl children, this has led to a marked gender imbalance in the populations of some countries (Momsen, 2010). In India, for example, it has been calculated that there are an estimated 23 million 'missing' females and in China the estimate is 30 million. Across the rest of world it has been estimated that 40 million women and girls are 'missing' (Seager, 2006, 40). As Seager explains:

> Son preference reflects the combined forces of economics, culture and religion. As smaller families become the norm, evidence suggests that the pressure to have sons accelerates. Girls are widely considered to have a lower socio–economic value than boys – a view often strengthened by marriage, dowry and inheritance practices. Son preference used to be thought of as a practice of the poor, but evidence suggests the opposite – increasing affluence magnifies perceptions of the greater worth of boys. (Seager, 2006, 40)

In the UK, certain cultural and legal traditions formally discriminating against women have, at least since the late nineteenth and early twentieth centuries, thankfully largely been relegated to history. Women in Britain are, for example, no longer legal property of and subject to the rule of their fathers and, subsequently, husbands. Women can now apply for divorce, have rights over their children, earn an independent living, own and inherit property in their own names and, of course, have the right to vote. In 1848, Elizabeth Cady Stanton wrote the following 'Declaration' for the first Women's Rights Convention in the USA. In it she sets out the ways in which women were treated by men at the time:

He has never permitted her to exercise her inalienable right to the elective franchize. He has made her, if married, civilly dead. He has taken from her all right in property, even to the wage she earns…becoming to all intents and purposes her master. He has so framed the laws of divorce…as to be wholly regardless of the happiness of women. He has monopolized nearly all the profitable employments. He has denied her the facilities for obtaining a thorough education. He has created a false public sentiment by giving to the world a different code of morals for men and women. (Cited in Miles, 1989, 223)

Nevertheless, while legal barriers to equality in both US and British society have largely been overturned, cultural norms live on which can convey the message to women that, as the poet Samuel Coleridge (1772–1834) wrote to his wife Sara: 'In Sex, Acquirements, and in the quantity and quality of natural endowments whether of Feeling or Intellect, you are the Inferior' (cited in Miles, 1989, 221). These cultural norms are, however, dissipating and rigid gender roles and expectations are becoming increasingly malleable. In a focus group discussion, a group of retired women, the eldest being 93, reflected on their experiences of the domestic divisions of labour:

'Mothers took responsibility for the house.'

'When I was ill one time my husband helped at home, wanted to be involved and actually baked a cake to take to the hospital and kept the house clean while I was in hospital once.'

'Father couldn't make tea.'

'My father used to check that the dusting had been done when he came home from work.'

'You had to have the meals ready, fire in hearth and Mother should be there to greet Father after work. Father only saw the children Saturday afternoon and Sunday, but he was in control.'

(Retired Women's Focus Group, West Yorkshire)

As discussed in more detail in Chapter Six, however, while such stereotypical divisions of labour and overt displays of masculine domination or symbolic violence (Bourdieu, 2001) may have become more flexible in recent years, they have by no means disappeared. In the survey data we asked who took prime responsibility for caring for, or arranging care for family members. A total of 273 women completed the questionnaire, 159 of whom answered this specific question: 67 per cent either agreed (26 per cent) or strongly agreed (41 per cent) that they took prime responsibility for caring for, or arranging care for family members. Of the 41 respondents who identified as male, 22 answered this question, of whom two agreed or strongly agreed that they took prime responsibility for caring for or arranging care for family members. When asked approximately what percentage of housework they believed they contributed to the household, of the 133 women who responded to this question, 88 per cent said they did more than 50 per cent of this work and 50 per cent said they did 75 per cent or more of this work. These trends echo findings of previous studies (see, for example, Oakley, 1974; Hochschild, 1990; Pilcher, 2000; Crompton et al, 2005; Gershuny et al, 2006) and were strongly underpinned by the qualitative data, as the following notes taken of the discussion during a focus group of women in their 20s and 30s illustrate:

> 'Women still have to do all or at least the majority of the housework. Many men don't help at all with anything around the house (it was noted that this does not apply to all men)…Jealousy if woman earns more – can lead to men losing self-esteem – could lead to arguments and domestic violence…One participant noted that men still often have unfair/unequal attitudes towards women's leisure time, for example, her male partner would complain if she went out after work to socialise, he would say, "But I haven't seen you all week." Now he goes out to work he often goes to the pub to socialise stating, "Well, I have been working all week, I deserve to go out and have a break."' (Focus Group Notes, Women users of community and voluntary services, Humberside)

Similarly, in focus group discussions with 16 women and men in their late teens studying for A levels, the majority said that women did most of the reproductive work in their own families and that they believed that it was easier to be male because there were fewer responsibilities, they usually earned more and had a higher status. Nevertheless they all expected to marry and have children in the future, although the women consciously understood that this would probably have a negative impact on their careers, which most of them expected to pursue in addition to their mothering roles.

While gendered divisions of labour, stereotypes and processes of gendering continue to be manifest today, as we can see, there have nevertheless been some positive shifts in cultural attitudes. Focusing, for example, on the institution of marriage, the cultural and symbolic practice of paternal ownership is repeated thousands of times every year across the UK as the father of the bride 'gives his daughter away' to the groom during a ceremony which commonly ends with her giving up her name and taking that of her husband. It is less common today, however, for the bride's father to be expected to pay for the wedding – a form of dowry – or for the bride to promise to 'honour and obey' her husband during the wedding vows. Indeed, though still relatively uncommon, it is no longer such a cause for scandal for a woman to retain her own surname rather than take that of her husband, and families are less likely to express a need to 'keep trying for a boy' if their first offspring are girls.

Nevertheless, an underlying, insidious but pervasive valorisation of boys and men continues to exist in Britain today, and this was something about which the women with whom we spoke were very much aware. One female professor of natural sciences told us recently, for example, that never mind any discrimination she may have encountered in the highly male dominated world she inhabited at work, even her own children did not believe she was a 'real' professor, and certainly not a professor of 'real' hard sciences, preferring to believe their father to have the senior professional role (which is not the case) rather than their rare and amazing mother.

Many women articulated that this male valorisation both within their family lives and beyond has a significant part to play in girl's identity formation and self-esteem. They felt that boys were still (despite any evidence to the contrary) assumed or expected to be, for example, more intelligent, better at sports, better able to negotiate the public arena, more confident, that boys' games are more exciting, that boys' subjects were better, harder and had a greater value, and that eventually their careers are more important. Inevitably these deep-rooted beliefs learned as children continue to have a significant impact on women's self-esteem. Alice, for example, describes how her father's preference for her brother affected her as a child and also continues to affect her understandings of her achievements today:

'I just always knew that my brother was cleverer than me, which is absolutely not true at all, um, as it's transpired [laughs], but it was always assumed that he would be cleverer than me. And also *my dad* had a very strong…he always tried to make it into a bit of a joke, but it wasn't a joke, *we had* a very strong attitude that sciences were boys' subjects and they were the only subjects that were taken seriously. And, everything that I did was waffle.' (Alice, late 30s, manager, education sector, volunteer, mother, West Yorkshire, emphasis added)

We highlight something of particular note in Alice's discourse here. Notice how she unconsciously slips from the views she attributes to her father and the views that suddenly in the space of a line become those of the whole family? We say this was unconscious because we asked Alice about this and she was quite surprised and not a little perturbed by what she had done. Her father's opinion *becomes* the opinion of the household, is the *only* opinion that counts, at such a deep level for Alice that she unconsciously slips between one and the other in recounting her childhood memories. This is an interesting illustration of these amorphous processes of gendering at work, and how their effects remain deep within us throughout our lives.

In addition, women noted that girls may learn that boys are not expected to help around the house to the same extent as girls tend to be. They also noted that the chores that boys are expected to do are different to the chores girls are expected to do, and that these gender divisions of labour command differential status. To illustrate this we can offer a possible scenario which is based on several women's reported experiences of growing up. Many girls are expected to clean inside the house, usually helping their mothers with housework, but may not be called upon, at least not as often, to help with certain kinds of work outside the house. Their brothers are more likely to be condoned for not helping with domestic labour inside the home but may be expected to help, usually their fathers, with chores outside the house, for example, washing the car. They may (as several women reported to us) get paid extra pocket money for this external labour.

What is a girl to learn from this scenario? She could learn that cleaning the house is a woman's responsibility but does not have monetary value, whereas washing the car is male work that deserves payment. She can also learn from this that the private space is where girls belong and the outside public arena is where boys belong. This plants a seed of understanding, however subconsciously, that certain kinds of work are associated with women, and that these do not have the same value placed on them as work associated with being a man. It is this kind of gradual inculcation of gendered values that we refer to as processes of gendering or gender socialisation (Bradley, 2013). These messages are not always consistent, and can appear to be contradictory, but the underlying effect remains, as Wendy articulates:

> 'Some of the messages I remember are my mother going back to work when I was about 12 and saying that she'd got this job at a local estate agent and the salary was "OK for a woman." I do remember asking her, I must have been about six, whether men were more intelligent than women because men were the ones that went out to work and she was horrified and said, "Absolutely not and you can do whatever you want to do," [but] there were the mixed messages about you can do whatever you want but this job's okay for me because I'm a woman and I accept that I'll be paid less, so it gave me a lot to think about…the gender roles were very defined between my mother and my father, she stayed at home, looked after the house, he went out to work, then she went back to work when my brother was well established at junior school, so that was fairly traditional.' (Wendy, late 30s, manager, community sector, volunteer, Humberside)

Wendy went on to explain that had she been born and raised male she thinks she would have experienced life differently:

> '[I] certainly would have, perhaps approached the world with a different level of confidence in my early years because of those reinforcing messages that boys get about "they can do anything, they can be anything, whatever they do is okay", you know, within certain limits, whereas as a woman, or a young woman, I think I got a lot of messages about "this isn't good enough, the way you look is more important really than what you do academically and what job you get" and I remember…at some point in my early twenties my mother said "I'd be happy if you had a job in Woolworths as long as" the underlying message was "as long as you were straight and you were thin" and I obviously didn't respond very well to that.' (Wendy, late 30s, manager, community sector, volunteer, Humberside)

Rosalind worked for over 20 years as a secondary school teacher in West Yorkshire, and now works as a self-employed painter and joiner. Having worked in a school for many years, she was fully aware of the power of gender stereotyping and the socialisation of young people into normative gender identities. She was also concerned about girls' levels of confidence in their own abilities:

> 'But it does strike me that women's confidence isn't any better in general…Aspiring to feeling able to be who they are. Er, I'm not even talking about aspiring to have certain status jobs but to feel okay about who they are. And, er, you know, whether it's their own physical image or the choice to be a mother or not to be a mother or to be a high flying financial consultant.' (Rosalind, early 50s, self-employed, non-traditional sector, West Yorkshire)

Gender, power and women's mental health

For Rosalind, women's levels of confidence have not appeared to improve in recent years despite popular notions that we now live in an egalitarian society. Linking directly here to themes developed in Chapter Two, that women continue to feel under-confident today, becomes all the more understandable, however, when we realise how long women have not just been told but also socialised into becoming the 'weaker sex'. As we have seen, connections between women and 'madness' have a long history. Women in western cultures have been construed as mentally fragile and prone to invalidity at least since around 400BC when Hippocrates developed the idea of women being biologically prone to 'hysteria' (meaning 'of the womb'). In more recent times, such notions were prevalent in the nineteenth century when gender roles and expectations, especially during the Victorian period, were particularly repressive for women (Ussher, 1991; Frick, 2002).

The links between psychiatry, constructions of mental illness and norms of femininity have been further analysed within feminist frameworks over the past three decades. Chesler (1972) did much to initiate and develop these ideas, arguing that the ways 'madness' is conceived maps onto normative constructions of femininity: in other words, all women could be construed as fitting the profile of mental illness. As Hockey explains:

> [t]he apparently ungendered profile of madness – passivity, emotionality, irrationality, dependency, lack of initiative, and need for support – is…also a profile of a 'normal' woman… Thus women are socialised into behaviour which, in men, would be categorised as mental illness. In effect, women are placed in a double bind in relation to psychiatry. Not only is madness a particularly extreme manifestation of the behaviour expected of a 'normal' woman, but women who display independence or an aggressive resistance to their social roles also risk receiving a psychiatric label. (Hockey, 1993, 254–5)

In line with feminist debates in the field, Sally, a health professional in a mental health unit, based on her professional experience, strongly believes 'gender to be a massively relevant factor within mental health'. She feels that for many of the women she treats 'a lot of the problems and distress they have in their lives are very much associated with their gender'. Sally believes that lack of confidence and poor mental wellbeing is linked to women's gender roles, power and women's socially ascribed and acquired roles as carers, as she explains:

> 'Women quite often feel that they have no control over anything and that they have no right to make decisions about anything and that they have no confidence to do anything or to make changes in their life or to get anywhere they want to and I think the gender role socialisation plays a massive part, as in, "My job here on earth is to care for other people and I'm not allowed to think about myself, I'm not allowed to prioritise what I need" and that they feel selfish if they do not do that…The socialisation of women as carers seems to go across all classes, ethnicities and ages and this idea that things are supposed to be better for women nowadays, I don't think it seems to be any less for younger women than older women.' (Sally, late 30s, manager, health sector, volunteer, West Yorkshire)

For Tanya, feeling she was not in control of her life and being brought up in a family context in which she felt undervalued has had a chronic impact on her mental wellbeing and on her subsequent choices of paid employment. She has self-harmed in the past and has suffered from panic attacks for many years, both problems she perceives as having their roots in her relationship with her father and subsequently with her husband, both of whom she feels undermined her self-esteem:

> 'So it was just like that, a downward spiral, and I ended up on tranquillisers, because they used to give them out quite freely then…I was borderline anorexic, and it's what they say, they say if you could actually talk to girls who self-harm and girls who diet, it's just control, you've just no control, nobody asked me what I thought, nobody looked at my life and thought, "Oh, my god"…I take it right back to my childhood, you know, "You'll never be anything, you'll never be anybody," it's just dogged me all the time, and then [husband] being like he was and I just actually got worse, which is probably why I've never got a better job because I think I'd be too terrified, there's been chances but there's always been good reason…but I actually take the bull by the horns now in these last two, three years, I still think I'm hiding in the job that I do, that took me a long time but I've been hiding there for maybe four years but I'm ready [to move on].' (Tanya, late 40s, part-time carer, mother, Humberside)

Both Sally, in her professional capacity, and Tanya's life experiences indicate the ways in which women's social roles and gendered power relations in society can have an impact on women's sense of mental wellbeing. Sally and Tanya are in good company; as we have demonstrated above, such experiences have a long history.

Gendering women: constructions of women's identities

> Does anyone know what the authentic voice of woman is?…The problem is, I suppose, that women have never been left alone to be themselves and to find out for themselves. (Jong, 1998, 44)

Here Jong talks about the myths women are told, about who they are and how they should behave, that are in themselves ways of controlling women's lives. She argues that these myths serve to prevent women from realising their own strengths, to obfuscate women's sense of self:

We were told we were weak; yet as we grew older, we increasingly knew that we were strong. We were told that men loved us for our dependency; yet as we grew older, we observed that, despite themselves, they loved us for our independence – and if they didn't, we found that we didn't always care. We found we could grow only by loving ourselves a little, and loving our strengths, and so, paradoxically, we found we could grow up only by doing the opposite of all the things our culture told us to do. We were told our charm lay in weakness, yet in order to survive, we had to be strong. We were told we were by nature indecisive, yet our survival often seemed to depend on our own decisions. We were told that certain mythic definitions of women were immutable, natural laws, biological 'facts', but often our very endurance depended upon changing those supposedly unchangeable things. (Jong, 1998, 44)

What we are suggesting is that there continues to be something more specific (and problematic) about the ways in which femininity is constructed in our society that leaves women in particular more prone to lower self-esteem and mental wellbeing issues than men. Of course, normative constructions of masculinities are also problematic, and much has been written about the problem of normative constructions of masculinities elsewhere (see, for example, Haddad, 1993; Glover and Kaplan, 2000; Alsop et al, 2002; Connell, 1995, 2000, 2005; Whitehead and Barrett, 2001; Whitehead, 2002; Connell and Messerschmidt, 2005).

Our theoretical standpoint here can be summarised by drawing again on the work of Meyers (2002) who rejects a false universalism of women's gender identity, but at the same time argues that to sever identity from gender is also a mistake. Rather, she argues that 'gender is internalized and does become a dimension of women's identities' (2002, 4). For Meyers, we develop simultaneously gendered and individualistic identities. While we are not passive victims of gendering, nevertheless '[g]ender worms its way into identity in ways that we may not be conscious of and in ways that we may not be able to change no matter how we try' (2002, 7). Gender also intersects with and cannot be extrapolated from other indices of difference such as ethnicity, age, sexuality and so on, a point Lawler makes clearly when she explains:

No one has only one identity, in the sense that everyone must, consciously or not, identify with more than one group, one identity. This is about more than combining multiple identities in an 'additive' way…identities impact on each other…race, gender and the rest interact…Different forms of identity, then, should be seen as interactive and mutually constitutive [and] dynamic. (Lawler, 2008, 3)

Just as we need to understand the impacts of intersectionality on identities, we must also not lose sight of the material impacts of patriarchy on gendered identities. However, to acknowledge and understand how identities can be constructed and experienced within particular gender regimes is not to dismiss the importance of individual difference and agency within those processes. As Meyers states, although '[t]hat women's identities are gendered in patriarchal cultures does impede women's ability to function as self-determining agents… subordination is internalized and becomes integral to individualized, subordinated identities' (2002, 5–6). Nevertheless, while 'gender does not exhaust any woman's identity and sense of self. Still…gender is constitutive of who we are – our personalities, our capabilities and liabilities, our aspirations, and how we feel about all of these dimensions of identity' (Meyers, 2002, 10). In this way, Meyers criticises those, particularly poststructuralist or postmodern, analyses of gender identity construction which she argues can appear to trivialise or fail to clearly acknowledge the materiality of the impacts of those identities on women's and men's lives. She is critical in particular of theorists such as Butler who, she argues, appear to suggest that one's gender identity can be cast on and off almost at will.

Meyers (2002, 8) points to Sandra Bartkey's essays on women's bodily self-discipline as significant in the literature exploring internalised oppression. Bartkey (1990) analyses the ways in which women internalise hegemonic codes of normative female embodiment through which notions of inferiority, objectification and subordinated value and desire are also simultaneously incorporated. For Bartkey, the result is that women are, ironically, led to feel competent and empowered by the very skills that reinforce their subordination. Bartkey points to the perpetual socio-cultural pressures placed on women to manage their bodies through, for example, constant dieting, controlling their movement and posture, covering their skin with make-up, eradicating body hair and so on, all of which serves to ensure that we are effective and disciplined performers of normative femininity. As Bartkey points out, however, we are playing a rigged game, for while an undisciplined female body is deficient, unruly and liable to sanction, a properly disciplined female body is a body with 'an inferior status inscribed' upon it (Barkey, 1990, 71 cited in Meyers, 2002, 8). Women who play the game well and adhere to a hegemonic feminine stereotype, rather than being praised for following the rules of the game, can find themselves ridiculed for their 'obsession' with clothes, makeup and other 'trivial' details of appearance (Bartkey, 1990, 70–3 cited in Meyers, 2002, 8).

A British television programme aired since 2008, ongoing in 2014 and running to six series unfortunately comes to mind here. Called 'Snog Marry Avoid?' (Remarkable Television, BBC 3, 2008–present), the premise is that women put themselves forward for scrutiny by selected young male judges – an overtly 'male gaze' to cite Mulvey (1975) – via a pseudo computer generated female host (the Personal Overhaul Device or POD). Purely on the basis of their appearance, these selected young men decide if they would 'snog' (kiss), marry or avoid the 'exhibits' as the title suggests. In this game, those women who are judged as too overtly 'feminine' – what might be described as caricatures of 'sexy' women (who might now be insultingly referred to as 'Chav-sexy': maybe their dress is too tight, their skirt too short, their make-up slightly too thick) – tend to be told they would be either 'snogged' or 'avoided', but not 'married' – which is assumed to be the ultimate goal.

They are then given a 'makeunder' to render them more acceptable for marriage, which tends to involve toning down any excesses of 'gaudiness'. Of course this performance is explicitly charged with multiple intersections of identity-based discrimination, not least on the basis of gender, class and sexuality (Skeggs, 1997; Lawler, 2005; Clisby, 2009). 'Snog Marry Avoid?' is a contemporary carnivalesque personification of the abjection of women who have tried too hard to play the game of hegemonic femininity. Women who may be deemed to be the wrong class, body shape, age or colour are placed on stage in a carnivalesque performance of the female grotesque, and as Russo has argued:

> an examination of the materials of carnival can also recall limitations, defeats, and indifferences generated by carnival's complicitous place in dominant culture…a redeployment of taboos around the female body as grotesque (the pregnant body, the ageing body, the irregular body) and as unruly when set loose in the public sphere. (Russo, 1995, 56 cited in Clisby, 2009, 55)

This may seem an extreme example, but that it has run for six years on mainstream television could suggest otherwise. For many women the dutiful performance of femininity is so effectively policed because

what they are doing and what they are making themselves
into seems entirely voluntary and natural. Indeed, when
feminists criticize these practices and urge women to
abandon them, most women give this suggestion a chilly
reception. [However,] [w]omen's reluctance to forgo
feminine self-discipline is not merely a result of the negative
sanctions women can anticipate. It also stems from the
embeddedness of the aesthetic of feminine beauty and
the routines of self-beautification in women's identities.
(Meyers, 2002, 9, drawing on Bartkey, 1990, 77)

As Meyers warns, however, we should not fall into the trap of inferring
from this that gender is some kind of 'toxic capsule' that we 'swallow
whole' (2002, 11). We see far too much diversity of experience of
genders for this to hold true, but at the same time we should not assume
that social and economic systems of constraints and rewards do not
influence individual identity, for, as she concludes:

The seeming naturalness of enacting gendered characteristics,
the passion with which people cling to their sense of their
own gender, and the intractability of many gendered
attributes when people seek to change them testify to the
embeddedness of gender identity. (Meyers, 2002, 11)

As explored in the previous chapter, there is a relatively long history
of similar arguments and over the past few decades in particular, a
significant body of work has developed exploring the relationships
between ill-health, constructions of femininity and socio-economic
and cultural conditions of women's lives. We are aware of these issues,
however, for all our knowing we have as yet failed to effect significant
change in dominant processes of gendering.

Moira Gatens (1996, 5) makes a similar point in her work on
'imaginary bodies' in which she is 'concerned with the (often
unconscious) imaginaries of a specific culture; those ready-made
images and symbols through which we make sense of social bodies
and which determine, in part, their value, their status and what will
be deemed their appropriate treatment'. Gatens (1996) suggests, even
if we are aware of the negativity of messages we hear about ourselves
and know that we should not believe them, processes of gendering still
have an impact on us precisely because, as Bourdieu (2001) has also
articulated, they are internalised in and through our bodies. In other

words we can simultaneously know we are not stupid, fat or ugly, but may at times feel stupid, fat and ugly nonetheless.

Thus even if we did see the kind of action needed to challenge and address the gendered dimensions of mental wellbeing through such things as enhanced service provision, this may do little to tackle a fundamental causal factor. Although policy reform can attempt to address functional issues of mental health, what our research suggests is that, for many women, their experience of mental ill health continues to be affected by deeply rooted socio-cultural identity constructions from an early age and throughout their lives in ways that are complex, difficult to quantify, embedded within and embodied in everyday gendered practices and experiences that cut across age and class differences.

To summarise, we argue that the ways in which women's gendered identities continue to be constructed, acquired and performed leaves them more prone to mental ill health in the broadest sense. The flaw, however, lies not with individual women but in the continued and pervasive normatively enforced patriarchal constructions of their gendered beings. So, while we are by no means claiming that the links between constructions of femininities and poorer mental wellbeing have not been made before, what we are saying is that this issue continues to be both pervasive and problematic – which in itself requires further analysis and discussion rather than acceptance. As Rosalind said:

> 'For all that we're supposed to be in the post-feminist era I'm not really sure that… It's almost not talked about these days…It's all taken for granted…we live in this egalitarian society now. And yet if you go into Toys R Us it [is] all still pink and blue, all still little vacuum cleaners…But it does strike me that women's confidence isn't any better in general.' (Rosalind, early 50s, self-employed, non-traditional sector, West Yorkshire)

FOUR

Gendering and engendering violence in women's everyday lives

'She was becoming really successful, you know, and then when she was getting too advanced for herself I suppose, then he would bring her back down sort of thing, you know, on the end of a fist, and eventually she did actually divorce him, but the damage was done, and even when she'd got a divorce he was being real nice and persuaded her to give him a lift home and by the end of the street he'd smashed her face.' (Octavia, mid-40s, volunteer, mother, Humberside)

Introduction

Gender-based violence (GBV), a broad term that includes violence against women and girls (VAWG), domestic abuse, or intimate partner violence and sexual violence,[1] has profound and complex effects on women's mental wellbeing in ways that can seriously affect them for the rest of their lives. The seriousness of the impacts makes the prevalence of such violence all the more alarming. Beginning with the narratives of women who participated in this study, this chapter explores some key experiences, issues and concepts concerning gender-based violence and violence against women and girls. We locate and contextualise the issues within both UK and international contexts, providing a brief statistical and policy overview in the UK context and consider responses to GBV within the international arena.

One key theoretical point we want to make in this chapter is that gender-based violence should be located along a broad, socio-culturally entrenched continuum of violence against women and girls, men and boys. Violence is so embedded within our cultural productions of masculinities and femininities that experiencing some form of GBV – be that through sexually objectifying images, sexual harassment, physical or emotional violence – is almost an ordinary – the mundane – rather than extraordinary life experience for many women and men in our society. Even the most extreme forms of GBV, such as violence arising within contexts of conflict, civil war, repression or revolution should also be seen as part of spatially and temporally contextual processes of gendering along a continuum of what we might call normative gender-based violence.

As such, any efforts to address GBV can only do so effectively, and sustainably, if that violence is viewed as arising from and fundamentally part of normative processes of gendering and gender relations in a given socio-cultural context. This calls for the clear location of these processes in the socio-economic, political and policy contexts of given gender regimes. Hearn and McKie call, for example, for a gender analysis of policy, arguing that 'it is necessary in policy analysis and development, and especially that on violence, to examine the assumptions that sustain gendered inequalities and gendered hierarchical processes' (2008, 75). In this way, a gender analysis of violence facilitates a greater understanding of the contexts of violence against women, men, girls and boys in ways that locate the extraordinary within the ordinary lived realities of people's everyday lives along a continuum of gendered experience.

Here we return to the framework we set out in Chapter One: that of the triad of violence played out along a long continuum. We can see how Bourdieu's 'symbolic violence, a gentle violence, imperceptible and invisible even to its victims, exerted for the most part through the purely symbolic channels of communication and cognition (more precisely misrecognition), recognition, or even feeling' (Bourdieu, 2001, 1–2), works alongside Farmer's use of the concept of structural violence, which he describes as the

> violence of 'sinful' structures characterized by poverty and steep grades of social inequality, including racism and gender inequality…In short, the concept of structural violence is intended to inform the study of the social machinery of oppression. Oppression is a result of many conditions, not least of which reside in the consciousness. (Farmer, 2004, 307)

Located within this framework we can also see how GBV provides a clear illustration of the ways in which processes of gendering can not only enact gentle, symbolic violence against us but also literal, physical, visceral violence, and moreover, that both are at opposing ends of the same unbroken continuum. This continuum can in turn be located within a broader frame of structural, and indeed infrastructural, violence that is manifest, yet not always easily identified, within particular gendered and social regimes. These symbolic, structural and visceral forms of violence create a powerful triad within which processes of gendering are informed and experienced.

A second key point to make is that this chapter arises from women's experiences as they recounted these to us in this research. We did not set out to ask about violence in our study. Rather the issue of domestic and sexual abuse emerged through women's narratives of their lives spontaneously. Approximately a quarter of the women we spoke with talked about some forms of violence which they had experienced during their lifecourse, and how these experiences of GBV had had an impact on their sense of self-esteem and mental wellbeing as well as having direct material impacts on their lives. Had we set out to focus on violence – had we explicitly asked women about their experiences of violence – we have no doubt that the numbers of women talking about their experiences of GBV would have been higher.

A third key point, as we argue throughout this book, is that women are aware of forms of gender-based subordination with which they live, and can articulate clearly the impacts of overt and covert gender inequalities and forms of subordination on the material conditions of their lives as well as on their sense of self and mental wellbeing. Recognising and identifying a problem, however, does not automatically equip us to eliminate that problem, especially when one understands those problems to have structural rather than personal roots. Nevertheless, in order to even begin to challenge subordination it is first necessary to recognise and locate it, which is exactly what the women in this study were able to do as situated knowers.

What is for us possibly the most important issue here is the mundanity of many forms of GBV as recounted by the women who participated in this study. Here we are not talking about 'mundanity' to mean 'unimportant' but to refer to forms of violence that are so deeply embedded in the everyday lived experiences of many women that they become easy to misrecognise, to almost overlook, and very difficult to extrapolate from healthy, non-violent relationships. It still tends to be the case, and understandably so, that the forms of violence that make headline news and become the focus of international attention are the extreme experiences of, for example, stranger-rape, paedophile rings, sex trafficking, or sexual torture in times of war and conflict – much of which is often incorrectly perceived as only being about 'other' women in 'other' non-western cultures. These extreme examples are not – thankfully of course – the experience of GBV for the majority of women and girls, nevertheless it is the very ordinariness of the violence and abuse which they do experience that can be even more difficult to challenge but which nevertheless has chronic negative impacts on women's lives.

Some tension exists between the terms 'gender-based violence' (GBV) and 'violence against women and girls' (VAWG) that is worth noting here. While both terms are useful and have slightly different meanings and foci, they are often used interchangeably, as if by 'gender' we really mean only 'women'. Gender-based violence is a broader term that refers to violence against adult women, men and trans-identified people, as well as girls and boys on grounds of their gender identity or sexual orientation. Globally, women and girls continue to be the main targets of and victims of violence on grounds of their gender, their femaleness, and as such there is a continued need for a focus on violence against women and girls specifically (VAGW). Nevertheless, much gender-based violence is of course experienced by people because of their male, or transgender identities or same-sex sexuality – including sexual abuse, forced conscription, homophobic and transphobic violence – often as a result of perceived transgressions of normative, hegemonic masculinities and culturally sustained heteronormativity. As Hoare (2007, 3) points out, 'just as it is used as a means of controlling the behaviour of women, gender-based violence can also be used as a means of controlling the behaviour of men and boys'.

Leach and Humphreys go further and avoid using the term 'gender-based violence' altogether because '[t]he term suggests that violence is not necessarily gendered and that forms of violence exist which are unrelated to processes of gender/sexual positioning' (Leach and Humphreys, 2007, 53). We need to take care not to fall into the trap of categorising gender-based violence in opposition to what might be seen as 'normal' violence, as if they are unrelated: much violence is, at some fundamental level, gendered – for example, street violence often involving young men emerges from constructions of hegemonic masculinities within particular cultural contexts, just as violence enacted against women can be located in the context of their femaleness.

Possibly the most perniciously 'mundane' form of violence is the coercive control experienced within domestic abuse. Domestic abuse is also often the most difficult form of GBV to encapsulate due to its relative intangibility, longevity and embeddedness within the fabric of our domestic lives. More so, it is usually played out behind closed doors. Escaping such violence is extremely difficult because to do so not only involves extricating oneself from the reach of the abusive partner, but can also lead to a dismantling of wider familial relations, losing your home, affecting children, grandparents and friendship networks. Here we outline two selected cases from our interviews, those of Miranda and Octavia, who finally escaped their abusive relationships, at no small emotional, social and financial cost, and began to rebuild their lives with their children. Both Octavia's and Miranda's experiences illustrate common patterns of domestic or intimate partner abuse and demonstrate the pernicious but often relatively intangible and amorphous scope of that abuse which can make it even harder for women to challenge and escape.

Miranda had a successful, professional career in a male-dominated 'non-traditional' sector, but after fleeing domestic violence, with her children, she lost her job, her home and many social and familial networks, effectively having to start again. Miranda is highly educated, and had a high status and well paid career but, after her experiences of domestic abuse, she was left feeling so lacking in self-worth and confidence that when we spoke with her she did not yet feel able to seek new employment or retraining. Through women's embodied infrastructures she had managed to access women's services, felt safe in that women-only space and she was slowly regaining some of her confidence, but even to begin taking some low-level classes and make her way to the women's centre at all had been a long and challenging process. Here Miranda illustrates the many forms domestic violence can take, from the persistent undermining of self-esteem to physical violence:

> 'He liked the image of being supportive but the undercurrent was that he did not believe in me at all…In front of other people he would talk the talk, at one point I was thinking of retraining and doing something like life-coaching, he would say in public, "Yeah you can do it," but in private he would say, "Why would anyone pay you for advice?"…There was violence in front of the children and I worry about that…He wanted me to do alright, but never brilliantly, that would be a problem…I used to have to give him money, but never in front of people, he didn't like it at all that I earned more than him…He used to tell me I was really up myself and that I elevated myself above other people and that other people were actually really uncomfortable around me, he did this to make me paranoid, which it did, it really upset me, as I would hate to think I made people feel bad – that's what he did to me, he always made me feel like it was me.' (Miranda, late 20s, non-traditional sector, mother, East Yorkshire)

Octavia and her children similarly escaped a long-term abusive relationship and, having lost many of their own familial and friendship networks through the course of the abuse, Octavia also eventually found her way to a women's centre. For Octavia the abuse had started at a much younger age, with her father being violent towards her mother and herself. This left her with little confidence as a child and she emerged into adulthood with limited educational, social and cultural capital. She articulated the ways in which her formative experiences were strongly connected to the abusive relationships she entered into as an adult. Through the women's centre she was encouraged to retrain and develop her confidence; she said that for the first time she felt that she was valued for who she was and began to recognise the contributions she could make to society through supporting other women. Here Octavia, like Miranda, explains the ways in which domestic abuse can take a variety of often insidious forms:

> 'My husband left me with very little money…he used to give me very little and it was his way of controlling me as well, although when I actually asked to learn, I wanted to have driving lessons, he wouldn't let me have them when I originally asked for them, then later on when we made these friends and we was in a circle and I'd said that I'd like to have lessons, he then, I only got the lessons because he felt that others knew that's what I wanted so he gave me a little bit of a leash, but he only let me have the lessons because he truthfully didn't think I'd ever pass my test, and then when I did pass my test came the issue of the car, we did have a car, it was paid for, but he got scared then because if I could go drive the car I could clear off then, so what he did was this car that was all paid for and in working good order, he put in then for part payment on a newer car, on finance, and for the first time he registered the car in his name, so again he had control of me.' (Miranda, late 20s, non-traditional sector, mother, East Yorkshire)

In a pattern typical in cases of domestic abuse, Octavia's husband attempted to isolate her from her support networks, making the family move from one place to another in the area and forbidding her to contact her family:

> 'Another thing what my ex-husband did with myself was he always wanted to live in areas where I was nowhere near

my family, so again I was isolated and I always made good friends, but you're still isolated because you had nobody to turn to.' (Octavia, mid–40s, volunteer, mother, Humberside)

A public facade obscured the abuse she and her children were suffering until Octavia finally felt able to leave him:

'When I actually said I was divorcing him my friends couldn't believe, "But he's such a nice person," and I said to them, "But the face he gives you is a different face than he gives me." He would be laid out and wouldn't do a thing and then as soon as he knew someone was walking down the path he would jump up, shove the blanket behind the couch, pick up the child and start playing with them, and the bairn would think, "Oh great, Dad's playing with me," enjoy every minute of it and then as soon as the company left, he'd sort of push them away, 'Don't want to know you no more', lay out on the couch, out come the blanket and then he'd be laid there all day doing nothing.' (Octavia, mid–40s, volunteer, mother, Humberside)

After finally seeking help from women's services and moving to a new environment to start afresh, when we got to know Octavia her life was really beginning to turn around. With the support of women's services she had secured part-time paid work helping other women who had suffered from domestic and sexual abuse, in addition to her community volunteering work, and she felt genuinely valuable, began to believe she was not stupid after all, that she was an independent and intelligent woman. Life can be unforgiving though, Octavia was diagnosed with a terminal illness shortly after we last spoke with her and she died in her late 40s.

Box 4.1: Escaping violence

Tessa talks about her experiences of domestic abuse and how she finally started a new life. Tessa had to leave with her child, spend six months in a woman's refuge and with the help of women's and children's services she was supported into a new home in a new town. Again through the embodied infrastructures of women's networks, Tessa rebuilt her confidence through working as a volunteer in a children's centre, and taking some training courses through women's services. Three years down the line she is now settled in her new life with her son and works part time.

'I mean, basically he changed as soon as we got married…our wedding night it was horrendous. He was really nasty to me and I thought, "Oh my god, what have I done?" Um, he was verbally abusive. Just…just nasty. Um, and as time went on he'd got violent and…just not nice.…he wanted me to get pregnant as soon as we met basically and I was saying, "Well, no, I'm not quite ready." You know, plus with losing my daughter in the first place I had to take vitamins and folic acid and things before I could even think about getting pregnant. Um, and then as soon as I was pregnant, because I mean I had quite a good job at the time, I was, err, assistant manager at [shop]. Quite well paid. Um, and he was…kept saying to me, "Oh, once you have this baby you'll never have to work again," and all this and I suppose, you know that isn't what I want and it was like…"Just wait until you have this baby," and, you know, and it was just like using it against me although he was the one that really wanted us to…I did really want to have a baby but I was…I really wanted some time just us before, you know. But…I got pregnant about a month after we got married so…it was all very quick and then it went severely downhill from there, the relationship.

'And I tried on several occasions to try and get us back on track and he just wasn't interested. He was just horrific and anything could set him off and he'd start smashing the house up and screaming and yelling and, you know, it…just not nice, so…as soon as I'd had my little boy he didn't want me to work. I could have gone back to work full time, part time. You know, and they were willing to accommodate whatever I wanted to do, and I said to him, you know, I'd really like to go back part time, but he says, "I don't want anybody else bringing our son up" and I said, "Well you can work shifts with your job", you know, "We could do it between us, you know" but, no, he didn't want me to go back to work. He really…it was just a controlling situation.

'I wasn't allowed any contact with my mum at all for the two years that I was with him. So, it was…just not a very nice time of my life really. [He controlled my contact with my family by taking] my mobile phone off me… and said you don't need a phone, but…you're stuck at home all day…and… he just, he…well he caused a lot of problems. He told me that my mum had tried it on with him. Um, you know so…to sort of break down the bond between us. Um, and if I ever saw my mum…you know, in the very beginning he…he would just cause a row…and then after I'd had my little boy, I said to him, you know, "I'd really like to get back in contact with my mum," and, err, and it was like, "Well if you do this is going to happen," and like painting a really black picture…and, you know, despite really wanting to I…I just daren't because, well I was more scared of him than…

'I wasn't allowed to go back to work. Although, you know, it was something I really wanted to do. [I had no contact with anybody] Just my health visitor who was a complete star and…eventually she put me in contact with, err, domestic abuse services. Err, and I used to sneak out of the house to go and see a counsellor every couple of weeks. Err, sometimes I couldn't get out. I'd even walked…we lived about an hour walk away…because I'd really needed to go and speak to her…because I needed that support. And, you know, he'd…he'd make sure that I didn't have any money to go out…

'When I started seeing the counsellor I realised that, you know, I could actually do it, I could actually get away from him and I wouldn't be completely on my own because my…my biggest fear was I've nowhere to go, I've nobody, you know, to help me…I realised that, yes, actually there were people out there that could help me and if I was really stuck they'd find me somewhere to be with and you know somewhere safe. Um, the first time I left him, um, I rang my dad and I said, "Dad will you come and get me, you know, I'm leaving him. I can't do it anymore," and basically told him some of the stuff that had been going on and, um, my step-mum said, "Well, you can't stay here" [laughs], err, but you know, she said I could and stay with my step-sister for a few days and, err, when I got there I found out that my step-sister was actually an alcoholic [laughs]. So, um, that was an even worse situation than being at home because at least at home although it was unpredictable I knew basically how it went [laughs]. She had different blokes and god knows at all times of the night and…so, err, after a couple of days of that and feeling really stressed I decided, you know, I couldn't do it and I went back because at first I was like I really don't want to go into a refuge…I went back for about six months and he just kicked off about the gas going. Um, we'd just moved into a new house…we moved in on the Wednesday and on the Sunday he just started kicking off…the gas was a meter and we didn't realise because it was outside and…we'd run out of gas and he…he started just going mental…he just started screaming and yelling and carrying on…I slept in my little boy's bedroom with, err, various items of furniture behind the door so that he couldn't come in.'
(Tessa, late 30s, part time, clerical, mother, North Yorkshire)

Tessa, with the help of an aunt and the counsellor with whom she made contact again, left her husband and was put in contact with women's services. She knew her husband was looking for her and she was afraid to stay in the same area:

'He was going to go mental. He was going to find me. You know, although he didn't know exactly where I was he would have been able to find me and I thought I can't risk it…I can't even walk down the street because

> he threatened to kill me. Um, so I rang her [counsellor] and I said, "Look I need to get away"…And, err, she got me a place in [city]. So…I travelled from [city to town] and, um, then I went back again and I'm not a very city person and at the time I was quite fragile as you can imagine [laughs]. Um, and I said I really can't stay in the city, it's too much for me, you know…I'm having panic attacks. I need to be somewhere calmer, um, and they gave me a list of options and I came to [another town]. I were in the refuge for about six months which wasn't very pleasant but it was somewhere to be…I got my house because Women's Aid and like Sure Start, you know, work together, um, and…my outreach worker contacted Sure Start and said, "I've got a new lady.'" (Tessa, late 30s, part time, clerical, mother, North Yorkshire)

Domestic violence in the UK claims the lives of two women each week (Women's Aid, 2013), and '[a]mong women aged between 15 and 44, acts of violence cause more death and disability than cancer, malaria, traffic accidents and war combined' (UN Women, 2014, np). In the UK, domestic violence accounts for between 16% and 25% of all recorded violent crime (Women's Aid, 2013), although issues of under-reporting and under-recording mean that this is likely to be a significant underestimate. Such violence is never far away, no matter where we are situated. Indeed, at the time of editing this chapter on violence, Dawn Warburton, a woman of a similar age to ourselves and who had two children, was strangled in a flat not a mile away from where we sat. The man, Mark Pickford, who was known to Dawn, has since been charged with manslaughter (Thompson, 2013).

To cite a few of the statistics concerning gender-based violence in England and Wales:

- Approximately 77 per cent of victims of domestic violence are women.
- Of the 1.2 million women who were reported to suffer domestic abuse in 2011–12, more than 400,000 were sexually assaulted, 60,000 were raped and thousands more women reported being stalked.
- One in four women will experience domestic violence in the course of their lifetime, but fewer than one in four of these women will report it to the police, even so, this amounts to one incidence of domestic violence being reported to the police every minute.
- It has more repeat victims than any other crime, and on average there will have been 35 assaults before a victim calls the police.

- In 2011–12 88 women and 17 men died at the hands of a partner or former partner and over half of all homicides against women are committed by a partner or ex-partner.
- The associated costs of gender-based violence to the state are huge. Walby's major study in 2004 estimated domestic violence to cost in excess of £23 billion a year through associated costs such as for social and health services. Recent Home Office estimates are that violence against women and girls (VAWG) costs the state £37.6 billion per year.

(Sources: Walby, 2004; Nicholason et al, 2007; Home Office, 2013; ONS, 2013c; Women's Aid, 2013; WRC, 2013a).

Official figures, however, represent the tip of the iceberg as the majority of cases are never reported and even fewer make it through the legal process. The notoriously low conviction rates for rape in the UK became headline news following a study of government crime statistics by Walby and Allen (2004) which stated that of the small minority of cases that are brought to court, there is a less than 6 per cent conviction rate, which does not encourage women to come forward in the first place. The negative media publicity surrounding this shocking indication of a failure of the criminal justice system led the government to take further action to address the persistence of GBV in the UK. Positive government responses have included allocating funding of almost £40m until 2015 to support specialist services such as Rape Crisis, widening the definition of domestic violence and abuse to include coercive control and to cover 16 and 17 year olds, and introducing new legislation to broaden police powers in cases of stalking (Home Office, 2013).

The Home Office also commissioned Baroness Stern to conduct 'The Stern Review' (Stern, 2010) into the handling of rape and sexual violence complaints by public authorities such as the police and criminal justice system. One of the report's comments was that the much-cited figure of the 6 per cent conviction rate can be misleading due to the complex way rape statistics have been calculated. The review recommended that these processes be amended to bring greater clarity to the figures. One of the problems raised with the counting of the statistics, for example, is that a charge that begins as rape may not result in a recorded conviction for rape if the perpetrator is charged with a different offence at the end of the criminal process.

In 2013 the Criminal Prosecution Service (CPS) released figures indicating that the conviction rate for rape prosecutions, if differently calculated, actually stood at 63 per cent, which is an all-time high.

CPS figures show that prosecutions for violence against women and girls in England and Wales rose from approximately 75,000 cases in 2007–08 to 91,000 in 2011–12 (Bowcott, 2013). Of rape and sexual abuse cases brought forward to the CPS by the police, however, 25 per cent end in no further action being taken, in part because it can be difficult to prove a rape case in court and the CPS will only take on cases which they feel have a chance of leading to conviction (Bowcott, 2013). There is also criticism of the ways in which the British Crime Survey (BCS) itself counts domestic and sexual abuse which can lead to misleading figures. In an interview on BBC Radio 4's *Woman's Hour* in 2013, Jane Keeper, director of operations at the domestic violence charity Refuge, explained this issue clearly. When asked if the BCS is accurate, she stated:

> 'No, sadly it's not at all accurate. What it does is it counts incidents of somebody in the household being abusive or violent to somebody else, so if your step dad's abusing you, your two brothers have had a fight or anyone else in your household's had a dispute with anyone else, all of that wrapped up together, together with what most of us would consider to be domestic violence. It then counts what it calls incidents, an incident might be a slap, so somebody might say, a husband might say "Yes, my wife slapped me last year," just the same as it might count attempted murder and it sets an arbitrary cap of five incidents, because for most crimes that would probably be about an average limit, whereas we know that domestic violence, sort of, acts of domestic terrorism, last for years and years and we know that women are far more likely to be victims of rape in marriage…There is no good national prevalence study [of levels of domestic violence] but the British Crime Survey has now so lost any definition of domestic violence that as a result there is a real distortion and minimisation of the scale of domestic violence. Millions of crimes are being buried by it.' (Jane Keeper, Refuge, BBC Radio 4, 2013)

Keeper raises a genuine issue here, there is a problem with counting all incidents in the same way – single incidents between couples or members of the same household are not the same as domestic violence and abuse perpetrated persistently over long periods of time. This is a point that was echoed by Catherine Donovan during the same programme when she was asked by the interviewer to respond to claims made by a US study that women perpetrate physical and emotional abuse at comparable rates as men:

> 'One of the problems with any of these kinds of studies is…they are based on incidents so what you miss out is context, meaning, impact, motives…now…we can think about there being different kinds of…interpersonal violence, so if you look at meanings for instance, there's a difference between somebody lashing out at somebody in anger or frustration or because they've have a bad day… you can now start to call that common couple violence. The difference being…that in domestic violence and abuse one person is being terrorised, so one person is living in fear. Often they're experiencing more than one incident and…the new government definition about coercive control really encapsulates that because it's focusing on not just one incident but a pattern of behaviours that can be physical violence, sexual violence, financial violence, emotional violence, that together build a picture of one person exerting power and control over the other. And if you look at that, and even with the British Crime Survey which is a crude measure, if you look at things like repeat victimisation or severity of impact, women are by far the largest group.' (Catherine Donovan, Sunderland University, BBC Radio 4, 2013)

Here Donovan is referring to a more nuanced way that is being developed to look at differences in the nature of GBV which would mean that what might be seen as relatively minor events could be categorised as 'common couple violence' and domestic abuse can be understood in terms of 'coercive control'. Using these concepts within the British Crime Survey would highlight incidences of longer term domestic abuse and reduce the numbers of single event intra-familial violence counted as domestic abuse, these cases would come under the category of 'common couple violence'. How statistics are calculated does make a difference, and it does matter.

There continues to be a relatively low reporting of and subsequent conviction rate for cases of GBV in the UK, and the vast majority of victims of GBV continue to be women and girls. Stating that women and girls continue to experience far higher rates of domestic abuse and sexual violence than men in both national and global contexts does not mean that violence against men and boys is not a serious issue. The one does not infer the other. What is important, though, is to understand that the gender imbalance in the ratio of perpetrators to victims of violence is not random, it is not some kind of unexplainable and unfortunate accident. As feminist theorists have clearly articulated for decades, GBV is a product of gender regimes and deeply embedded in hegemonic constructions of masculinities and femininities (see, for example, McKinnon, 1979; L. Kelly, 1988; Dobash and Dobash, 1992; Radford and Russell, 1992; Hester et al, 1996; Maynard and Winn, 1997; Hearn and McKie, 2008; True, 2012). As Banyard states:

> Look beneath the surface and you find the roots of all these individual acts connected in a tangle of gender inequality that is planted firmly in the heart of normal, everyday society – in behaviours deemed 'manly', in cultures deemed 'traditional'. Rape, domestic violence, harassment, stalking: uncomfortable as it may be to acknowledge, while these are all deeply personal acts, they are also profoundly political acts drawing on a common ideology. They express and bolster the power assumed by one social group over another. The only way we will ever be able to uproot violence against women – what Amnesty International have declared as 'the greatest human rights scandal of our times' – is by changing the cultural landscape that nurtures it. (Banyard, 2010, 107)

The cultural landscape that nurtures GBV has been the focus of greater national and international attention in recent years. Over the past two decades in particular we have seen some dramatic and positive shifts in the ways that powerful bodies such as international development institutions and national governments view both gender-based violence (GBV) in general and violence against women and girls (VAWG) in particular. We have seen considerable advances in the international acceptance of gender-based violence as development and human rights issues, and as structural and gendered issues that states have a responsibility to address. There have been a range of key events and declarations with which we are now quite familiar, for example, the UN Conference on Women's Rights in Vienna in 1993, followed by the 1993 UN Declaration on the Elimination of Violence Against Women which were pivotal in placing violence against women within an international human rights framework (Mathur, 2004). The Cairo Programme of Action emerging from the UN International Conference on Population and Development (ICPD) in 1994 located violence against women within a more holistic development framework, including recognising it as an obstacle to women's reproductive and sexual rights (UN, 1995), and the 1995 Beijing Platform for Action pledged countries to eliminate it.

Indeed a range of international, regional and national declarations were drawn up in the late 1990s and into the 2000s, often led by the work of the UN, which committed states to addressing gender-based violence and violence against women and girls (Hoare, 2007, 1; UNIFEM, 2003, 6). As Carillo wrote in 2000, commenting on the progress made in the 1990s, '[i]t is remarkable that in less than a decade, the political climate surrounding the rights of women has shifted from refusing to admit that violence against women is a problem to an almost universal understanding that it is the ultimate expression of the subordination of women globally' (Carillo, 2000, 14).

The advances made during the 1990s have subsequently been further embedded into institutional structures and practices in the 2000s, particularly supported by the ongoing work of UN bodies such as UNIFEM and UNHCR as well as a range of global and local feminist and human rights organisations. All this means that we are now working, at least ideologically, within a more positive context. One in which there is a greater fundamental acceptance of the importance of violence as a global human rights and *gendered* development concern coupled with a far more sophisticated understanding of how violence is underpinned by gender norms and processes at various levels.

In order to both acknowledge and better understand the achievements made during the 1990s and early 2000s, UNIFEM commissioned an important review of work being done to combat violence against women in a range of regional contexts. The subsequent report, 'Not a Minute More' (UNIFEM, 2003), concluded that there had been some positive advances made and more services were available for women, more programmes addressing violence existed, but that women did 'not appear to be substantively freer from the ravages of violence than they were when the work began' (UNIFEM, 2003, 6). In this report, Noeleen Heyzer, the executive director of UNIFEM at the time, posed the question: '[w]hy does gender-based violence continue seemingly unabated?' Her response remains as accurate today as it was just over a decade ago, as she said, '[t]he answer is deceptively simple, but the solution is deeply complex: gender inequality fuels violence against women and the power imbalances it creates are not easily rectified'. Heyzer goes on to make the point that we reiterate here because it continues to be of fundamental importance:

> [G]ender-based violence is part of an intricate web of violence. The trafficking of women is linked to the trafficking of drugs and arms, and an increase in criminality. Rape and sexual abuse are tied to the devastation caused by HIV/AIDS and the destruction of families. Impunity for violence against women suggests impunity for criminal behaviour and the disintegration of the rule of law. Violence against women is tied also to the brutality of war. (UNIFEM, 2003, 7)

We emphasise here that violence needs to be seen not only as an intricate web that plays out along an extended and intrinsically inter-connected continuum, but also as a fundamental part of processes of gendering, of the constructions of masculinities and femininities across a whole range of social contexts and cultures. We are referring to a long continuum of structural and symbolic violence that ranges from the sexualisation of girls in popular culture, to sexual comments and gestures made by men to women walking by in the street, any street, anywhere, to the insidious undermining of one's sense of self that characterises domestic abuse, to the rape and sexual abuse of both girls and boys, and to the use of rape and the widespread sexual humiliation and abuse of both male and female combatants and civilians as a weapon of war.

As we are well aware, women who have been victims of violence experience lifelong consequences, including most commonly, anxiety disorders, depression, post-traumatic stress disorder, antisocial behaviour, low self-esteem, body image issues, self-perceived poor health, and fear of intimacy (Lees, 2000; Croghan and Miell, 2000; Fanslow and Robinson, 2004). The health consequences have been widely noted, to the extent that, in 2002 the World Bank estimated that globally, violence against women was 'as serious a cause of death and incapacity among women of reproductive age as cancer and a greater cause of ill-health than traffic accidents and malaria combined' (UNIFEM, 2003, 8). The costs to society are also huge, with the annual economic costs of picking up the pieces, through legal, social and educational services, running into the billions.

Box 4.2: The coordinator of Hull Rape Crisis talks about working with women who have been raped

As part of this research we asked a coordinator of Hull Rape Crisis and Sexual Assault Service (HRCSAS), to write a short piece for us about her perceptions and experiences of the impacts of GBV for women's wellbeing and we want to reproduce it for you here:

> Rape is a terrifying, violent and humiliating experience that no woman wants or asks for. Different women have different ways of reacting to any experience in their lives. An experience such as rape or sexual assault, which will have affected a women's whole life by taking away her feelings of safety and trust, will similarly produce many different reactions and feelings. An important task for HRCSAS working with a woman following a rape or sexual assault is to reassure her that whatever way she is feeling is valid – there is no 'right' way of reacting.
>
> Many women fear they are 'going mad' because they are being overwhelmed by different emotions. It is helpful for us to reassure the woman that she is not going mad but simply reacting to a very traumatic event. Fear can paralyse a woman after being raped. She may find it impossible to go into a place which resembles where she was raped, or to be in a situation which she associates with the rape in any way. Certain words, phrases, films, books, smells etc may bring the fear flooding back. She may be scared of going out or of staying in depending on individual women's circumstances. Nightmares are also very common after an assault. These can be specific details or vague terrifying shapes or feelings. These nightmares can make the woman too scared to go to sleep.
>
> During a rape or sexual assault a woman has no control over her body or what is happening to her. The feeling of the violence and lack of control over your body can stay with the woman for a long time after the assault. As a result women may strive to have control over various other aspects of their life, eg constant cleaning or a need for things to be in order.
>
> Friends, family and workers will often try to make decisions for the woman, but it is important that she is allowed the time and support to make decisions for herself. This is vital around the decision of reporting the assault to the police. A woman will have to weigh up what she will go through with the police and the legal system, against how she will feel if she gets no recognition from society for the crime which has been committed

against her. The woman will have to live with the consequences of that decision and only she should make it.

Most women feel physically dirty following an assault and will spend a lot of time washing and cleaning themselves and their homes. Some women may feel they are not worth cleaning any more, and neglect their appearance. Realising that it was nothing in her personally that made him rape her can help. After an attack women frequently think of something they believe they could have done to avoid being raped: 'If only I'd locked the door/hadn't spoken to him' etc. The list is endless and society often reinforces this by saying that women shouldn't dress in certain ways, or that women lie about rape etc. She may say that she was out alone, or that she had been drinking, or that she let the man into her house, or that she should have known what he was 'like, etc, reminding a women that there is nothing 'wrong' with being out alone, or having a drink, or trusting someone and discussing how difficult it is to tell what someone is 'like' just by looking at them, can be very useful in helping a women realise that she cannot be responsible for someone else's actions. Sexual violence is always the responsibility of the perpetrator. It is *never* the victim's fault.

Women's experiences of domestic and sexual violence not only have long-term impacts on their self-esteem and mental wellbeing, but these experiences also form a common thread of experience in women's lives, cutting across geographic, cultural and socio-economic boundaries. Numerous studies in recent years have identified clear links between experiences of sexual or domestic violence, mental ill health and self-harming health behaviours throughout the world (McCauley et al, 1998; Stewart and Robinson, 1998; McMahon et al, 2000). Tomasulo and McNamara (2007) surveyed 148 women accessing a community health clinic in the Midwest of the United States and found a significant correlation between exposure to abuse and poorer physical and mental health. Chrisler and Ferguson (2006) similarly found in a review of principally US and UK literature, that:

> Among the problems commonly diagnosed in women who have been victims of violence are anxiety disorders, depression, post-traumatic stress disorder, and antisocial behaviour. In addition, women often complain of low self-esteem, body image issues, self-perceived poor health, fear of intimacy and an inability to trust men...Behavioural and substance abuse problems often develop after an experience of violence, perhaps in an effort to cope with overwhelming

anxiety, in an attempt to distance themselves from their damaged bodies, or in reaction to a belief that the victims themselves are now worthless. Higher than average rates of alcohol and drug abuse and eating disorders are often reported among victims, as are risky sexual behaviours. (Chrisler and Ferguson, 2006, 8)

In the UK, National Children's Home (NCH) Action for Children conducted research in 1999 focusing on adults who had been victims of sexual abuse in their childhood and found that '58 per cent of respondents reported a lifetime of difficulty and distress following childhood abuse, including low self-esteem, fear, eating disorders, [and] alcohol problems' (cited in Ibson, 2007, 130). Closer to home, Ibson (2007) conducted an ethnographic study of women accessing services for drug misusers in the Yorkshire and Humber Region over a ten-year period. Within this she conducted life-history case studies with 15 women and found that of these, 11 had experienced serious levels of domestic violence and/or sexual abuse throughout their childhood and into their adult lives, with one woman having also been subjected to torture. In this extract from Ibson's work, we can see how these patterns of abuse, poor mental wellbeing and subsequent self-harm through drug misuse can develop:

> In another case, Kay and her sister were placed into care by their mother when the latter's marriage broke up; both of the children were under three years of age. Her natural father had a severe drink problem and her mother could not cope with the domestic violence. Kay did not see her mother again until she was eight years old. Her mother had remarried and Kay and her sister moved out of Local Authority care to live with their mother and stepfather. Kay reported no good memories of her early life:
>
>> My mother failed me big time; she left me and my sister in an orphanage and disappeared. When she turned up again, we did not know who she was, she had re-married and had another daughter. She expected us to be a family, what a joke. My so-called step father sexually abused me from a young age, I never had a childhood. Why do you think I take drugs? To forget the bastard and to blank out the nightmares, that's why. (Ibson, 2007, 128)

Based on our qualitative data, we also found a significant link between women's experiences of sexual and/or domestic violence and negative impacts on their mental wellbeing. For example, as Sally explains:

'The majority of people coming through mental health services have experienced some kind of abuse or violence or trauma that has affected them for a long time and women disproportionately more than men.' (Sally, late 30s, manager, health sector, volunteer, West Yorkshire)

Similarly, a professional psychotherapist with many years of experience in the field talked about the connections between violence and women's self-esteem and the harmful impacts of violence on women's lives:

'In my experience from working with clients and also supervising the work of other therapists, the impact of GBV, sexual abuse and rape on women's self-esteem and confidence cannot be underestimated. I suppose the predominant issue can be feelings of shame which can be paralysing, making it difficult for the person to talk to, or trust another with their experiences...longer-term effects [include] feelings of inadequacy, "I should have stopped it", inferiority, worthlessness, "It was my fault," isolation and withdrawal, depression, disphoria, body dismorphia, self-harm, cutting, eating disorders, [feeling] suicidal, complex PTS [post-traumatic stress] – disassociation, flashbacks, nightmares, OCD [obsessive compulsive disorder], lack of trust in others, anger issues, addictions. I work a lot with adult survivors of child abuse – physical, sexual and emotional and it always seems that the younger the person was when it started the more severe are the long-term effects, which is obvious of course. There often is a pattern of ending up in abusive relationships as adults and repeating the experience. Then of course the knock-on effects of their children...I am continually in awe of women's courage in confronting these issues and ability to survive.' (Harriet, late 50s, professional, health sector, Humberside).

In conclusion, in the same way as it is not a coincidental correlation that women statistically experience higher levels of mental ill health, it is not a random fact that gender-based violence disproportionately affects women and girls the world over. Domestic and sexual violence perpetrated by men and boys against women and girls is a consequence of unequal power structures and processes of gendering within patriarchal gender regimes. Recognising this is the first step, the easy step, the next is far harder because it calls for us to challenge and change 'the societal conditions that produce and sustain men's violence to women and children' (Hearn and McKie, 2008, 85).

The impacts on women and children who experience such violence are profound, affecting not only their mental and physical health, but also their educational and career aspirations and life chances. In order to address violence/gender-based violence we have to not only locate it within a long continuum, but this should inform policy and practice. We need to simultaneously recognise the ways in which normative patriarchal constructions of masculinities and femininities, played out differently within many and varied cultural contexts, underpin structural and symbolic violence at any point on that continuum, from the ordinary to the extraordinary.

To understand this clearly we should make links between seemingly diverse experiences of GBV the world over – from the everyday to the extreme. Drawing on just a few contemporary international news reports, we can look at, for example, the US clothing company who were criticised in 2013 for producing t-shirts with slogans such as 'Keep Calm and Rape Her' and 'Keep Calm and Hit Her'. They claimed they were randomly computer generated which is highly unlikely and does not explain why they were approved for production and sale, nor why Amazon felt that they were suitable to sell through their website (McVeigh, 2013). We connect this then to the sale in major supermarkets in Western Europe of toy pole dancing kits and pole dancing dolls, and lacy lingerie and padded bras aimed at young girls.

This we in turn connect with the trials that took place in Delhi in 2013 of men accused of gang raping and murdering the 23-year-old woman whom they dragged from a public bus in December 2012. We should consider why some public figures in India implied that she brought it on herself because of her Western dress and lifestyle. We have to also link this to the Indian governmental panel that joined women's rights advocates in 2013 in calling for some of the more degrading elements of the sexual assault examination to be stopped. The state examination they want to amend includes the 'two finger' exam in which a doctor inserts two fingers into the vagina of the woman who has been raped in what amounts to further abuse, to see if she is used to having sexual intercourse. Presumably this is meant to indicate that women who have consensual sex as a normal and healthy part of their lives cannot then be raped (Burke, 2013).

We have to link this to the woman in Somalia who said she was raped in an internally displaced person's camp in Mogadishu, who, along with a local journalist who interviewed her, was jailed for insulting the nation after the story was reported in the British *Guardian* newspaper. She was released on appeal but the journalist was not (Ahmed and Smith, 2013). This we can link to a similar case in 2013 of the Norwegian woman who claimed that she was raped by a male colleague in a hotel room in Dubai and who was jailed for 16 months for having sexual intercourse outside of marriage. Following international outcry she was released and pardoned, however her alleged attacker was also released without being charged for rape (BBC News Online, 2013a). We have to link this to the rise of the neo-Nazi group 'Golden Dawn' in Greece, who have become synonymous with homophobic and racial violence, with alleged complicity on the part of some members of the police (Savaricus, 2013), and in turn link this to the rise in homophobic violence and homophobic repression the world over. Then we have to link this to the widespread femicide that continues in Mexico and Central America (Prieto-Carrón et al, 2007), to the sexual abuse of children by humanitarian workers in West Africa (Hyder and MacVeigh, 2007), to 'corrective rape' of lesbian women in South Africa (Human Rights Watch, 2011) and to the rape and violence to which women and men in Syria have been subjected during the civil war that shows little sign of ending in 2014 (Proudman, 2013).

Finally, to bring us right back along that continuum to the perpetuation of 'mundane', symbolic, structural and visceral violence in the UK, we can end with the cases of Caroline Criado-Perez and of 'S' and 'E', just two examples from the many women who have written in to *The Everyday Sexism Project*.[2] In the first illustration, Caroline Criado-Perez successfully campaigned in 2013 for one woman's face (Jane Austen's was selected) to be added to those of all the famous men displayed on British banknotes. This seemingly innocuous act was met with a barrage of systematic sexist and violent abuse via Twitter, including threats to rape and kill her. Two of the Twitter 'trolls', one young man and one young woman, were subsequently arrested (BBC News Online, 2013b; Taylor and Quinn, 2013). In a final illustration of this continuum of violence, on *The Everyday Sexism Project* webpage, established in 2012 to collect experiences of 'mundane' sexism, one young woman reported that:

'I'm 17 now, and just had to quit my job because when I handed a man his change, he felt my arms and turned to my boss saying, "How much?" to which my boss just laughed and said I could choose the price.' ('S', Everyday Sexism Project, June, 2013)

And another young girl reported that;

'At 12, a boy in my class repeatedly stroked my arm, legs and my hair in the middle of class and at assembly...He also called me a cow, bitch and other things to my face. Even though my teacher saw this, she just told him to sit somewhere else. When I told my dad and stepmother, I was told that he liked me and that I should feel happy about it, and even encourage him. This happened under six months ago.' ('E', Everyday Sexism Project, June 2013)

And so it goes.

In terms of future work on gender-based violence there are now numerous examples of good practice and we should recognise the wealth of analyses and data to which we have access, thanks largely to the work of organisations such as the UN, national governmental and non-governmental agencies, and the work of human rights and feminist activists and practitioners at local and global levels. To draw on one example, the seven key principles underlying the Department for International Development's (DfID) 'Theory of change on tackling violence against women and girls' (2012) make very good sense, and we summarise these here:

1. Context is critical
2. The state has primary responsibility for action on violence against women and girls (VAWG)
3. Holistic and multi-sectoral approaches are more likely to have impact
4. Sustained reduction in VAWG will only occur through processes of significant social change, including social norms, at all levels
5. Backlash is inevitable but can and should be manageable
6. Women's rights organisations (WROs) create and sustain change
7. Empowering women is both the means and the end: focusing on the rights of, and being accountable to, women and girls is the most effective way of tackling gender inequality as the root cause of VAWG.

To consider the question of why GBV violence continues to persist at such high levels despite all that we understand and all that has already been done, we would suggest that it is not a case of not knowing why and how or even what can be done in particular cases at the project level. Rather, it is a problem of scaling both up and down: of embedding those understandings at national, local and individual levels to the extent that the powerful can no longer support such violence, either through action or inaction, because it is fundamentally unacceptable within the national consciousness. To reach that place we would need to see a widespread shift in normative gender constructs in any cultural context so that gender-based violence is not, and could not, be perceived or sanctioned as a mundane and everyday part of women's and men's lives. That process has already come a long way, but we are calling for a revolutionary change in gender norms and clearly that will take a great deal more time.

Finally we want to return to the women's voices in this study and end by reiterating the significance of the pernicious and often 'mundane' domestic violence that does not grab headlines, but is possibly the most insidiously damaging to millions of women's emotional and material wellbeing. We end with a quote from Tessa, who had spent years in a violent relationship before eventually leaving, again with the support of women's voluntary services (see Box 4.2). Here Tessa talks about how domestic abuse left her with such low self-confidence that completing even relatively simple tasks were huge achievements for her. For us this quote speaks volumes about the long-term, serious and yet simultaneously 'mundane' impacts of abuse:

> 'Do you know, and it's…and it takes a lot to, sort of, say, yes, I am going to go there and I am…I mean I…I took my little boy to Flamingo Land one Sunday and I was just like, "Oh my god, I've actually done it." You know, and I felt so proud of myself. Something so silly that's…other people would just take for granted doing, it was such a big achievement. We went on the bus and, you know, and we actually went on our own and went to Flamingo Land and it was like, wow, we did it, do you know, and that was like, you know sort of a bit of breakthrough. It was like, yes I can go and do things.' (Tessa, late 30s, part time, clerical, mother, North Yorkshire)

FIVE

Gendering education:
the paradox of success versus status

Introduction

Our experiences of schooling and education have far-reaching impacts on our lives. Educational institutions are profoundly gendered arenas and also key sites through which the effects of the symbolic, structural and physical violence of gendering can be felt. In this chapter we explore the intersections between education, aspiration, achievement and wellbeing. In considering education we address a range of different areas, from formal school and institutionally-based education to the more subtle forms of education that girls and women receive through processes of socialisation that teach them, for example, appropriate ways of carrying their bodies and expressing their thoughts. Considering education in relation to wellbeing and confidence allows us to see that, for many girls and women, as well as boys and men, experiences of formal education are both shaped by, and shape, female and male identities and beings. This means that it is important to pay attention to the gender regimes that structure educational systems.

A significant range of research has demonstrated the ways in which the institution of education is deeply implicated in processes of gendering (Arnot et al, 1999; Ringrose and Epstein, 2008; Bradley, 2013). Given that schools perform a large portion of the task of moulding good citizens it is critical that we understand how gender relations are reflected and reproduced in education at different levels. At an ideological and symbolic level messages about gender, along with other significant identifiers such as race, class and ethnicity serve to socialise young people into expecting and accepting their future roles. At structural and organisational levels, overt and covert practices inform young people about the relative power of different groups and individuals, as well as what kinds of knowledge and ability are deemed most valuable (Murphy, 1996; Ringrose and Epstein, 2008). This means that sites of education provide key spaces within which gendered roles and practices are learned, rehearsed and enacted. The main focus of this discussion is on the ways that formal and informal education teaches girls and women to adopt roles and strategies that influence their lifelong attitudes, aspirations and achievements. We also consider how personal and individual experiences of wellbeing and confidence are central to women's experiences of education and attainment, expanding and limiting the opportunities open to them.

In the first part of this chapter we briefly outline some of the main changes in education that have taken place in the UK over the last 100 years and that have resulted in much greater formal equality in education. We then turn to explore processes of schooling, examining the ways that structural, symbolic, spatial, ideological and cultural practices operate to sideline and diminish girls next to boys.

We start, as we state above, with a brief commentary on changes in the education of girls and boys. Arnot et al (1999), note that women's experiences of education have changed dramatically in the last few decades and women have achieved previously unimaginable levels of success in many areas of education, meaning that, '[o]f all the educational inequalities which form the terrain of policy-making since the Second World War, gender has shown the most dramatic shift' (Arnot et al, 1999, 30). It is only fairly recently, however, that laws have been introduced that require girls to be treated the same as boys in education. The Elementary Education Act of 1880 made schooling compulsory up to age 10 and this was raised in successive Acts to the current school leaving age of 16 by the Children Act (1972). These *implicitly* included girls alongside boys. The introduction of the Sex Discrimination Act 1975 (amended 2005) means that women and girls cannot be formally discriminated against in admission to education and once pupils, they must be given the same opportunities to access facilities and services. In addition to this, the 2006 Equality Act ensures that all public authorities have a duty under the Gender Equality Duty (2007)[1] not only to *eliminate* unlawful discrimination and harassment, but also (and significantly) to *promote* equality of opportunity between women and men.

So far so good; changes in education for women have been swift and, largely, positive, and in spite of the inevitable gap between policy, rhetoric and practice the positive equality measures that have taken place in schooling, the wider range of opportunities available to women and girls, as well as the fact of many girls' higher attainment, have filtered through into women's consciousness. This is echoed in the lived experiences of women to whom we spoke, many of whom stated that the opportunities open to women and girls are significantly broader than even a few years ago.

Any measures to improve gender equality take place within specific economic, cultural, social and political contexts and, as Arnot notes;

'[h]istorical analysis of the gender reform movement exposes the complex interface between economic and political structures, macro and micro educational structures and processes and cultural movements, and the nuanced engagements between social class, ethnicity and gender inequalities' (2007, 207). Over the last few decades women's movements and the 'educational feminism' movement have achieved significant advances in developing more 'girl friendly' schooling (Arnot, 2007; Ringrose, 2007) by focusing attention, beginning during the 1970s and 1980s on the ways girls were 'marginalized and belittled in the classroom, the victims of systematic discrimination from male classmates and teachers, and the school system itself' (Francis, 2002, 4). Liberal educational feminists proposed that certain measures could be used to measure inequality, including:

- different attainment patterns in certain subject areas (especially maths, science and technology)
- sex stereotyping in optional subject areas and in careers advice, bias in examination and test construction and marking
- sex differences in role models (especially school staffing patterns)
- a lack of self-esteem and confidence among girls which reduced their expectations and narrowed their horizons
- a lack of gender awareness (gender blindness) among parents, teachers and society generally about the failure to develop women's potential. (Arnot, 2007, 211)

These could also be used to measure the different treatment and attainment of boys and girls. In spite of criticism from the popular press and others, much of the gains in girls' education, feminists would argue, have been through advocating equal opportunities rather than a more radical programme that addresses fundamental issues in schooling (Weiner, 1985, 9; 1986; Ringrose, 2007). As discussed above, however, this has left many of the patriarchal assumptions leading to women's subordination in wider society largely unchallenged, and may have even done some unintentional harm. As Ringrose and Epstein argue, '[t]he very aims of educational parity by gender sought by educational feminists have created measures of "equality" that could be used in the reverse' (2008, 153) to shift focus away from girls.

Women have succeeded in gaining parity to the extent that they have moved from being excluded from whole areas of education, to out-performing boys; gaining better overall grades at all levels, including Higher Education (DCSF, 2009). Today, girls do better than boys at GCSE level, a trend that has been developing in recent years (DfES,

2007; DfE, 2013) and continues to grow with 2013 GCSE results showing the largest gap between boys and girls (Paton, 2013). Even so, gendered patterns remain and the gap is smaller in subjects that are perceived as traditionally 'male'. Girls are also more likely to stay on in post-compulsory education and to perform better at A-level and beyond.[2] More women are now applying to university[3] (UCAS, 2011) and, in 2012, young women were a third more likely to progress to Higher Education at 18 than men (UCAS, 2012). Once studying at university, women also perform better at undergraduate level with 66 per cent of women compared to 61 per cent of men gaining first or upper second class degrees (HESA, 2012).

This 'out-performance' of boys by girls first became apparent in the early 1990s when national league tables, disaggregated by gender, were published. Girls had been doing as well or better in many subjects before then, but as these were in less prestigious (feminine) subjects they did not merit much public attention (Arnot et al, 1999). It was the introduction of the National Curriculum, requiring girls to take science subjects at schools and leading to girls doing well in these more prestigious (and traditionally masculine) subjects that called national attention to the relative achievements of girls and boys (Francis, 2006). It should be noted, however, that the picture of attainment is more complex than 'girls do better'; not all girls out-perform all boys and other factors such as socio-economic status and ethnic identity can be more marked than simple gender-based differences (Batho, 2009; DCSF, 2009). Similarly, other critical indices of difference such as class, ethnicity and culture can be obscured and this 'distorts issues involved with school achievement' (Ringrose and Epstein, 2008, 153). Recent evidence highlights, for example, that socio-economic class is the strongest predictor of educational attainment in the UK (Francis, 2002; Perry and Francis, 2010). Indeed:

> Education Secretary Michael Gove recently told a Commons education committee that 'rich, thick kids' do better than 'poor, clever' children, even before they start school. Although the blunt and emotive language provoked criticism…there is a broad agreement with Gove's essential message, that of the clear connection between poverty and educational (under)achievement. (Perry and Francis, 2010, 5)

There are also some marked differences in attainment based on ethnicity, for example:

Chinese pupils remain the highest attaining ethnic group. Pupils of any black background remain the lowest attaining group although the percentage making expected progress is above the national average. Pupils eligible for free school meals (FSM), pupils whose first language is other than English and pupils with Special Educational Needs continue to perform less well than their peers (DfE, 2013, 1).

Department for Education statistics reveal these differences in educational attainment are clear by the time children take Key Stage 2 assessments at 11 years old. A detailed examination of the levels of attainment by ethnicity at GCSE level, based on 2010–11 figures, reveals that girls of all ethnic groups outperform their male counterparts in every category of ethnicity (for example, Asian, black, white, Chinese) *except* in just two small sub-categories. Comparing 'like with like', of those children categorised specifically as 'Traveller of Irish Heritage who receive free school meals', boys slightly outperformed their female counterparts (35 per cent gaining five or more GCSE grades A★ to C compared with 31 per cent of girls in the same ethnic category), and for pupils categorised as 'Gypsy/Roma', 19 per cent of boys compared with 16 per cent of girls gained five or more GCSEs at A★ to C. In *all* the other 15 ethnic sub-categories girls outperform boys. Pakistani girls, for example outperformed Pakistani boys at this level by 8 per cent, black African girls outperformed their male counterparts by 11 per cent and white British girls outperformed white British boys by 7 per cent (DfE, 2012b).

One effect of this framing of the statistics in terms of 'boys versus girls' has been to encourage a view that 'girls are "not a problem" in spaces of school' and this 'has resulted in a massive neglect of girls' experiences, and a failure to allocate resources to girls' needs in school' (Ringrose and Epstein, 2008, 153). Indeed, the gains that have been made in gender equality in the area of education have led some to believe that, if gender in education needs to be addressed at all, the issue of boys' underachievement is most pressing. Rather than celebrating the achievements of girls, increasing concern has arisen in recent years over the comparative under-achievements of boys. As Ringrose and Epstein explain:

> There has been a general failure to conceive of gender as a relational category, and a refusal among policy makers to differentiate gender analysis and categories of girl/woman and boy/man so that resources could be allocated

> to girls and those who fall outside this convenient rhetoric
> of feminine success and boy's failure. The educational
> failing boys' discourse of male disadvantage…inculcates…
> the widespread belief that women have achieved equality
> with men in society. These sets of presumptions orienting
> educational debates bolster the quintessential *postfeminist*
> argument 'that girls and women are doing fine, feminism
> is unnecessary…the movement is over…girls have attained
> all the power they could ever want' and may actually 'have
> too much power in the world'. (Ringrose and Epstein, 2008,
> 153–4, replicated as the original)

Many of the concerns about boy's underachievement may, in fact, be myths but, as Weaver-Hightower (2003) suggests, this 'boy turn' means policy and research is more narrowly focused on boys' attainment, and masculinities have become, over the course of the past two decades, the subject of education research, presenting a deficiency model of the education system that is 'failing' boys. Newspaper headlines such as the *Daily Mail*'s 'Boys are being failed by our schools' (Clark, 13 June 2006), the ***Observer***'s 'Generation of boys "being failed" by the school system' (Hill, 3 May 2009), the *Guardian*'s 'Feminised curriculum "has thrown boys out with bathwater"' (Smith, 13 June 2006) or the *Times Educational Supplement*'s 'Failing boys: "public burden number one"' (Dean, 27 November 1998) fuel a 'moral panic' (Cohen, 1972) that develops around boys regarding their disadvantaged status relative to girls', representing them as 'victims' whose 'interests are set against those of girls' (Martino and Meyenn, 2001, x; Francis, 2006; Ringrose and Epstein, 2008). Epstein et al (1998a, 6) argue that three discourses have developed to explain and understand the performance of boys: 'poor boys', 'failing schools' and 'boys will be boys' which addresses issues of 'biology, psychology and traditional notions of masculinity' (Lloyd, 2011, 37).

The most damaging to girls and women is the 'poor boys' discourse that sets boys and girls in competition and sees the success of girls to be due to changes made to education systems as a result of feminist pressures to benefit girls at the cost of boys. In this discourse the blame for boys' failure lies squarely with women, whether mothers, teachers or, more broadly, 'feminists' (Epstein et al, 1998b; Ringrose and Epstein, 2008). This discourse serves not only to blame women and girls but also to undermine their educational success by questioning the bases of these achievements and celebrating the achievements of boys and girls in very different ways.[4] We see the move to eradicate coursework from GCSEs and assess students solely on the basis of exams as part of this concern with the relative success of girls, and therefore potentially damaging not just to attainment but also to girls' confidence. As women absorb these messages about differential achievement they also absorb messages about the relative merit and intelligence of boys and girls, as Helen notes here:

> 'Now they're scrapping course work, girls do better at course work than boys, at GCSE they're scrapping course work now, and it always makes me wonder if that's because girls are doing better than boys at school and I find that interesting that course work's been successful for years for girls and now they're scrapping it.' (Helen, early 20s, student, Humberside)

What we have seen, however, is that while schooling practices moved ahead in terms of parity, societal expectations still tended to place women in traditional areas and girls' educational success has not usually translated into career and earnings successes. As Arnot notes, 'the greater female educational achievement, the greater the gap between women's qualifications and their employment; the higher the level of female achievement, the more we witness a moral panic over male achievement levels' (Arnot, 2007, 208).

Occupational segregation on the basis of gender remains a significant aspect of modern society (Blackburn, 2009; Jarman et al, 2012) with women concentrated in feminised subject areas and less able than their male counterparts to convert their qualifications into career success, professional advancement and earnings (Skelton et al, 2007; EOC, 2007a). Studies of gender segregation in employment over the past 70 years repeatedly find similar patterns of horizontal and vertical segregation by gender to the extent that 'women and men are concentrated in different industries and that within the same industry women are over-represented in the least-skilled and lowest-paid jobs' (Charles, 2002, 23). Expectations about what constitute appropriate female work and remuneration remain (Dale et al, 2005). Further, women, in general, continue to earn less than men and 'women's occupations' attract lower financial, cultural and status rewards than men's outside the home, just as they do inside (Grimshaw and Rubery, 2007). Figures from the ONS show that the gender pay gap has actually widened from 14.8 per cent to 15.7 per cent recently (Fawcett, 2013d).

Expectations and aspirations are linked, not only to gender but are interwoven with class-based norms and expectations (Charles,

2002). Women in our study articulated clearly how their aspirations were further restricted by the limited expectations of others in their communities. Fiona's sense of the possible futures available to her are clearly related to both class and gender:

> 'It was expected and that's what I did, that I'd probably go into secretarial work...or hairdressing or nursing because they seemed to be the only options at the time...It was never even considered that I'd go onto university...never... never even...it was something that I didn't think about.' (Fiona, late 40s, manager, community sector, volunteer, mother, Humberside)

While other socio-economic factors, such as class, culture and ethnicity, are significant influencers of educational choices and achievement, and we should not fall into the trap of only looking at the gender binary as Ringrose and Epstein (2008) warn, nevertheless gender remains 'an independent and significant predictor of attainment' (DfES, 2007, 4). Since the introduction of the National Curriculum in 1988 which formalised equality opportunities policy (Ringrose, 2007), a legitimate space has been provided for girls to take on traditionally 'male' subjects and vice versa (Arnot et al, 1996; EOC, 2001). Evidence from the EOC suggests that subject selection at GCSE continues to be determined by gender stereotypical influences, and these in turn determine the kind of career paths embarked on following school. Similarly, we found that only 37 per cent of respondents in our study agreed or strongly agreed that 'at school boys and girls were encouraged to take the same subjects regardless of gender' and, more significantly for women's self-confidence and wellbeing 72 per cent of people agreed that 'subjects traditionally taken by boys are valued more than those traditionally taken by girls'.

Currently, as highlighted in Chapter One, as soon as subject choice is introduced, extreme gendered divisions appear, with young men typically pursuing technical and science oriented subjects and young women typically pursuing caring, or arts/humanities/social science subjects, a trend that occurs whether in academic or more vocational courses (Fuller et al, 2005a; Skelton et al, 2007; Wenchao et al, 2010). As Miller et al (2004) note, '[t]he making of early educational choices that effectively close off certain career options remains one of the prevailing barriers to the entry of women into areas of non-traditional work' (p 15).

While we might argue that there is nothing intrinsically wrong with young people pursuing subjects and careers which interest them, we must question both the causes of these choices and the impact that they have on future life chances and opportunities. The differential value afforded to male and female subjects was clearly recognised by the women in our study. Carol, whose schooling experiences are very recent makes clear associations between intelligence and 'male' subjects, echoing value judgements held within society that masculine subjects are intrinsically more difficult:

> 'I think, because I've always worked in the top classes in school, I think I was just encouraged by everyone to go for, you know, like science or maths, or something like that.' (Carol, late teens, student, Humberside)

Throughout this study, women we spoke to recognised that gendered opportunities in education are broader than even a few years ago but, at the same time, many told us that these opportunities had not been *personally* experienced. They narrated tales of their own individual achievements and the many and varied ways that they felt that their choices were constrained, their expectations lowered, and their confidence shaken within education. These findings echo those of others who have argued for several decades that 'the nature of women's socialisation guarantees our oppression and that schooling is an important part of that process of socialisation' (Mitchell, 1971, cited in Foster, 1985; see also Gillborn, 1990; Skelton et al, 2007).

Early socialisation into appropriate gendered behaviours for both males and females is an important factor in gender segregation in education and beyond, drawing girls and boys to different areas of the curriculum (Gillborn, 1990; Skelton et al, 2007). This means that 'pools of talent for some occupations are influenced from a young age, this can in turn restrict the opportunities for young men and women to fulfil their potential when they enter the world of work' (Women and Equality Unit, 2004, 1). The continuing gender disparities are so marked that policy interventions remain of critical importance. As Prosser argues, 'there are a variety of ways in which the government can influence women's opportunity through taking a gendered approach to education and training, infrastructure, supporting families or regulation where appropriate' (Prosser, 2005, 3). The Gender Equality Duty requires schools to take a proactive approach to tackling gender inequalities in subject segregated achievement. This presents guidance on gender and equality in schools and identifies a number of key remaining equality issues:

- challenging gender stereotypes in subject choice and careers advice
- pupil attainment
- health, sport and obesity
- sexual and sexist bullying and violence. (EOC, 2007b, 4)

Legislation and policy change are welcome for the protection they provide, and, as we have seen, have helped to create much greater parity between girls and boys, women and men. We need to be cautious, however, as we know that in themselves they do not necessarily bring about rapid cultural change and consequently, for the majority of men and women, roles in the home, education and work remain organised along traditional gendered lines (Madden, 2000). Each of the above categories of concern have an impact on girls' sense of their own competence and on their self-esteem, as well as teaching girls, through daily interactions, the expectations they can have of their future social role and status, as we explore below.

Where does girls' confidence go? The transformation of girls in schooling

In earlier chapters we have articulated the damage to women's sense of self-worth that is caused through processes of gendering. We now examine school as a key site in this creation and maintenance of (albeit not uniform) hegemonic notions of dominant, confident males and subordinate, under-confident women. Schools themselves remain highly gendered contexts and, crucially, young people are most involved in the school system at a time they are developing their own identities, friendships and independence. This interplay of individual, familial, friendship and wider socio-cultural expectations of behaviour is crucial as gendered behaviours can be seen to be relational; we perform gender by what we are not and do not, as much as by what we are and do.

Naturalising gender discourses, presenting the idea that there are some behaviours and traits that are 'male' or 'female' create and constrain ways of thinking. This means that boys and girls differ markedly in how they feel about themselves, their aptitudes and their achievements. Rosalind, whom we first introduced in Chapter Three, worked in a secondary school for over 20 years, experiencing the effects of gendering and stereotyping of young people into normative gender identities on a daily basis. Her concerns about the connection between girl's levels of confidence and the impact on their aspirations are clear:

'I think the main thing would be issues to do with women's confidence in the first place. I think barriers always seem bigger if your own self-esteem's lower don't they?…And maybe the barriers wouldn't be there at all if the self-esteem bar was raised. And so I would imagine that it's something that's very fundamental in terms of bringing up young girls still.' (Rosalind, early 50s, self-employed, non-traditional sector, West Yorkshire)

Studies have repeatedly shown that, '[b]oys are more prone to identify self-enhancing patterns in their self-descriptions of their aptitudes and achievements while girls are more prone to demonstrate self-derogating patterns in their self-descriptions of their aptitudes and achievements and that men typically have greater self-confidence than women in social and professional situations' (Tavarni and Losh, 2003, 142). Further, 'Judgements of personal efficacy affect what students do by influencing the choices they make, the effort they expend, the persistence and perseverance they exert when obstacles arise, and the thought patterns and emotional reactions they experience' (Pajares, 2003, 140). We can easily imagine, then, how women become self-limiting, seeking more qualifications than men because they lack confidence, and never feel that they have achieved enough, as Rachel explains:

'I think what you might find is that women tend to do even more training…to do more before they actually get into employment…the brightest of brightest young women that there are, to get into [university] they still, when asked, didn't feel competent enough to move onto the next stage. These are the brightest of bright young women and still felt they hadn't quite made the [grade] and it's like they made every grade…I think it's to do with the way women view themselves, that they need…not everybody, but there's a sense of always needing to, "You must need something more," I think it's about something in the psyche.' (Rachel, early 40s, community sector manager, Humberside)

Best describes three areas in school where students are taught about gender: the

actual academic curriculum, with its sexist materials and gender typing of academic skills; the behavioural curriculum, wherein boys and girls played different roles and engaged in different activities and the sexual curriculum, which emphasised different roles for males and females (for example 'getting it' for boys, 'being careful' for girls). (Best, 1983 cited in Basow, 2004, 118))

While some of the worst forms of sexism in the curriculum have been addressed in the UK since Best was writing, other issues have arisen and these three areas continue to provide a useful framework for this discussion and so in the following sections we will address each of these broadly in turn to explore how schooling can be damaging to girls.

The interplay of structural and symbolic violence: gendering the academic curriculum

Drawing on Bourdieu's (2001) and Farmer's (2004) concepts of structural and symbolic violence as a way of framing our understanding of the effects of the academic curriculum on processes of gendering we can see how these effects take many forms which are often simultaneously structural and symbolic: from the organisation of the school day and the options commonly chosen by boys and girls to the materials used in classrooms and the gendered expectations of key figures such as teachers and classroom assistants. The ways in which children encounter ideas and subjects affect the degree to which they feel these are realistic and appropriate choices for them and open up or close off possible futures. While it may be unrealistic to expect schools to be able to cater for the specific individual needs and preferences of every child, it is the case that within formal school structures gender is a significant predictor of choice and involvement.

In spite of significant attention having been paid in recent decades to developing greater levels of gender-equal images children continue to be subjected to strictly demarcated gendered roles within their own families, in the aisles of toy stores and clothes shops and through advertising, children's television and wider socio-cultural settings. Gender roles are developed and enforced as children's subject and behaviour choices reflect a desire to align themselves with gender appropriate pathways. While there may be some disagreement about whether these gendered preferences are the result of socialisation or predicated on 'natural' individual differences, there is general agreement that children differentiate by gender from an early age (Wharton, 2005; Bradley, 2013). One teacher in our study reflects this:

'You usually find that a lot of the girls will still choose the arty crafty subjects and the boys don't as much although some do…role play areas and things, boys still tend to want to be soldiers and knights and have pretend weapons and girls want the fairy palace and…You still find that and as much as you try and address that they naturally tend to choose certain activities.' (Frances, mid–40s, manager, education sector, mother, North Yorkshire)

However genuinely such lamentations may be expressed, it has been shown repeatedly that the assumptions made by both formal school organisational structures and by teachers themselves are highly gendered and serve to reproduce patterns of gendered behaviour and disadvantage. In schools, the materials available to children frequently re-inscribe gender roles as children and teachers make choices about play and learning (Skelton, 1993). To take one example: books are significant sources of gendered messages and expectations of gendered behaviour (Turner-Bowker, 1996; Taylor, 2003) as 'characters portrayed in children's literature mould a child's conception of socially accepted roles and values, and indicate how males and females are supposed to act' (Kortenhaus and Demerest, 1993, 220) and provide 'symbolic representation of the world and of society' (Sleeter and Grant, 2010, 185). Studies of children's books throughout the twentieth century all reached similar findings; that males are frequently represented as more important, more commonly occupy the central role or title of the book and are more commonly found in children's stories. We need only to recall the passivity of Rapunzel, waiting to be rescued from her tower, or Sleeping Beauty (who doesn't even merit a name of her own) to recognise the continued relevance of such arguments. Lobhan (1975, cited in Skelton, 1993, 334) found that in reading schemes adult males had 33 occupations while adult women only merited eight which were; 'mum, granny, princess, queen, witch, handywoman about the house, teacher and shop assistant'. In general men are active while women are passive (Clark, 1999) leading Bender and Leone (1989, 36) to declare that reading books written for young children provide clear gendered messages, '[b]oys live exciting and independent lives, whereas girls are primarily auxiliaries to boys. To put it more bluntly: It's a man's world, kids!' (cited in Gooden and Gooden, 2001, 92).

These same studies also show, however, that things have changed somewhat towards a position of greater gender equity into the twenty-first century, with the growth of central female characters, a wider set of occupations for women and girls, and girls taking more active roles in the stories,[5] but overall, boys and girls continue to be portrayed differently, with girls more likely to be passive and dependent (Kortenhaus and Demerest, 1993). Alongside the gendered messages contained within children's stories and reading books, text books also convey messages to boys and girls about gender roles (Skelton et al, 2007). Ziegler and Heller (2000), researching the lack of girls within chemistry, note, for example, that girls are under-represented and those who do opt for chemistry are often more anxious and show less self-confidence partly 'as a consequence of gender-specific socialisation processes already existent in introductory chemistry courses' (Ziegler and Heller, 2000, np). Such stereotyping is not limited to traditionally male areas, however, studies of language textbooks in the 1970s and 1980s show that 'gender bias is rife in terms of both relative visibility and occupational and personal stereotyping of female characters' with girls and women again being more passive (Jones et al, 1997, 469). Though progress has been made, gender bias in textbooks around the world continues to be 'one of the best camouflaged – and hardest to budge' obstacles to gender equality in education (Blumberg, 2007).

Popular cultural beliefs about gender are reflected in the structures of educational systems that may require children to make choices early in their academic career that effectively set boys and girls onto different and lifelong pathways. These are not just present in textbooks and learning materials but in the structural and physical organisation of schools. Gillborn's research in a Midlands school notes timetabling structures meant that at 14 years old 'students who might otherwise have been tempted to study a non-traditional choice in addition to a more traditional one, were forced to choose between them' (1990, np). Gillborn (1990) goes further to describe how staff queried subject choices which were not seen as gender appropriate, sometimes causing students to change their choices. Discouragement may be subtle and those doing it may not even be acting with deliberate intent (a form of 'gentle', symbolic violence) but researchers have repeatedly found that teachers' expectations for pupils differ dramatically according to their gender: expectations tended to be gender-stereotypical and were more ambitious in the case of boys (see for example, Stanworth, 1983; 1997; Walkerdine, 1989; Rees, 1992). Stanworth's (1997) classic study showed, for example, how teachers are more likely to imagine futures that involve marriage and family even for highly achieving girls and professional careers even for less highly achieving boys.

Herbert and Stipek (2005) found, in their study on children's beliefs about academic ability that girls rate their abilities in maths lower than boys from an early age, even when there are no actual differences in attainment. As competency in maths is generally seen as a pre-requisite for science subjects it is easy to see how these self-assessments have long-lasting implications. Ulrica describes how the different presentations of confidence between boys and girls can lead girls to undervalue their achievements:

> 'It always appeared that the boys knew quite a lot of things, it took me quite a long time to realise, I could never work out why they didn't seem to do better in exams. Eventually I decided they are just better at bullshitting than the girls.' (Ulrica, early 50s, manager, non-traditional sector, Humberside)

As Erica notes, the patterns that are developed for boys and girls are different and reflect different ideas about future aspiration and expectation,

> 'Yes, I think boys were veered off towards maths, physics, chemistry very much so and the girls were sort of moved into biology for some reason and the languages and there was typing still, you did typing…"Do the typing, that'll be really nice for you" [but] I managed to keep out of typing.' (Erica, mid-30s, self-employed, mother, North Yorkshire)

Such gender streaming has an instant impact on girls' and women's sense of their own capabilities, as is shown in Erica's assessment of 'Do the typing, that'll be really nice for you', a subject she 'managed to keep out of'. Typing continues to be an extremely valuable skill in contemporary society, but because it has become feminised it commands little status as Erica clearly understood even as a child. Hidden curricula effects began early for many women in our study and the gendering of choice was a 'normal' part of the school organisation, as Becky describes:

> 'You had of course the timetabling issues, so you had that kind of hidden curricula effect where you couldn't physically take a feminised subject and a, er, a kind of a subject that was seen as more masculine, because they were timetabled against each other.' (Becky, late 30s, part-time administrator, mother, East Yorkshire)

Rhona, who ended up in a traditionally 'male' area of work notes similar limitations to the options available to her:

'at that school you had to choose. Um, you had to fight to do all three sciences, to be honest…I couldn't have done home economics, I couldn't have done art. It didn't fit with the timetables.' (Rhona, mid-30s, engineer, West Yorkshire)

Messages such as these in schools mean that girls come to understand clearly what their present and future expectations should be. Dale et al (2005), researching women in non-traditional occupations, found that a 'majority had been dissuaded by schools – because they were girls, because they were clever, or simply because at girls' schools the topic had never been raised. As one woman said, "I just didn't know it was a possibility"' (Dale et al, 2005, 16).

The careers advice that girls receive in schools has also been the subject of concern for failing to offer a broad enough choice for girls. The Women and Work Commission (2005, np) note concern about 'girls' access to information and support to make informed choices about educational subjects, training, jobs and careers' and argued that future developments in careers advice provision should take concerns around constraints to girls' and women's choices seriously in order that 'their horizons are broadened and aspirations raised' (Women and Work Commission, 2005, 11). A 2005 study funded by the EOC found that few students receive advice about non-traditional work placements and that work placements can operate to perpetuate stereotyping by leading boys and girls into traditional areas (Francis et al, 2005). More recent reports have continued to show that many girls feel that they get poor careers advice at school, are steered into stereotypical female jobs (Youth Work Now, 2007) and denied better job prospects because they lack all-round careers advice (Fuller et al, 2005a). Though these issues are being tackled, for example through the implementation of the Education Act (2008), though the requirement set out within this for schools to deliver 'impartial careers education free from institutional or individual bias' (Hutchinson et al, 2011, viii) seems to have had limited impact to date.

The internalisation of differential symbolic socio-cultural values is revealed in the ways in which women repeat the differential assessments of male and female subjects. Women in our research talked about being 'forced' to do cooking while being 'jealous' of boys who were 'lucky' to be doing subjects such as technical drawing. Such comments demonstrate the ways in which complex gendered assumptions and valorisations operate to enact symbolic violence that serves to undermine 'female' areas and accomplishments, leading to lower sense of self-worth and personal value. Martin (1996) argues that boys' 'domephobia' – the diminishing and 'morbid anxiety' of things related to the domestic sphere is problematic for girls' self-esteem as the very things that boys scorn are those most closely associated with traditional girls' roles in the future.

Elizabeth's assessment of the subjects she took at school shows not only how little value she felt was attached to them but also how they were clearly directing her and other girls towards the domestic sphere;

> And, erm, a lot of it was compulsory. And I *ended up in,* erm, needlework and cookery. Skills that a woman needs…It was…all gender geared. All your subjects, girls were *pushed into* domestic science and needlework. And the boys were *allowed to do* woodwork and metalwork. (Elizabeth, late 30s, part-time student, mother, Humberside, emphasis added)

Polly shows similar assessments of subjects associated with feminine pastimes, while valorising boys' subjects:

> 'I used to be very jealous of the boys at the boys' school down the road because they did – was it called technical drawing, or something? They did things like that and we *weren't allowed* to do that; *just* cooking.' (Polly, early 40s, part time, community sector, mother, North Yorkshire, emphasis added)

Research clearly shows the differential valuations that different subject choices attract. The preferencing of rationality and 'maleness' in modernity means that issues of confidence and mental wellbeing are rooted in the ways that girls are socialised into being girls, and becoming women (Bradley, 2013). The structural and symbolic roots of this gendered and 'gentle' violence that underpin processes of female socialisation can have a significant impact on how women and girls feel about themselves, their abilities and their rights to achieve success as individuals. These deeply held positions are played out daily in classrooms around the country as subjects such as 'hard' sciences and maths are valorised over others such as English and social sciences (the 'soft' sciences). The impact of the academic curriculum, then, is to teach girls that feminine subjects are of lower value, that girls' destinies are to be sidelined to the projects of boys and that they are themselves, ultimately, of lower value.

The structural and symbolic gendered violence of the behavioural curriculum

Other answers to how girls become under-confident can be found in the attributes and characteristics that are encouraged and valued in girls and the ways that these can lead to unwillingness to push boundaries, disagree with authority and risk exposing oneself to ridicule by challenging expectations. We examine these in more detail in the section below.

Basow (2004, 117) argues, speaking of the USA, that in spite of some greater equity in boys' and girls' achievements at school, such as graduation rates, 'boys and girls in general still learn, and are reinforced for, traditional gendered behaviours'. Similarly, Kevin Stannard, the director of Innovation and Learning at the Girls' Day School Trust, suggests that girls are praised for traits and characteristics such as 'sitting nicely and making sure their margins are aligned' that do not necessarily equip them for success beyond school (Barker, 2013, np). Opal, for example, summed up what she thought the purpose of her schooling had been:

> 'Well, to teach you how to behave properly. You know…
> to read and write and, um, sort of like the basic skills of
> knitting and sewing…You just do this, you know, add up,
> read, write, um, sew things, cook, domestic sciences, how to
> use a washing machine.' (Opal, late 50s, volunteer, mother,
> Humberside)

Through both classroom and family socialisation girls can also absorb messages that their male associates are assumed to be, or expected to be, 'better' in a range of ways; more intelligent, better at sports, better able to negotiate the public arena, more confident, be more likely to eventually have a better career and so on. This is confirmed by interactions in the classroom as boys are more likely to get attention from teachers. A Kelly's 1988 meta-analysis of the literature reveals that studies find consistently that boys receive more attention, but also that girls volunteered to take part more than boys (for example, by putting their hand up) and suggests that 'this implies that girls were willing to take an equal part in lessons, but were not allowed to do so' (1988, 6). As Orenstein (2004) explains in her study of 'schoolgirls' in the US educational system, boys demand attention and become disruptive when teachers attempt to direct attention elsewhere, boys are more likely to answer questions, and to be called on to do so, less concerned when they make mistakes and, through all of this:

> Speaking out in class – and being acknowledged for it – is a constant reinforcement of a student's right to be heard, to take academic risks. Students who talk in class have more opportunity to enhance self-esteem through exposure to praise; they have the luxury of learning from mistakes and they develop the perspective to see failure as an educational tool. (Orenstein, 1994, 12)

There is some evidence that the ways that girls behave in classrooms, conforming to gendered expectations of 'good' behaviour, mean that teachers are less likely to pay them attention or to understand them as individuals. As Stanworth famously put it, girls risk becoming a 'faceless bunch' (1983) that blends into the background and, in addition, the less dominant behaviours girls display means that their abilities are also often underestimated.

Girls can also learn that boys control public spaces in the school, with a greater share of the playground during free time (Holly, 1985), occupying the central spaces while girls occupy the periphery. For boys 'the physical school is a more spacious place' than for girls (Gordon, 1996, 39) and boys' activities 'tend to be more spatially invasive than girls' (Kelle, 2000, 170). Here Alice describes how she was very conscious of the gender differences in space and movement in her primary school playground:

> 'I remember in primary school there was a girl's playground…and that was at the bottom, and the boy's playground at the top…and we weren't allowed to cross over. But the boy's space was massive and ours was about a third of the size. I complained to the headmaster one day, asked why girls couldn't play football at the top with the boys. He said we would get hurt [laughs]. But then after that he did, as a special treat, let the girls play on the boy's playground for one day. Only once though…we were all really excited and felt important because we got to join in with the boys' games one time.' (Alice, late 30s, manager, education sector, volunteer, mother, West Yorkshire)

Alice was clearly aware, even as a young girl, of the spatial and symbolic gender differences at work in her school. She even did something about it, raising the issue with the headmaster, which no doubt took courage. The gender boundaries were overtly marked, boys were physically located 'at the top' and girls 'at the bottom'. That she recounts understanding it was a 'special treat' to join in with the boys' games in their far larger outdoor space and that it made the girls feel 'important' clearly illustrates the power of the symbolic and structural gender violence that seeps into the everyday lives of women and girls, placing clearly demarcated gendered values on boys and girls.

We are not suggesting here that all teachers intentionally perpetuate gender stereotypes, many teachers think that they treat boys and girls the same (A Kelly, 1988; Beaman et al, 2006) and many actively challenge biased behaviours in the classroom. Moreover, as Skelton (1993) argues, teachers are not necessarily aware of the gender stereotyping they perform as much is done on a sub-conscious level. Educational research during the 1980s and 1990s found, for example, that teachers would pit boys and girls against each other, praising girls for being the quiet ones which 'promotes the notion that girls are valued for their abilities to be passive and non-vocal [and] "punish" boys who misbehaved by making them sit with the girls. There can be no greater insult to a boy's sense of masculinity than by referring to him as a "girl"' (Skelton, 1997, 309). Girls learn early in their lives that girls and boys who adopt behaviours which are not perceived as appropriately feminine or masculine can be sanctioned by teachers (Stanworth, 1983; Walkerdine, 1989). As Charles (2002) notes, in both Stanworth's (1983) study on gender and schooling and Walkerdine's (1989) study on gender and maths, they found that 'if girls exhibited challenging and intellectually questioning behaviour it was regarded negatively in marked contrast to the same behaviour in boys...and that being noisy and demanding is perceived as inappropriate behaviour for girls but for boys is a sign of intelligence' (Charles, 2002, 98).

A further finding of a range of educational studies was that girls are more likely to interpret failure as their own failure due to lack of ability, while boys are more likely to blame others, or their own lack of effort (but not lack of ability) (Stanworth, 1983; A Kelly, 1988; Jones and Jones, 1989, cited in Skelton and Francis, 2003). As Orenstein (1994, 16) argues, '[t]oday's girls fall into traditional patterns of low self-image, self-doubt, and self-censorship of their creative and intellectual potential. Although all children experience confusion and a faltering sense of self at adolescence, girls' self-regard drops further than boys and never catches up'.

Processes of gendering within schools must of course be understood as inextricable from similar processes of socialisation within wider family and community life. As well as teachers' overt or subconscious gendered attitudes, and the impacts of educational structures such as gendered timetabling constraints, family and the influence of friendship networks are also important factors that influence subject choices at school and particular ways of behaving (Fuller et al, 2005b). Heather's story reveals how, even when teachers and family are supportive towards girls pursuing non-traditional areas, the power of social pressures and gendered identifications of what is 'appropriate' still operate to constrain the options which women/girls perceive are open to them:

> 'I always remember as well, um, which is a bit strange, um, one of my teachers thinking I was really, really exceptional at metalwork, but I refused to take it as an option because, for me, it was a boys' subject…I absolutely was adamant I wasn't doing a boys' subject…But, um, I think I just didn't want to leave the group of girls I was with probably. I don't know. But at school there was no way I was going to be seen to be doing it at school…So they probably influenced my thinking back then a lot as well.' (Heather, late 30s, self-employed, mother, North Yorkshire)

Visceral violence: the impact of sexism, sexualisation and sexual violence for girls in school

We have explored the ways in which academic, behavioural, formal and hidden curriculum factors – structural and symbolic forms of 'gentle' violence – can have an impact on boys' and girls' specifically gendered educational experiences. Another critical gendered issue that can have serious impacts, in particular, although not exclusively, on girls' lives, is that of actual, visceral violence through sexism, sexualisation and even sexual assault within the school environment. Alongside messages about what types of subjects are appropriate for girls, and what types of behaviour attract positive and negative sanctions, schools are also a key site in which girls and boys learn about sexual politics and the ways in which their developing sexualities are perceived by peers and others.

Gender-based violence within schools in the UK (as it does worldwide) includes heterosexual harassment, homophobic violence and stigmatisation, bullying, sexual comments and even direct sexual attacks. Many of these gendered performances are played out to enhance and reinforce hegemonic, negative cultures of femininities and masculinities, leaving little safe space in which children can choose not to conform to these practices.

Jones (1985), for example details the various and numerous types of sexual harassment that girls and female teachers were subjected to in her study of a school on the outskirts of London. These include being called names (cunt, slag, pro, bitch), having their physical appearance commented on by boys, suggestive talk and a general normalisation of sexual treatment of women and girls. Research by the National Union of Teachers finds similar results: almost 20 per cent of primary teachers and two thirds of secondary teachers have suffered sexually abusive language from pupils while nearly 75 per cent of secondary teachers and 30 per cent of primary teachers have come across this language being used between pupils (cited in EOC, 2007b). In 2010 a YouGov poll found that 29 per cent of 16–18 year old girls (compared to 14 per cent of boys) had 'experienced unwanted sexual touching' while at school (YouGov, 2010, np).

Martin (1996, 28) suggests 'girls of all ages are experiencing a degree of harassment and hostility in their in-school interactions with boys that is almost unimaginable to their elders'. This finding is echoed by Leach and Humphreys (2007, 51) who also warn that 'recognition that schools can be violent places has tended to ignore the fact that many such acts originate in unequal and antagonistic gender relations, which are tolerated and "normalised" by everyday school structures and processes'. Such violence and harassment can now also follow girls beyond the public sphere and into their private spaces with abuse, coercion and exploitation through media such as sexting: 'the creating, sharing and forwarding of sexually suggestive nude or nearly nude images by minor teens' (Lenhart, 2009, 3). While both boys and girls engage in sexting it is 'not a gender-neutral practice' but 'shaped by the gender dynamics of the peer group in which, primarily, boys harass girls, and it is exacerbated by the gendered norms of popular culture' (Ringrose et al, 2012, 7).[6]

Here Alice talks about some of her experiences of a co-educational comprehensive school in West Yorkshire:

> 'There was a lot of sexual harassment and violence at my [secondary] school. I hated being there. I was seen as quite pretty and so some girls bullied me because I was popular with boys. One girl terrorised me for ages…I was scared to go to school. She finally attacked me in the street outside school, beat me up…After, though, she was criticised by other kids because I was so small and quiet and she was really

big…so she said she did it because she saw me "snogging" a boy she liked. It wasn't true, but it could have been because I did get attention from boys. A lot of the time I didn't want it but you are taught to want it, I learned to think that I had to please boys and just laugh if they grabbed my body and made rude comments. One day a boy in my class grabbed me on the way home from school, dragged me down a [pathway] and assaulted me. He pushed me against a wall, held me by my throat and really hurt me…touched me, pushed his face…and hands into me…They called it fingering back then. But he was violent. It hurt, I was only 13. I managed to get away before he raped me. But I guess what he did was rape, kind of. I never told anyone that. I just had to see him every day in class, smirking at me and bragging to his mates…I would never send my daughter to a co-ed high school.' (Alice, late 30s, manager, education sector, volunteer, mother, West Yorkshire)

How could this level of gender-based and sexual violence in schools not make a difference to both girls' self-esteem and academic achievement?

Conclusion

Our research confirms research conducted elsewhere that by the time young women leave school, the majority, for a variety of complex interlocking social and structural reasons, have opted for more feminised subject areas that attract, in the future, lower earnings and lower status. The lower status of these ambitions are clear to the girls and women themselves and shines through in the ways that women in our study speak of their ambitions in deprecating and disparaging ways when they relate to feminised pathways. As Pamela notes, many women's experiences of schooling have been that:

> 'the girls would be slotted off somewhere along the way for something nice and easy.' (Pamela, mid-40s, community sector manager, volunteer, Humberside)

They have also learned that girls are rewarded for particular behaviours such as 'being good' and not being disruptive and that more outgoing behaviours such as speaking out and being disruptive attract censure from both peers and adults. We do not intend to imply here that all girls are quiet, demure and self-effacing, there are, of course, girls who break the mould and who actively struggle against gendered norms and expectations. Girls in general, though, have learned that they should not expect the same levels of attention as boys, and that their access to public space, whether in the classroom or at play, is achieved through negotiation with and the agreement of boys, a trend that will continue throughout their lives when, as grown women they will be counselled not to walk home alone, not to walk through parks and to live their lives in continual recognition of potential physical and sexual attack from men, whose freedom of movement is not recommended to be restricted in the same ways.

This research found that most women we spoke with recognised coercive elements in the way their schooling was directed. They saw the valorisation of boys' subjects, and internalised these perceptions while being simultaneously aware and critical of them. As situated knowers they talked explicitly about the ways it was made clear to them the sorts of things they should expect from their future lives. This included strong messages received by women during their schooling that they were not as clever as boys, that girls' subjects were not as academically challenging and they should not raise their aspirations too high. From talking with the women in this study it seems that Delamont's presentation of schools as conservative spaces which 'reinforce [gender roles] in tougher form than they actually exist in the world outside' (1980, 10) continues to be the case today and that this has long-lasting impacts on children's futures.

It is often no longer conscious discrimination that is the main barrier to girls' aspiration and success, but rather it seems to be rooted in forms of symbolic violence: deeply held social and cultural beliefs about 'appropriate' behaviours and interests for males and females, which then translate into 'appropriate' ambitions and occupational aspirations. While women enjoy *de jure* equality, the *de facto* reality is that the differential values attached to 'male' and 'female' subjects – which subsequently translates into occupations – means that women can experience life-long economic and status disadvantage resulting from educational 'choices'. Tackling this necessitates a more strategic as well as practical approach to such gender needs.

Women themselves are aware of these processes and a number of women in our study actively volunteered aspirations for their daughters that would see them living different kinds of lives from their mothers, lives that were not bound by lack of confidence, by gendered aspiration and traditional expectations of women's place.

Ella, who works with young parents, talks about what she perceives as motivations for mothers to return to education, again this makes clear that women's motivations are not entirely for personal development:

> 'I spoke to young women who've said, 'Oh, I hated school, I hate reading, I hate writing, but I have to learn' and it's like it's a real shame you couldn't have got that before the baby was around, which is a bit of a shame, but they only start having aspirations because they want something good for their child, not for them.' (Ella, late 30s, manager, community sector, volunteer, Humberside)

As Martin (1996, 32) argues, 'To treat issues such as girls' low self-esteem, boy-hostile girls, and the curricular misrepresentations of women as unrelated, isolated phenomena instead of as interrelated by-products of one and the same education-gender system, is to allow that large organization of beliefs and practices to remain hidden and to go unchallenged.' Things have moved on, but there is more moving to do, and a need for continued vigilance to monitor that process.

SIX

Gendering reproduction: women's experiences of motherhood and mental wellbeing

Introduction: women and mothering

This chapter discusses motherhood,[1] which we understand to be one of the defining or 'enduring' (Hartman, 2004) features of women's lives, whether or not they choose, or are able, to become mothers themselves. Women in British society have progressed in ways our mothers and grandmothers could not have imagined. The advent of reliable and available contraception means that for many women motherhood has become a matter of choice in a way that was inconceivable even 50 years ago. This new freedom comes, though, with additional pressures and costs as individual women must now try to negotiate an acceptable line between personal choice and wider social pressures within cultures that are overwhelmingly pronatalist.

While many feminists have had a problematic relationship with motherhood, being critical of the role mothering plays in women's oppression as an obstacle to equality and personal autonomy, here we develop an understanding of motherhood that explores the different ways women both benefit from and are constrained by ideals and practices of motherhood. We can understand the position held by de Beauvoir that woman's 'misfortune is to have been biologically destined for the repetition of life' ([1949] 1997) and Allen's more radical position that motherhood is 'dangerous to women' and should be rejected (1996, 28). The reality remains that most women either are mothers, become mothers or live with and around motherhood at some point in their lives. Rather than decrying and rejecting motherhood we follow work such as that of Oakley (1974) that explores the stresses and isolation of mothering and the consequences for women as a group and as individuals.

This chapter is divided into two parts, in the first part we explore how different constructions of mothering have an impact on women's construction of self and, consequently, how conflicting cultural demands and expectations have an impact on women's wellbeing. We begin by setting out the multiple pressures women face when making decisions concerning whether or not to become mothers. Building on this we explore popular constructions of 'good' and 'bad' mothering and the impact that these have on women's self-confidence. We show how naturalising discourses of motherhood serve to make mothering look 'easy' (Coward, 1992, 117) and cause women themselves to underestimate the range of skills required to raise children, valuations that are echoed by those around them and within wider society. We explore how women's intimate association with child rearing leads to their association with other areas of domestic life that are also of low value. Finally, we argue that the adoption of mothering into the public arena subjects women to confusing and contradictory messages about the status and value of mothering, undermines women and causes them to adopt a 'not-good-enough' image of their own mothering. We do not wish to suggest that women are passive subjects or 'docile bodies' (Foucault, 1979, 138), but that hegemonic patriarchal regimes, in which women themselves are complicit, act in numerous and often under-recognised ways to diminish both mothers and mothering. We argue that these processes have negative consequences for how mothers construct their life narratives and their sense of self.

The second part of this chapter builds on these arguments but moves further beyond the home to explore intersections between motherhood and the public sphere, focusing on the complex and interwoven connections between motherhood, education and employment. While typical men's working patterns are full time and continuous, typical women's patterns are reduced and discontinuous due to caring commitments (Warren et al, 2001) and women are concentrated in low-status and low-paid work. Our research found that requirements on women to juggle multiple roles often leave women feeling inadequate in all of them. In this study, women to whom we spoke, whether mothers or not, talked about mothering as a deeply personal and formative experience, but worried about conflicting messages and ideas about how they should 'do' mothering and how to combine work, womanhood and mothering successfully for themselves and others.

Gender regimes, womanhood and motherhood: unpicking the Gordian knot

In western societies 'womanhood' is often still equated with 'motherhood' (Oakley, 1979; Nicolson, 1997; Gillespie, 1999; Dykstra and Hagestad, 2007; Loftus and Andriot, 2012), considered as 'central to feminine identity' (Gillespie, 1999, 43) and to be fulfilling for women. In our broadly pronatalistic societies married couples, and women in particular, are expected to both want and have children (Veevers, 1973). For those women who either cannot or choose not to have children full adult status can be problematic and women who are not mothers may well be perceived by themselves and others as both incomplete and unfulfilled (Gillespie, 1999; Letherby, 2002).

In spite of this strong cultural and social imperative, the conflicting pressures that many women feel in relation to mothering are indicated by the general decline in fertility rates in almost every part of the 'developed' world, including Europe, in the last few decades. Within the 27 countries of the European Union fertility rates in 2009 were recorded as 1.59 live births per woman, below the 2.1 live births per woman needed to replace the population through birth alone (Eurostat, 2012). In the UK the total fertility rate has risen slightly over the last decade and is currently around 2 children per woman (ONS, 2011a). To bring this back to the local context, the total fertility rate in 2007 in the Yorkshire and Humber region was 1.89, the sixth highest in England (ONS, 2009) and Hull has tended to record rates of teenage (under 18) pregnancy which are 'significantly worse than the England average' (DH, 2010, np), although rates have recently declined. Women are delaying the age at which they have children with the mean age of mother rising to 29.5 years in 2010 compared with 28.5 years in 2000 (ONS, 2011a), one of the highest ages in OECD countries (OECD, 2011).

It is apparent that in situations where women, in general, have a greater range of choices available to them there are increases in delayed fertility, smaller family sizes and in absolute childlessness (Nicoletti and Tanturri, 2005; Schober, 2007; ONS, 2011c). This is especially the case for women with career/professional aspirations who fear that having children early could have a negative impact on career prospects. This suggests to us that women clearly understand the structural limitations of their lives and the fact that they have to make choices between family and work in ways men do not (Kelly, 2009). Women, for example, continue to bear the major responsibilities for childcare regardless of their other working commitments (Dench et al, 2002). As Ina noted:

> 'I don't think for one minute that my partner has considered sacrificing anything in terms of fitting around family life, I think he's taking it as a given that he can go on and just do what he needs to do, and I'll be the one who shuffle around

and fit in with everything, and that's not disrespect that he has for me, it's all down to your paradigm, it's preconceived ideas you don't even realise that you've got, and he doesn't even realise he's acting on them.' (Ina, mid-20s, student, mother, Humberside)

Voluntary childlessness[2] is seen to be affected by three main areas: female education, female labour employment and culture (Houseknecht, 1982, cited in Gobbi, 2011, 3). Since the 1970s it has tended to be women with higher levels of education who are deferring the birth of their first child or remaining voluntarily childless (Gillespie, 1999; Joshi, 2002). The centrality of motherhood to legitimate women's identities can be revealed through attitudes to those who do not become mothers. Women who do not have children are viewed negatively or with suspicion, the object of sympathy and support if their lack of children is not voluntary (Gillespie, 1999, 44) but constructed as 'selfish' and 'deviant' if they are childless by choice (Gillespie, 1999; Hird, 2003). Repeated research findings suggest that 'nearly all childless women felt that they faced some disapproval from friends and family' (Kelly, 2009, 165) meaning that being without children is almost always seen negatively.

Kelly (2009) lists a range of different ways women come to make choices around whether to have children describing them as 'transitional', 'postponers', 'ambivalent' or 'passive' decision makers who may end up not having children but may have done if circumstances had been different. Veevers (1980) found that two-thirds of the voluntarily childless couples she interviewed kept putting off having children, meaning that the 'right time' just didn't arrive. Indeed, some women who delay having children may find it more difficult or even impossible to conceive once they wish to. Helen succinctly sums up the tension between her own career aspirations and the pressures she imagines would be felt to stop work if she has children:

'I don't think that's my role but society does…' (Helen, early 20s, student, Humberside)

Ella, who works with young women in education, reveals some of the dilemmas women face between cultural constructions of 'good mothering' and their own aspirations:

'We had a young woman in…who asked to be re-housed away from there because she was actually getting hassled for being a bad mother for going to college. The people who lived there, they were stopping her in the street and saying, "Oh, we've heard about you, you go off to college, you want to be staying at home and raising that baby properly."' (Ella, late 30s, manager, community sector, volunteer, East Yorkshire)

For those women who follow the expected course the path is just as problematic with myriad pressures over when and how to have children (Bennet, 1996 cited in Letherby, 2002), how many children to have, how their bodies should look and how children are best raised. For some women, the cultural expectation that being a mother is 'enough' for women's fulfilment is also problematic. Erica describes how she loves being a mother, but still has ambitions that go beyond her children:

'You know, I would never not be a mum, you know, I just love being a mum, I love my kids and everything, but I just think, um, I just want something else for me as well and I've got to have that other sort of aspect in my life.' (Erica, mid–30s, self-employed, mother, North Yorkshire)

Alongside concern that certain groups of women are delaying or refusing motherhood, is a parallel concern that women from some groups, especially those from less advantaged backgrounds, tend to have children in early adulthood (Joshi et al, 2004). Such decisions about early motherhood can be seen by the women themselves as ways to demonstrate their value as women and to provide a sense of purpose, self-respect and adult status to their lives (Hallam and Creech, 2007). Early motherhood, however, is often interpreted by others as problematic, especially for those with lower aspirations or expectations, associated with problematic types of parenting and often evoking 'disgust' among the middle classes (Lawler, 2005; I. Tyler, 2008; Clisby, 2009). In 2013, for example, the 40 Group of Conservative MPs[3] proposed that teenage mothers only be allowed to claim benefits if they are living either with parents or in a supervised hostel (New Statesman, 2013). Women make motherhood choices within a social context in which 'children and motherhood are valued rhetorically and not structurally supported' (Letherby, 1999, 361). Mothering itself is often treated as if it has no financial value (Crittenden, 2001) and popular models of good mothering frequently pit work and mothering against each other as dichotomous (Johnston and Swanson, 2004) while increasingly exhorting mothers to be economically active.

This leads to contradictory expectations as women are simultaneously expected to be both a perfect mother, willing to engage in 'intensive mothering' (Brydon, 2009) and to enter public life to become full citizens. Being a mother requires then that the woman 'devote her entire physical, emotional, and intellectual being, 24/7, to her children' (Douglas and Michaels, 2004, 4) and, as Collett emphasises, she must also 'enjoy every minute of it' (2005, 329) on top of engaging in paid work outside the home. Women who do have children must, therefore perform motherhood in sanctioned ways and find strategies to fit other aspects of their identities into this confusing and contradictory framework. Furthermore, women are often hardest on themselves; a recent survey of over 3,700 women in the United States found that women 'overwhelmingly say, "I am my own worst critic", the option selected by 49 per cent of working and 47 per cent of stay-at-home mothers' (Working Mother Research Institute, 2011, 9).

Such ideals lead many women to feel ambivalent about mothering. As Parker suggests there is 'a complex and contradictory state of mind, shared variously by all mothers, in which loving and hating feelings for children exist side by side' (Parker, 1997, 17). Or, as Boulton puts it, 'On the one hand, "everyone knows" that it is "depressing" to stay at home with young children. On the other hand, "everyone knows" that children are "naturally rewarding" to their mothers' (1983, 2). Knowledge of these contradictions is not new, and such sentiments were clearly drawn in Oakley's work on housewives in the 1970s (Oakley, 1974). Parker goes on to argue that mothers' ambivalence to their children and mothering roles causes them to experience feelings of guilt partly from 'weathering the painful feelings evoked by experiencing maternal ambivalence in a culture that shies away from the very existence of something it has helped to produce' (1997, 17). This shows clearly how gender regimes are implicated in the constructions of women's sense of self at even the most intimate levels.

The reasons women choose to have children or not to have children are complex, and of course each individual woman will have personal reasons for such a decision. There is no doubt, however, that these reasons are influenced by wider social factors in ways which diminish a woman's autonomy, instead subjecting women's decisions and bodies to gendered scrutinies and patriarchal surveillance systems. Through hegemonic constructions of gender identities motherhood becomes romanticised and viewed as the normal and appropriate occupation for women which, therefore, needs little attention and few support systems. Through the close associations between mothering and women, caring for children comes to be seen as something that women do and mothers come to be seen as something that women are (Gillespie, 1999, 44). Such representations are deeply damaging to women who struggle to have their 'mother-work' recognised and rewarded, and may consequently struggle to maintain a positive sense of their own selves.

Mothering in the public realm: understanding messages of good and bad mothering

As we see above, it is almost impossible for women's decisions about whether and when to have children to be wholly personal, individual ones. Instead, through numerous different means women are held to account for their decisions to partners, families, workplaces, friends and even strangers. This leaves many women feeling that they are constantly being measured against ideal standards of motherhood, womanhood and citizenship that are, themselves, incompatible.

Clare talked to us about how she feels that she constantly has to explain her own childlessness in order to manage the expectations of others:

> 'I spent years smiling politely and making jokes, deflecting the discomfort I feel every time someone asked me why I don't have children or made comments about it "being your turn next"...er, after that I began to tell people that I am not planning to have children...no one really seems to believe me. I've given up with that now and tell anyone who asks, and it happens much more than you would think, that I would love to have children but my partner can't. That usually embarrasses them into not asking any more. Though some people seem to think it's an invitation to discuss fertility options...I think some people just can't accept it... and it is everywhere, at work, family, with strangers, people just seem to think it's their business...but it does make it much harder for me.' (Clare, late 30s, manager, education sector, volunteer, Yorkshire)

Clare's comments also reveal her desire to avoid confrontation or discomforting the people who are asking about her choices and her eventual adoption, after years of 'smiling politely', of a more challenging approach. It seems that Clare's experiences suggest that others cannot imagine her feeling complete or comfortable without children. As she says, 'some people just can't accept it'. Such representations of the incompleteness of women who don't have children are common in the media, and are even portrayed by women themselves as in this interview excerpt with Gwyneth Paltrow:

> She won an Oscar and married a rock star, but Gwyneth Paltrow's life didn't truly have meaning until she became a parent. 'I never feel like I don't know what my purpose is anymore. They [my children] have given me a real life. The mom has to be there and put time into every relationship in the house. Once you're a mother, you see everything in a different light.' (interview with Gwyneth Paltrow, *In Touch* magazine, June 23, 2008 cited in, Gentile, 2011, 38)

The point, Gentile notes, is that it is difficult for any woman to transcend these romanticised, naturalised images and so many women are left feeling that they are a failure.

Once they become mothers, however, women may feel overwhelmed by the change in their circumstance and their attempts to learn new skills and adapt to their new position. Medicalised models seek to inform women that these symptoms need naming and treating and seek to deal with the individual rather than the social, cultural and material conditions of their lives (Hockey, 1993). Sally, whose work involves supporting new mothers, talks about the way women who may be struggling after the birth of a child are treated, suggesting women experiencing problems are made to feel that their issues are individualised and, to some extent, that they themselves are to blame:

> 'Quite often women will be encouraged to see it as their individual problem rather than a reaction to circumstances they are in...I really worry that women are encouraged to individualise and diagnose their problems rather than look at the situations they are in.' (Sally, late 30s, manager, health sector, volunteer, West Yorkshire)

In the next part of this discussion we explore some of the messages to which women are subjected concerning 'good mothering' from the media, local communities and from their own families. Such public interest means that parents in general, and mothers in particular, are exposed to a pervasive set of ideals and images of what constitutes 'good' parenting rather than being left to develop their own parenting strategies.

Idealised images of mothering which 'in white Western society is of the ever-bountiful, ever-giving, self-sacrificing mother' (Bassin et al,

1994, 2) closely linked with idealised images of family life predominant during the 1950s remain powerful images for women and families today. Thompson (1996, 388) argues that as adults, women born after the Second World War continue to 'grapple with an array of conflicting social expectations, gender ideals, cultural values and interpersonal demands'.

As we have demonstrated in previous chapters women grow up absorbing, learning and replicating gendered patterns that gain them approval and acceptance. No wonder then, that as most women in this study grew up in what might be termed a 'traditional' family structure, with the mother staying at home, at least while the children are small, and then taking on a mixture of part-time and temporary posts once their children had started school, many feel that this is the model to replicate. Both Lynne and Gayle talk about this here:

> 'She gave up her work to bring up me and my sister, as most women did then…and she went back to work when my sister and I went to school.' (Lynne, late 30s, manager, civil service, Humberside)

> 'She worked on and off, but my dad, he never put his foot down, but he used to say "I'm the bread winner, I like to bring the money in." But she went out to work, he never stopped her, but she was mainly a housewife.' (Gayle, mid-30s, education sector, mother, Humberside)

For many women decisions around if and when to return to work are realised as a complex negotiation between the often contradictory expectations that exist of women and mothers. The adoption of child rearing choices into public debates, and the concomitant sense of social and public interest and, to some degree, control, over women's decisions in how they organise their time meant that many women we spoke to absolutely felt that they were subject to unfair external pressures, based on what other people thought were appropriate ways of behaving. Modern media carry huge numbers of stories about celebrity mothers that present unrealistic and unobtainable targets for normal women, but, as Douglas and Michaels (2004, 3) note, 'Even mothers who deliberately avoid TV and magazines, or who pride themselves on seeing through them, have trouble escaping the standards of perfection, and the sense of threat, that the media ceaselessly atomise into the air we breathe.'

It is clear in the language Gayle uses above that the patterns of male dominance and control ring loud in many women's memories, even if they are not conscious of them. This is reflected in the phrases, 'He never stopped her,' and, 'He never put his foot down,' making clear that her mother's freedom to choose between home and public life was negotiated and ultimately dependent on the agreement of her father. It is not just messages from men but also those from other women that can serve to undermine women. Here, Dawn talks about her mother's attitude to her going out to work and how her mother repeatedly made her feel guilty about working:

> 'I think I was very much influenced by my mother and I know when I first started talking about going back to work she was quite disapproving. If [daughter] was poorly or anything she would say, 'Oh well, I'm sure she wouldn't have been ill if you were at home with her'; what difference that would have made I don't know.' (Dawn, late 50s, civil service, mother, West Yorkshire)

While women are influenced by family, societal pressures also play a large part. Polly recounts feeling judged by other people whose conflicting demands and expectations meant that she could not avoid disapprobation – as both by staying at home or by working she attracted criticism:

> 'In other circles that I'm in, I find it's almost the opposite. It's kind of like, "Oh, you go out to work." You know, "You're not at home for your family." Not so much now that they're older, but certainly before my youngest started school. I suppose you kind of feel like it [working] is part of your identity…I don't know. I suppose it just makes you feel like you've got some worth. But, at the same time, it's not really that worth that's most important to me. I don't know.' (Polly, early 40s, part-time community sector, mother, North Yorkshire)

Polly's comment above is full of qualifications and equivocations which may reveal her own sense of conflict and dis-ease with the attempts she has made to juggle work and family.

Most working women who have children take a period of time out of paid work when the children are young, seeing this as the 'best' or 'normal' thing to do. These individual and family choices are supported by legislation that provides for both women and men to take parental leave, but gendered expectations are made clear within this provision.

Men are entitled to one or two weeks' statutory (paid) paternity leave while women are entitled to 26 weeks.[4] This confirms women's connection to the private sphere and, while having children can be a source of pleasure and satisfaction to women, many told us that they had underestimated the negative impact being at home with children would have on their own wellbeing. Mothers in our study reported feeling isolated and losing their individuality within what some felt was an overwhelming 'mother' identity. Octavia's experiences were echoed by many women in this study:

> 'I did feel very isolated, I was very isolated and although I did, I make friends very easily, but you know people have still got their own lives to lead, you know, and I hated being stuck at home…so I needed something different, and something else to focus on, because I found that you end up going down in a spiral, and you know you start losing your self-worth, and I needed something else.' (Octavia, mid–40s, volunteer, mother, Humberside)

Fiona's experience encapsulates the contradictions that many women experience between the mothering myth and the lived realities of becoming and being a mother:

> 'So I was very lonely for the first year and I thought it was going to be wonderful and I was so lonely.' (Fiona, late 40s, manager, community sector, volunteer, mother, Humberside)

What we found was that, for many women, being a mother was just not enough. As much as they love their children the majority of women in this study felt that they were diminished in important ways once they had children, that their worlds shrunk and that their primary identity became 'mother' rather than 'me'. This loss of individual identity might not be such an issue if we lived in a gender regime in which mothering itself was accorded a higher status and subjected to less structural and symbolic violence.

Mothers and public sanction: good and bad bodies

The process of becoming a mother is a personal, social, cultural and medicalised one. While women make personal journeys and adaptations to engage in mothering roles, gendered norms operate to survey women's bodies, behaviours and practices. These pressures on all sides can leave many women feeling that, even in fulfilling the most 'natural' of gender roles – the coincidence of fertility and femininity in motherhood – they can never quite get it right. These pressures to look and act in particular ways serve to further undermine women and mothers' confidence as they are surrounded by media images of celebrity bodies that we are told 'do' pregnancy, birth and mothering well.

In the UK, as in many other cultural contexts, women become mothers in a social arena that places huge importance on women's appearance, a pressure which, Wolf (2002) argues, has increased as women have gained success and power in other arenas. Pressure is further increased by the images presented in different media of the 'perfect mother' figures whether these are 'Yummy Mummies' or celebrities, praised for re-gaining their pre-pregnancy figure and even for the speed at which they lose 'baby-weight' after childbirth. Here 'good' bodies that return to pre-pregnancy states can 'signal the fact that having children did not spell the end of an exciting or sexual life' (Coward, 1992, 117).

Model Heidi Klum was 'celebrated' when she modelled on a cat walk only six weeks after the birth of her child, a record that was subsequently broken by model Natalia Vodianova who did so after only two weeks while other celebrity women's post-baby weight loss plans regularly make the front pages of magazines (Gentile, 2011, 49; O'Brien Hallstein, 2011). A recent example of such pressure on women to conform to body norms can be seen on the *OK!* magazine front cover, released the day Kate Middleton, the Duchess of Cambridge, came out of hospital after giving birth in July 2013. This cover headlines 'Kate's post-baby weight loss regime. Exclusive *OK!* talks to Kate's trainer 'She's super-fit – her stomach will shrink straight back' and inside there are several pages of diet and exercise plans to ensure this happens (*OK!* 30 July 2013).

Such pressures are unhealthy for all women as they teach us that our bodies are problematic when they do not confirm to realistically unobtainable standards and that we should be more concerned with how we look to others than how we feel, what we can do or even what is healthy.[5] Physical change is an experience common to all mothers as their bodies alter during and after pregnancy, unfortunately few women now feel able to embrace these changes positively. We now move to explore the consequences of this physicality of mothering and the attention given to women's bodies.

Pregnant and mothering bodies: public possessions?

Almost every pregnant woman finds themselves subjected to ongoing commentary about their physical appearance from family, friends, colleagues and even people they do not know. Such comments reflect the ways people feel able to partake in a collective 'mothering process'. Gottlieb suggests, 'the discretion of strangers disappears as soon as you have a child – in fact, it disappears as soon as you are visibly pregnant' (2010, 371) and women find themselves subjected to unsolicited advice, physical contact and judgements on how closely their bodies conform to cultural and medical expectations of pregnant bodies. As Veevers (1980, 47) notes, 'A woman carries her pregnancy "well" if she happens not to show until well advanced, and then to remain relatively small.' Pregnant bodies cease, in many ways, to be the property of the women themselves and become 'public bodies' as women lose their individuality and the focus shifts to them as good or bad 'hosts' for new members of society. Such attention causes women to engage in 'self-objectification' which not only affect women's attitudes to bodily functions such as breast-feeding and menstruation, but are also 'associated with negative attitudes towards the physical changes associated with pregnancy, including weight gain' (Gow et al, 2012, 178). Women's control over their own bodies is further reduced through engaging with patriarchal medical systems that judge women's bodies and pregnancies against pre-defined 'normal' ranges and serve to medicalise the process of pregnancy, birth and childrearing.

Birth requires other dangerous choices for women, such as whether to breastfeed their new baby, and if so for how long. The adoption of breastfeeding into public discourse means that women are evaluated and judged according to the decisions they make around feeding. It is commonly recognised by health practitioners that breastfeeding is best for both mother and baby, and pro-breastfeeding messages promote benefits to present and future physical and mental health as well as the importance of bonding time for both mother and child (NHS Choices, nd). Globally, the importance of breastfeeding is recognised by international bodies such as UNICEF and the WHO through the 'Innocenti Declaration' first issued in 1990 and updated in 2005 (UNICEF Innocenti Research Centre, 2005). In the UK the numbers of women who persist with breastfeeding remains low, however, with just over half of mothers (55 per cent) breastfeeding by the time the baby is six weeks old.[6] In spite of low rates of breastfeeding, it is usually presented as an essential part of 'proper' mothering and '[b]reastfeeding, like being pregnant, is a state in which the body is in some ways a public good and thus open for public comment' (Stearns, 1999, 308).

Breastfeeding choices, however, are complicated for many women and, in recent years, rates of breastfeeding have been falling in spite of numerous campaigns to increase them. The reasons for this are various but for social, cultural and biological reasons 'breastfeeding is not always easy to do' (Boyer, 2011, 430). For some women breastfeeding removes too great a degree of autonomy and independence (Stewart-Knox et al, 2003; Friedman, 2009) and begins a process through which they, much more than the child's father, become responsible for parenting. Some women struggle with the desexualisation which they feel is associated with using breasts for feeding or feel disgust at the idea (Earle, 2002). For others the practicalities of breastfeeding in a society that promotes the act while not really supporting it leads them to 'choose' formula over breast milk.

Women who choose to breastfeed, doing what is 'best' for themselves and their babies find themselves at risk in public spaces; able to do so only through the sanction of others (Stearns, 1999). These 'others' who may well be surrounded by bare breasts on billboards and in magazines, on television and in films, are not supposed to be inconvenienced by the confusion and embarrassment of the dichotomous roles of maternity/ sexuality combined in women's breasts when they are breastfeeding. Public dis-ease with the breastfeeding breast means that women may have to put planning and time into adopting discrete breastfeeding practices and associate breastfeeding with confusion and embarrassment (Stewart-Knox et al, 2003) rather than comfort and relaxation. Women are placed literally in liminal and problematic positions, often resorting to feeding babies in public toilets or deciding to stay in the house rather than risk feeding in public (Boyer, 2011).

This public intolerance of breastfeeding has been the subject of recent work 'Embarrassed' that spoken word poet Holly McNish released on YouTube[7] in July 2013. This quickly 'went viral' attracting huge amounts of support from over the globe, as well as some of the abuse women have come to expect when they speak up about the things that matter to them. The words in McNish's poem have reawakened debate about women breastfeeding in public as she eloquently deals with everything from other people's sensibilities, her sense of embarrassment and the lengths she went to in order to avoid upsetting others, for example as she refers to below, sitting in toilet cubicles to breastfeed, as well as the impact of global formula milk markets on women's choice. McNish's poem is a polemic against the double standards of our society as these two short excerpts demonstrate:

So I whispered and tiptoed with nervous discretion.
But after six months of her life sat sitting on lids
Sipping on her milk nostrils sniffing up piss
Trying not to bang her head on toilet roll dispensers
I wonder whether these public loo feeds offend her?
'Cos I'm getting tired of discretion and being 'polite' as my
baby's first sips are drenched in shite
[…]
'Cos in this country of billboards covered in 'tits'
And family newsagent's magazines full of it
WH Smith top shelves out for the men, I'm getting
embarrassed
In case a small flash of flesh might offend.

Discriminating against a woman breastfeeding in public has been illegal since the 1975 Sex Discrimination Act but this has been further strengthened by the 2010 Equalities Act which makes it clear that it is illegal to expect women and their babies to leave public places such as cafés, shops, parks and public transport. Newspapers, however, still run regular stories of women being asked to leave public spaces or called names while breastfeeding, meaning that women are constantly reminded of the risks of doing so in public. Breastfeeding is, then, encouraged within society but breastfeeding in public remains problematic (Stearns, 1999; Smyth, 2008; Friedman, 2009) while breastmilk itself may be seen as polluting. Reflecting on her own experiences, Friedman's comments articulate the confusion mothers feel: 'Before I had the baby, I was already vaguely concerned…the strange contradictions between the fervency with which breast was presented as best and the outright hostility to breastfeeding that I perceived the rest of the time' (2009, 27).

Such experiences were clearly articulated by women in our study. Miranda was still breastfeeding when she returned to work after maternity leave and so wanted a safe place to express milk, a request that produced a problematic response:

'When I was breastfeeding I asked if there was somewhere private I could express my milk, I was told I could use the first aid room but if there was an emergency I would have to get out straight away, or I could use the toilet, I said to them, would you make a cup of tea in a toilet?…There was [hundreds] people working there, many of them women, surely this problem has been raised before, but nothing was

done ever about it. [I] never wanted to be treated differently;
I just wanted to have the resources to be able to do my job
to the best of my ability.' (Miranda, late 20s, non-traditional
sector, mother, East Yorkshire)

Such problematic associations with breastfeeding cause women to doubt
their legitimate participation in public arenas, to feel uncomfortable
about their own bodies and contribute to them feeling that their
mothering choices are problematic. Such messages serve to teach
women once again that their entry into public spheres must be
negotiated and is subject to sanction by others. No wonder then that
most women who initiate breastfeeding give up in the first few weeks
or months, or that large numbers of younger women do not even try
to breast feed at all.[8]

Family, domesticity and the 'good' mother: how to be a proper woman (and have a clean, tidy house)

This discussion now moves on to explore the different ways mothering
and domestic labour come to be linked, with much research confirming
that mothering is closely associated with taking responsibility for
other types of domestic labour, which are in turn, afforded low status
and value. Women then, take responsibility for, as well as perform, the
majority of reproductive work involved in childcare and domestic
labour but also take responsibility for and perform the majority of
social reproductive work (Momsen, 2010) spending time and effort on
the emotional labour that binds families, friendships and communities.

There has been an array of feminist writing since the 1960s that points
to the problems women face in leading unfulfilling domestic lives. In
The Feminine Mystique, Friedan (1963) clearly showed the unfulfilling
nature of domestic labour and the 'melancholy' that arises from it while
Oakley's famous study of housework (1974) found similar patterns of
women's labour, under-appreciation and discontent.

Although domestic labour is not, these days, as clearly demarcated as
women's work as in the past,[9] there are still great discrepancies between
what men and women do in the home. More recent research shows
that, in heterosexual households, even where women work, they still
tend to do the majority of the domestic labour (Bianchi et al, 2000;
Hochschild, 1990, cited in Crompton et al, 2005) although estimates
of just how big the gap between men and women's household labour
contributions vary.[10] What is fundamentally important for women is
that, as Pilcher notes, 'women's increased participation in paid work

during the twentieth century has not been matched by men's increased participation in unpaid household and caring work' (2000, 774).

Additionally, even when men do perform domestic labour, two key facts remain; that this is often seen as 'helping' with overall responsibility remaining with women and that women continue to perform more of the routine and dull house work (Pilcher, 2000). Duncan's (2003) work on women in Leeds reveals that even women who consider themselves feminists can also believe that being a good mother means that they should be in the home for their children to a greater extent than the father/husband. Many women in our study were fully aware of the ways inequality in the private sphere is central to women's wider subjugation, as Helen shows here:

> 'I don't think there'll be like gender [equality] until…I think just the concepts themselves of like masculinity and femininity…until we've broken down those roles and men can accept, society can accept that men can take care of kids, it's childcare, it's the work at home that nobody recognises… you can't even get into the labour market until you've sorted out the home, I think, I think it has to start in the home.' (Helen, early 20s, student, Humberside)

Research has repeatedly shown that this commitment to the household results in much more than physical pressures and demonstrates how women's domestic lives are emotionally demanding and often marked by experiences of guilt, frustration and being overwhelmed (Oakley, 1974; Hochschild, 1990).

The inequitable division of household labour becomes even more marked when a couple have children as many other 'household' tasks come to be associated with 'mother-work'. Historically, motherhood has been imagined as the primary source of emotional labour and childcare in family life (Thompson, 1996). Oakley argues that this means huge pressures are placed on the modern woman as 'she has to make decisions and choices, decide what is best for her child nutritionally, aesthetically, educationally, physically, psychologically, emotionally' (1979, 12). Women's lives change a great deal more than their male partner's as a result of having children, meaning 'balancing work and family is inherently, although not exclusively, a gender issue' (Lewis and Campbell, 2007, 5). While in a partnership it may seem that decisions around sharing labour are made between individuals, in reality they are shaped by expectations of appropriate gender performances and these operate to diminish and undervalue women's contributions making inequitable shares appear natural (Schober, 2007; Armstrong, 2006). Becky, for example, notes how her husband's expectations of their roles in marriage changed after having their first child. He quickly switched to criticising her cleaning rather than taking on some of it himself:

> 'When I'm cleaning he's "Oh, you missed that bit." Before [daughter] was born we used to share these things fifty–fifty you see.' (Becky, late 30s, part-time administrator, mother, East Yorkshire)

Feminists have been calling for the economic value of domestic labour to be recognised since Rowbotham's seminal work in the 1970s. Dex (2003) suggests that the lack of pay for domestic labour also leads to it being undervalued and largely unrecognised, something that is explicitly discussed by some women in our study, as Becky continues:

> 'I think we are sometimes, especially if you have children, in a no-win situation, because society doesn't value motherhood as much as it should... months ago [husband] was on about getting life insurance, and I said, "Maybe you'll have to get life insurance for me as well." He said, "Why?," I said, "Well, if I drop dead"...do you know how much it's going to cost you to get the cleaner, the nanny?... And he was like, "Oh. Oh well, I'd have to take off all the times when she's asleep and I'd have to take off all the times when you're at work, so it wouldn't cost that much." And I thought, "You have no idea."' (Becky, late 30s, part-time administrator, mother, East Yorkshire)

There is also evidence that shows greater equity in household divisions of labour is, as we might expect, at the behest of men, meaning women in heterosexual relationships are dependent on their partner's good will. In addition, men and women often report that the division of labour is fair, even while simultaneously admitting that it is not divided equally – that women do the lions' share, with both men and women making excuses for why this is so. While men and women continue to take unequal proportions of household work, the overall time spent on work (including paid and unpaid work) is more equal. It is no surprise then that women feel that they are performing a second shift and are suffering the emotional and psychological strains associated with doing so.

Women enjoy less leisure time overall (Bittman and Wajcman, 2000; OECD, 2010) and, what is important, find that this is of shorter periods, more interrupted and often associated with performing another task at the same time (Bittman and Wajcman, 2000). Consequently, women in our study made frequent use of the term 'juggling' to describe the multitasking that they undertook, including emotional labour, organisational labour, possibly paid work and looking after the children as well as taking on the majority of the housework. For some women this pressure to bear the majority of physical and emotional labour means that they can feel that they are always 'on duty' and rarely have time to pursue their own interests. Here Elaine talks about her additional responsibility for the management of her children's schedules and needs as well as housework:

> 'Yes, if I'm the one at home, I mean, I don't feel that I'm spending a lot of time cleaning and things at home. I mean, [husband]…is as equally likely, to do that kind of cleaning at home as I am, or it just doesn't get done. Um, but because I'm there with the children, of course I'm cooking their tea and I'm sorting out their stuff for school. I'm the one who's keeping all that stuff in my head on top of, um, going to work. So I know when they've got to take their recorders to school or they need their swimming stuff or what they do after school.' (Elaine, late 40s, civil service, mother, North Yorkshire)

Tracey clearly relates her experience of being at home for several years with her children to her losing self-confidence and becoming introverted, an issue commonly raised by the mothers with whom we spoke:

> 'I just, I didn't go anywhere, I just stayed at home, went up to school, it's just you get in the comfort zone where my confidence was like totally zero, I hadn't got any, used to walk with my head down hoping nobody would notice me, which is really horrible because I was never like that, that's just not me, and I think it's because I spent so much time at home just me and the kids and [husband] and not really got out and met new people.' (Tracy, early 30s, part time, community sector, mother, North Yorkshire)

In addition to the pressures to conform to appropriate gendered performances at home, women are under increasing pressure to perform in the public arena as well. While many women want to work after having children this is not always, for them, a good experience or easy to fit with the expectations people have of their home role.

Understanding the impact of motherhood choices in the public arena: thinking through work and play

Alongside mothering decisions there is clear evidence that mothering has a significant and detrimental impact on women's earnings,[11] career choices, career success, time use and leisure time. Parents' roles in childcare and the household are closely linked to their labour market status, and that this has particularly problematic impacts on women, is well known (Joshi, 2002; Women and Work Commission, 2006; Grimshaw and Rubery, 2007). Decisions about returning to work again clearly show us how women's lives are marshalled and controlled by the real or imagined censure of others. In order to address the question of why women feel such conflicting pressures we argue that it is vital to explore the ways in which male and female roles are negotiated within the context of micro level relations and interactions as well as macro level structures and expectations.

Ina's experience recounted below is typical of many of the narratives of the mothers in our study. In it she clearly shows how for her, being a woman has affected how her partner sees their respective home and work roles. It also shows how women's freedom to choose is constricted by powerful gendered norms that still, often, place men in greater positions of power in relationships:

> 'I think he does, I think he thinks I should just make that sacrifice because that's how life is, he's made it clear to me that I'm not going to be able to pursue a career until [daughter] starts school because of childcare, which I wouldn't have wanted to do anyway, but the fact that he's put forward…actually while we were having the debate it slipped out of his mouth and he knew the minute that he said it because he put his hand over his mouth, he said, "But yes, you're the woman."' (Ina, mid-20s, student, mother, Humberside)

The interesting question is, why does this inequitable situation continue in so many households? Ina felt that her relationship with her partner was a good one, and that they saw themselves as equals, but even in such situations gender regimes serve to influence individual attitudes to the ways they organise their lives.

Jane's experiences were a little different, as she eventually decided she wanted to be at home with her baby, but again, she shows high levels of concern about how others will judge her decisions. Before having her daughter Jane was quite certain she would return to work, at least part time, after her maternity leave and she and her husband planned financially for her to take a year off with their daughter. During this period Jane realised that she wanted to stay at home with her daughter for longer, but she suffered intense internal conflicts about her decision:

> 'I found it a really difficult decision to make to not go back to work…as I said I had thought I would go back part time, by the time she was about six months I really started thinking about what I wanted to do and I think that deep down I actually knew that I wanted to stay at home, but I think that I felt that I ought to be returning to work. I felt that there was a real expectation that you have your children and you go back to work and you go back to work full time and you are a success at work and you're a marvellous mother and…I found it really difficult to almost justify to myself that decision to stay at home…I felt there was a lot of pressure and expectation…[not so much from her husband] from society itself…but then, conversely my parents were very much against me going back to work which very much conflicts with the way they brought me up.' (Jane, early 30s, full-time mother, West Yorkshire)

'Mothers' are one of the groups that is being encouraged to be economically active. Active participation in paid work is increasingly being used as a measure of social citizenship, meaning that working is seen as an essential condition for full participation in society. Women's paid work is also seen as a major strategy for reducing the incidence of child poverty. These initiatives and broader social trends (for example, the high costs involved in home ownership) mean increasing numbers of women with dependent children are opting to work.

Economic activity rates have changed little in the last 40 years, but there have been markedly different gender patterns. The economically inactive female population decreased from 45 per cent in the middle of 1971 to 29 per cent in the first quarter of 2011 while for men there has been an increase from 5 per cent to 17 per cent during the same period. This looks positive for women but the picture becomes clearer when we explore the figures more carefully. Men and women are found to be economically inactive for very different reasons; men are more likely than women to be students (33 per cent compared to 19 per cent), or long-term sick (33 per cent compared to 17 per cent), while women are several times more likely than men to be economically inactive due to family or home commitments (35 per cent compared to 6 per cent) (ONS, 2011b).

Mothers are, in general, showing higher rates of return to employment following maternity leave, and diminishing lengths of time out of the employment market (Dex and Ward, 2007, 5–6) with large numbers of women taking no more time out than their maternity leave provision (Hansen et al, 2006). Of those mothers with dependent children, on average 68 per cent work, however the age of the youngest child affects mothers' employment rates: 56 per cent of those with children under 5 work, 71 per cent whose youngest child was between 5 and 10 work, and 77 per cent whose youngest child was between 11 and 15 work (ONS, 2006). More recently, the 2008 European Labour Force Survey found that the employment rate for women across Europe aged 25–49 with children under 12 was 67 per cent, compared to 79 per cent for those without children under 12. Conversely, men with children under 12 were more likely to be employed than those without; 92 per cent compared to 85 per cent (European Commission, 2010, cited in EHRC, 2011). Mothers are more than four times as likely as fathers with children under 16 to be economically inactive whereas men and women without children have similar rates of inactivity (Smeaton et al, 2010 cited in EHRC, 2011).

As we have shown above, however, choices to work or not bring the possibility of social censure and personal feelings of inadequacy. Women both recognise their own oppression and struggle to act against it. Author, Shirley Conran, noted that guilt over work is something which only mothers feel, not fathers, and that women need to stop worrying and follow her advice: 'All working mothers feel guilt. Working women don't tend to feel guilt, only working mothers. The second you feel guilt say, 'Does my partner feel guilt?' Then you'll be rolling around on the floor laughing merrily at the very idea' (D. Tyler, 2008, 81).

In spite of economic and social developments over the last few decades, the UK still operates with assumptions within policy making organisations that the family is a private sphere 'framing responsibility for childrearing and familial care as a private household concern' (MacLeavy, 2011, 2). Family oriented policy developments are not necessarily the answer as they elide gendered issues and rarely mention gender equality. They talk instead about the need for 'parents' to make choices about how to balance work and family (Lewis and Campbell, 2007) and reconcile paid work with unpaid caring work with little consideration for the structural and cultural factors that constrain choice.

As we discuss above, changing policy does not necessarily change behaviour, and the cultural context in which mothers' employment is supported to a greater or lesser degree also has an impact on individual decisions (Budig et al, 2012). Such constructions serve to weaken women's position within households by attempting to use both sticks and carrots to persuade women into work. Government policies have focused on three main mechanisms for creating a better balance for people caring for children:

- introducing new forms of leave and extending existing ones
- investing in childcare provision
- addressing people's working hours through a statutory 'right to request' flexible working and a campaign to persuade employers to adopt best practice. (Lewis and Campbell, 2007)

Motherhood has well documented economic penalties for women, not least because of the impact which career breaks have on overall lifetime earnings and subsequently on pensions. Joshi et al (1999) note one of the significant reasons for the low earning power of mothers compared to others is that they take a career break. Estimates suggest that all women lose out due to motherhood as mothers have significantly lower earnings than both non-mothers and men in the UK (Harkness and Waldfogel, 1999; Joshi et al, 1999; Joshi, 2002; Bennet, 2005). Over the lifecourse an average women who works full time could lose over £300,000, which increases if she takes a career break to care for children or undertakes low paid part-time work (Cabinet Office, 2000; EOC, 2007a). Gregg (1998, cited in Bennet, 2005) notes that, on average, women experience a drop in pay of about 16 per cent (twice that of men) after taking a year out of the labour market, while others point to the downward mobility that is faced by many women after an employment break (Warren et al, 2001; Smeaton, 2006).

Women, it seems, face *disproportionate* costs for taking a career break. The time at which women may take career breaks or reduce working hours to have children may well be at a crucial point in promotion structures, often linked to age and expectations that all staff can be treated equally in assessment for promotion at a particular age or after a certain number of years of service. This means that '[t]he cumulative impact of this small break in career can be expected to far outweigh any real difference in actual, and certainly in potential, ability' (Grimshaw and Rubery, 2007, 45). Structural gendered inequalities such as these mean that it often makes economic, as well as culturally sanctioned, sense for women in a partnership to give up work or work part time (Dench et al, 2002). Moreover, such assumptions lead women's work to be undervalued and women themselves to underestimate the importance of their role within the family (Harkness et al, 1997; Barrett and McIntosh, 1990; Andersen, 1993).

This research confirms previous findings that an important barrier to career advancement for women can be employers' perceptions that balancing responsibilities of work and home equates with women being less productive in or less committed to their employment (Walby, 2007). This was certainly Erica's experience who felt that her employers devalued her, asked her to hide her pregnancy from clients, stopped inviting her to key meetings and viewed her as less competent and committed overall:

> 'I told them I was having a baby and woah, off you were, "Off you go." Yeah. It was like overnight, they just…yeah I told them I was pregnant and it was all of a sudden…and then it was you weren't invited to meetings as often.' (Erica, mid-30s, self-employed, mother, North Yorkshire)

Moving back into work after having a baby can also lead women to feel labelled, as if they are being asked to prove their worth all over again as demonstrated by the way Miranda felt when she returned to work:

> 'I took a career break for maternity leave for around eight months, it does really hold you back and I think this is more so in male dominated careers…When I came back from maternity it was like being on probation all over again…I felt like I had to prove I could still do the job.' (Miranda, late 20s, non-traditional sector, mother, East Yorkshire)

Having to prove yourself in a situation where you were previously considered competent was common for many women to whom we spoke who returned to the same work after having children. Common themes that emerged from our interviews included not being considered as seriously committed to their work and feeling that colleagues/bosses believe that they constantly think about their children resulting in being passed over for promotion or positions of responsibility. While the women in our study generally argued that these characterisations were unfair, one would not be surprised, given normalised gender roles if, as Hakim (1995) argues, women in fact *do* display greater levels of commitment to the domestic sphere than men. Women, as situated knowers are clear that paid employment is often structured in ways that situate 'male' needs as the norm and women's/mothers' needs as problematic aberrations, but struggle to find ways to address this situation to their benefit.

Patti returned after a 12-month period of paid and unpaid maternity leave to find that her job had been downgraded in her absence. The work she was expected to do, her working conditions, and the status of her job had changed for the worse. The manner in which this was done left her feeling disillusioned, alienated and angry. She did not, however, feel able to challenge these decisions and instead of confronting her employers, devoted time and energy to finding alternative employment:

> 'My new contract stated I was now holding an administrator's post, rather than the academic-related post I had applied for back in [date]. My job had been evaluated...while I was on leave. I had not been consulted. [I] feel increasingly dissatisfied with my working life. After nine years' experience working in [education], after a degree and a doctorate, I am doing a job I could have done when I left school.' (Patti, late 30s, education sector, mother, West Yorkshire)

Erica similarly felt undervalued and downgraded upon her return to work:

> 'I think it's like what so many women go through when they go back to work, you know, you go back you've had a baby and all of a sudden, you're no use to them.' (Erica, mid–30s, self-employed, mother, North Yorkshire)

Such experiences can clearly have serious consequences for the career progression and self-esteem of the women involved. From an employer's perspective, however, such behaviour, whether that is actual or perceived on the part of the employee, has direct and negative implications for their business. By downgrading a woman's job, employing her at a lower scale which does not utilise all her skills and experience, businesses are not using their human capital as effectively as they might.

Although these experiences are clearly related to gendered understandings of appropriate working conditions and practices, some women also noted the lack of support and understanding that they felt from female colleagues, especially those without children. It is noticeable how gendered stereotypes are played out in such situations though, as women seemed to expect a greater degree of solidarity and understanding from female colleagues than male ones. Polly's experiences reveal how such understanding was not always forthcoming:

> 'I felt there were some people higher up in the company or one particular person who was the PA to the chief executive, she didn't have children and her attitude could be quite scathing of people that needed to look after children and things.' (Polly, early 40s, part time, community sector, mother, North Yorkshire)

When women do work the implicit understanding that women's careers are less important or less serious than men's is revealed through women being expected to take time off when children are ill or have appointments, or even during school holidays. Women are themselves complicit in accepting these situations while at the same time recognising the injustice of family and work patterns. Justine's description of arrangements should one of her children be ill and absent from school clearly shifts the blame from the individual and places it within a structural context that does not support women:

> 'If he's [husband] not working that day fine I can go to work but he doesn't actually, they're [husband's work] not very good at giving them time off for children.' (Justine, late 20s, part-time manager, civil service, Humberside)

Kirsty echoes similar thoughts in talking about the way she and her partner organise work and childcare during school holidays:

> 'When it comes to school holidays my husband just goes to work, whatever he has to do on his rota he just does it, and I've got to work out what days I can work and school holidays I've got to organise, "Are they going to their grandma's?", you know, "What day off I can have to fit around his shifts?" He has to go to work and I have to work around him.' (Kirsty, early 30s, catering sector, mother, North Yorkshire)

The isolation and reductions in self-confidence that many women experience alongside the devaluation of 'mother–work' means that women seeking to return to work often underestimate the range and depth of skills they have which can be utilised in the job market:

> 'I remember saying exactly the same thing, well I don't have any skills, you know, I think we've all said it at some time, you are a mother, you go shopping, you do all these things but you just don't see it…and that's because it's just not recognised here that looking after children is an important role and it is a job…they think you're just doing nothing.' (Carla, mid–40s, manager, community sector, mother, North Yorkshire)

Jackie, whose work involves assisting parents into work, notes:

> 'Erm, confidence…is a big thing. Er, feeling they've got a lack of skills, if they've been out of work and been at home for a number of years, they don't feel they've got any skills.' (Jackie, early 40s, civil service, mother, North Yorkshire)

These thoughts are echoed by other professionals working in similar fields:

> 'A lot of the women do suffer from the confidence, a lack of self-confidence and self-belief and that usually emanates from having time away from work because of responsibility with children, or through a bad relationship, or through a bad work and bad employers.' (Edward, early 40s, manager, education sector, father, North Yorkshire)

Such complex responsibilities mean that women themselves may feel that they are not doing a 'good enough' job either at home or at work. Women who choose to work while having children are, then, seen simultaneously as both heroines and as betrayers of their natural instincts. Such decisions – to return to work or stay at home with children – are, as we have seen, made within patriarchal gender regimes that locate women firmly in the domestic sphere, require them to negotiate their access to the public sphere with others and undervalue the work that women do both inside and outside the home. As Duncan (2003) notes, mothers' decisions to take paid work are not necessarily made according to economic rationality, but 'with reference to moral and socially negotiated (not individual) views about what behaviour is right and proper, and this varies between particular social groups, neighbourhoods and welfare states' (2003, 5). Duncan et al (2003) note further that, although women's choices around mothering are diverse, they are uniform in that a mother's 'gendered moral rationalities still involve their primary responsibility for their children' (2003, 327).

Within capitalist systems, patriarchy and capitalism are closely linked. This means that women become 'othered' through the casting of men into the role of breadwinners causing women's work in general and 'mother-work' in particular to become not only 'other' but also of lower value. Motherhood may still be necessary for many women to establish their status as women and their femininity, but the effort that goes into these projects is undervalued and often unrecognised. Women's low feelings of self-esteem as mothers reflects this.

Ultimately, what is important to women is the chance to make choices for themselves in which they can realise their own ambitions in the private and public spheres:

> 'You know, like, you get these feminists who say women shouldn't be housewives, they should all go out to work and that? I suppose I used to be like that; thinking that all women should strive to get a career and everything. But I think now it's more, like, people should have a choice to do what they want rather than, because I think that's just sorting people into another stereotype really, isn't it?' (Carol, late teens, student, Humberside)

SEVEN

Gendering women's labour: status, esteem and inequality in paid and unpaid work

Introduction

In this chapter we explore women's experiences of work, developing a particular focus on the ways in which issues of confidence and wellbeing affect and are affected by women's working choices and experiences. In earlier chapters we have explored the ways in which women's association with the private sphere has an impact on their ability to take on paid work in equal conditions to men and so this will not be a focus of this discussion. Here, we explore the socio–cultural impact on women as individuals, and as a group, of the intersections of confidence and employment opportunities. We examine in detail the complexity and diversity of women's experiences of work, bringing clearly into focus some of the opportunities and barriers women face throughout their working lives.

As in other chapters our discussion is led by the empirical data, we present the issues which women themselves feel hinder their participation and progression in the labour market and explore some of the strategies that they suggest help them succeed. As this research demonstrates, the choices that women make and the meanings they attach to work vary enormously and may change for individuals over the lifecourse. Our data reveals the tightly interwoven patterns of women's lives and teases out the range of structural and individual factors that influence women's opportunity and choice in the labour market.

We open this chapter by presenting some detail about the current situation for women's labour participation in the UK. Patterns of employment in the UK remain highly gendered and, in spite of legal equality men's and women's experiences differ dramatically. These differences have their roots in the development of capitalism and modern industry which saw the growth of factories that separated the workplace from the home-based family unit. This led to a pattern of male employment outside the home, leaving women to care for children within the home (Rowbotham, 1973; Andersen, 1993). Banyard notes, however, that while '[i]t is true that unequal gender relations are intimately connected with capitalism. Yet gender inequality cannot simply be designated an unfortunate by-product. It predates capitalism…because at some point in human history the concept of female inferiority was woven into the very fabric of how we see ourselves, how we treat each other, and how we organise society' (Banyard, 2010, 8). It is these deep-seated assumptions that serve to structure work and work patterns which serve to 'other' women and problematise their experiences of paid work against men's.

The women's equality movements in the 1970s and beyond, that have influenced the introduction of sex discrimination legislation, theoretically opened up equal opportunities in employment for all. As we have shown throughout this book, however, legislative and policy change do not automatically bring cultural change and many women's lives continue to be built around traditional roles both at home and at work. A 2009 IPSOS Mori poll reveals that there is general public recognition of workplace discrimination against women: 44 per cent of men and 59 per cent of women disagreed with the statement that 'in Britain, men and women on the whole receive equal pay for doing jobs of equal value' (EHRC, 2011, 35).

Women now form a major part of the UK workforce and, since the Sex Discrimination Act (1975) this has increased steadily from around 56 per cent in 1971 to around 70 per cent in 2005 (ONS, 2009). These figures, however, do not tell us much about the types of work that women do or the financial and social recognition they receive for doing them. Research repeatedly shows us that despite the introduction of the Equal Pay Act as far back as 1970 and, more recently, the Gender Equality Duty in 2007, expectations about what is appropriate female work and remuneration remain (Dale et al, 2005). Vertical and horizontal gender segregation in the workplace is still marked across countries with high levels of economic development (Blackburn et al, 2002; Blackburn and Jarman, 2006; Jarman et al, 2012). Women continue to be over-represented in poorly paid, low-status work such as caring and service industries (Grimshaw and Rubery, 2007), to be more likely to take on part-time work and less likely to reach the 'top' of their chosen profession than men (Centre for Women and Democracy, 2013).

Women do not earn the same as men; women experience a full-time pay gap of around 15 per cent based on mean hourly earnings (ONS, 2011b; Fawcett, 2013d), but for the 43 per cent of women who work part time (Eurostat, 2013) the inequality is even more pronounced.

The gender pay gap continues to show the largest level of difference for women in part-time employment (ONS, 2007; Women and Work Commission, 2007; EHRC, 2011) and is one of the widest in advanced economies (Connelly and Gregory, 2009). Average hourly part-time earnings are 37 per cent per hour lower than full-time earnings (Fawcett, 2012) a figure that has changed little and remains about the same as when the Equal Pay Act was introduced over 30 years ago. More than two-thirds of women work part time at some point in their careers and though many return to full-time working, they are likely to suffer both occupational downgrading and long-term financial penalties (Connelly and Gregory, 2008; 2009). Women who become mothers suffer an even greater economic penalty. Mothers with children under 16 are four times more likely to be economically inactive than fathers (EHRC, 2011).

At 40 years old, men's salaries, on average, are 27 per cent higher than women's (EHRC, 2011) and recent figures from the Trade Unions Congress (TUC) reveal that these disadvantages are lifelong. Women in their 50s earn nearly a fifth less than men for full-time work and around a third less than the average full-time wage for part-time work (WRC, 2013b). Women's lower earnings in work have lifelong consequences, for example, women's average personal pensions are only 62 per cent of the average for men (Hills et al, 2010, cited in Fawcett, 2012). This discrepancy arises from the ways our lives are structured by gender and are the result of a mixture of women's lower incomes, part-time working and career breaks during which women cannot contribute to pension schemes.

Women who opt for part-time work not only suffer financially but are also often seen to be of lower status than full-time workers (Fawcett, 2013a), and have fewer opportunities for progression and development (Fagan and Burchell, 2002, 81). Moreover, many women working in part-time positions have previously worked in positions that were more highly qualified, skilled and required greater experience, expertise and responsibility (EOC, 2005b; Yeandle et al, 2006). Women are using part-time work to 'combine continuing labour market participation with home and family responsibilities particularly during the childcare years' (Connelly and Gregory, 2008, 52).

Occupational gender segregation remains pronounced with the majority of workers pursuing masculinised or feminised careers (EOC, 2005b). Men are still more likely to opt for apprenticeships in engineering and manufacturing, motor vehicle maintenance and construction while women opt for hairdressing, health and social care, childcare and travel (Fuller et al, 2005a) with only 2 per cent of childcare workers being men and less than 1 per cent of plumbers being women (EOC, 2006). These trends continue with 83 per cent of people employed in personal services being women; and over 40 per cent of female jobs compared to 15 per cent of male jobs being in the public sector, meaning that women are especially vulnerable to changes and cuts in the public sector (EHRC, 2011).

All of this amounts to a considerable status gap as well as a financial gap between men and women. The 'power gap' between men and women is pronounced, with women representing only 10 per cent of directors in FTSE 100 companies, just under 23 per cent of Members of Parliament, 22 per cent of peers and only 12 per cent of local authority leaders (Centre for Women and Democracy, 2013). Things have improved over the last 40 years, in 1974, for example, just 2 per cent of managers were women compared with 33 per cent in 2006 and less than 1 per cent of directors were women, compared to 14 per cent in 2006 (EOC, 2006). There is still a long way to travel before women are equally represented in positions of power. In 2009 it was still the case that only a third of managerial posts were taken by women (EHRC, 2011, 422).

The number of women in decision making and powerful positions does seem to make a difference to the ways that gender and family issues are dealt with. The election of New Labour in 1997, for example, brought a large number of new female MPs to parliament. Walter (2010) argues that this increase in the number of women in power[1] led to an increase in feminist arguments being heard and brought about real and lasting change in legislation. In relation to work this included the introduction of a national minimum wage, a move that had a much greater impact on women's lives than men's, increases in maternity pay, paid paternity leave and the introduction of flexible working. In recent years, however, the pace of change has slowed and the 2013 'Sex and Power 2013: Who Runs Britain' report is fairly damning, arguing that in spite of recent progress, 'Britain is a country run largely by men' (Centre for Women and Democracy, 2013, 13).

What is clear, is that women enter into and take part in the job market under different conditions to men and that women's participation is contingent on a number of factors including availability of jobs or possibilities of fitting work with childcare. This can be seen repeatedly, for example in the mass exodus of women from the workplace and back into the home following the First and Second World Wars and the fact that women are losing jobs more quickly than men in the current recession. Women, for example, make up 65 per cent of public sector workers, an area of large numbers of job losses (TUC, 2010). The current period of austerity is having long-term and damaging impacts on women's lives as economic arguments are used as justification for the lowering of focus on developing family-friendly and women-friendly policies. As the Fawcett Society (Fawcett, 2012) argue here:

> Over time, the impact of austerity will not only be calculated through the money in women's pockets and their spending power relative to men's. It will result in a society in which women's voice and choices are diminished, where women's access to employment, justice and safety are undermined and where women become more, rather than less, dependent on the state or their families for support (p 4)…[suggesting that this represents a] tipping point for women's equality.' (p 13)

Having presented a basic picture of women's employment in the UK, along with some of the risks posed by current economic policies the remainder of this chapter explores some of the ways that women's sense of wellbeing and confidence link to these stark facts. The question which we explore is, is there a relationship between women's life experiences, their levels of wellbeing and the nature, type and value of their employment?

As discussed in previous chapters, there are numerous deeply ingrained factors influencing women's place in the labour market. These include: expectations of women's roles in the home, choices and constraints that take place during schooling and afterwards and women's self-assessments of their own abilities and strengths. Central to understanding the ways that women's employment is constructed is an understanding of ideas of what constitutes 'women's work'; something that, as we have seen, has not changed much over the last few decades. The welfare system built on the Beveridge Report (1942) relied on the notion of 'the family wage' and supported the idea of men as 'providers' and women as 'dependents'. Women's wages came, then, to be seen as of secondary importance or 'pin money' reducing the significance of both women's work to their personal status and the contribution made to household finances (Barrett and McIntosh, 1990; Andersen, 1993). This deeply ingrained cultural assumption has long lasting impacts on women in our study, not only on the kinds of jobs they take and the kinds of hours they work, but is also reflected in the ways that family decisions, such as where to live, are made. It is, for example, still more common for women to follow their male partners' jobs as was the case with Gabriel:

'I worked in a bank for far too long [laughs], erm, basically thinking that was the probably the only thing I was capable of and also that my husband, erm, transferred around the country and it was easier to get a transfer – leave one job on Friday and start another on Monday.' (Gabriel, early 40s, part-time administrator, mother, Humberside)

Elaine's understanding of the relative status of her and her husband's work led her to give up a career with higher occupational status and higher earnings, because the shift work it involved meant that her work cycles clashed with her husband's. Elaine seemed surprised when we asked if her husband would have considered changing his job as she was the higher earner, but crucially, had not even had the confidence to discuss the possibility with him, saying:

'Oh, no, no. I don't think I would have considered asking him. Erm, it seemed the obvious thing [for me] to actually find another job and work, erm, normal hours. He was in a factory environment…I had the better job…I think it was just upbringing really, erm, what women were expected to do at that time really.' (Elaine, late 40s, civil service, mother, North Yorkshire)

As we have discussed above, the areas of work that women 'traditionally' do are generally undervalued compared to those done by their male counterparts (Grimshaw and Rubery, 2007) and, following on from this, women's work in general comes to be undervalued. We have seen in previous chapters the close association between women and childcare; women are expected to be caring and nurturing and so outside the home are seen to be fit for jobs that are associated with such 'naturally' perceived female attributes (Elson and Pearson, 1981; McDowell and Pringle, 1992). As Ashleigh describes her assessment of opinions of nursery work:

'It has a very low status, rated poorly, low on the agenda. People think children come and just play and don't realise what we do in terms of learning and development and planning and training, and meeting all the government requirements. This is reflected in the low pay.' (Ashleigh, early 40s, manager, caring sector, East Yorkshire)

Huppatz, developing Bourdieu's ideas of capital, argues that women are attracted to feminised occupations involving caring or emotional labour because they anticipate a 'feminine advantage' (2009, 53) in these occupations. She argues that these may well be helpful to women but that this becomes problematic when these forms of capital come to be represented as 'natural and innate' (2009, 53). While caring and nurturing come to be closely associated with femaleness and femininity they are also constructed in opposition to hegemonic constructions of masculinity and so ultimately serve as limitations to women. In effect, 'women's conceptualization of their skills as traits and instinct also works against them' (2009, 55) as, given the dichotomous nature of gender constructions, for women to be naturally good at one thing means that they may also have 'diminished confidence in less stereotypical capacities thereby limiting their practice' (2009, 55). This is held out in the evidence that repeatedly shows that, even in occupations that are overwhelmingly feminised, men are frequently over-represented in the highest positions.

Powerful gendered expectations and practices pervade all aspects of society influencing attitudes and the choices we make throughout our lives. Stepping outside expected gendered roles can bring disapproval, ridicule or feelings of isolation, thus the process of changing gendered norms tends to be long and difficult. Huppatz and Goodwin (2013) show how men who work in feminised occupations such as nursing may well emphasise their own feminine characteristics that mean they are suited to such work but do so 'at a cost' (2013, 304), noting that many men feel that their 'relationships with family and friends have suffered because they do feminised work' (2013, 304). Thus, gender segregation plays a part in limiting opportunities for women in the workplace if they conform to 'gender normalcy' (Skeggs, 2004, 22) as feminine capital is more limited and of less value than masculine. Women and others tend to associate their participation in such work as an extension of their natural abilities and, by extension, exclude themselves from the possibility of having other, more masculine abilities that are more highly valued.

In the sections below we explore the different ways that self-belief, confidence and wellbeing all have an impact on different areas of women's working and professional lives. We acknowledge the differences in experience and expectation that women themselves, as well as others, bring to issues of employment and we seek here to explore women's own understandings of these issues. We will show how confidence and self-esteem can affect women negatively in all areas of their professional lives from the kinds of jobs they do to the kinds of reward they seek and how they are able to negotiate relations with colleagues. Levels of self-esteem, estimation of ability and assertiveness, all positively associated with masculine traits, are more likely to encourage people to enter into masculine dominated areas. Heather echoes extensive research evidence that shows that women lack confidence in their own abilities compared to men and need to be actively encouraged (Maccoby and Jacklin, 1978):

> 'With men the norm is towards slightly over-selling yourself, being over-confident and, I think, with women it's the other way…It is that underestimation of your ability and that inability to sell yourself.' (Heather, late 30s, self-employed, mother, North Yorkshire)

Zaima spoke about the ways in which cultural and femininised constructions of behaviour intersect with class and ethnicity to damage confidence levels:

> 'It's about women in general, we don't really – I mean, I don't know about you – but I wasn't brought up to, kind of, say to everybody, "I'm wonderful. Employ me." It was always, "You have to be modest."…And I think it is a class issue because when I, kind of, look at, sort of, the people getting on, they know how to say the right things, they know who to talk to. Do you know what I mean? They know how to talk to people.' (Zaima, mid–30s, civil service, human resources, Humberside)

Women's experiences of processes of gendering, their socialisation as women, teaches them to expect less, to aspire to less, to doubt themselves more and, ultimately perhaps, even to settle for less (Sandberg, 2013). Here Lynne is commenting on how she feels that men are more likely to apply for jobs even if they do not have all the requirements outlined in the job specification, whereas women, she believes, are more likely to lack confidence to apply in the first place:

> 'Men seem to think, "Oh well, I'll be okay and I'll learn the rest that I don't know when I get there" sort of thing, whereas women feel as though they've got to have 100 per cent of the skills to go for it in the first place.' (Lynne, late 30s, manager, civil service, East Yorkshire)

The role of advice and guidance for women

That women are socialised into adopting roles of lower value, and to be less likely to challenge organisational structures means that we must pay attention to the kinds of support and encouragement available to women. Women's interactions with the employment sphere begin in schools with careers advice when girls begin to imagine possible and appropriate futures for themselves. At school, as we have seen in previous chapters, gendered regimes in the academic and behavioural curricula combine with peer and wider social pressures to educate girls on what expectations they can reasonably have for their own futures. Recent reports have continued to demonstrate that careers advice is structured to reflect gendered norms (Fuller et al, 2005a; 2005b; Hutchinson et al, 2011), and has steered young women into feminised professions and away from non-traditional areas (Youth Work Now, 2007; O'Donnell, 2008).

Women in this study who reflected on the careers advice they received at school mentioned similar problems to those found by O'Donnell (2008) in her study in Northumberland. Women frequently mentioned the stereotypical options suggested to them alongside what they felt were lower expectations for girls compared to their male classmates. Pamela and Christine's memories both evoke these two interlocking strands clearly:

> 'I think the expectations, when I look back, were stereotypical in terms of boys would be engineers, girls would be caring roles, hairdressers, perhaps a teacher. But boys would be looking at going on to university to study engineering or study science or accounting or whatever, and the girls would be slotted off somewhere along the way for something nice and easy.' (Pamela, mid-40s, manager, community sector, volunteer, Humberside)

> 'Careers advice [was] very different to the [advice of] teachers at school who wanted me to stay and do A Levels and who had encouraged me to do sciences because they wanted more girls to do sciences. Teachers were proactive with regard to this imbalance. Whereas I remember distinctly the careers advice was, "Oh, you're a girl with quite good results, you can be a dental receptionist, or why don't you go for this office job?"' (Christine, late 40s, self-employed, mother, North Yorkshire)

Moreover, many of the women also felt that unless girls were considered to excel at school, expectations for their futures were low and relied on women's associations with caring and nurturing as much as individual aptitude and more formal skills.

> 'Girls, maybe the bright ones, that were maybe going on to teach and girls that might go on to do medicine...but there wasn't the same for us, the thought was that you still went into secretarial work, nursing, teaching, you know, there weren't any other areas you were encouraged to go into then.' (Fern, mid–40s, manager, agricultural sector, mother, North Yorkshire)

Time and again, women's accounts of their own lives reveal that aiming low, playing safe and fulfilling traditional expectations were organising principles for themselves and for those around them. While Pamela felt that girls were 'slotted off along the way for something nice and easy,' Pippa, who works as a nanny, commented on her own choices:

> 'It was kind of safe and predictable and yes it's a nice thing to do isn't it?' (Pippa, late 30s, caring sector, East Yorkshire)

This was a recurring theme among our respondents whose levels of confidence seemed, time and again, to lead them into the types of roles others expected of them. As Drexler puts it, 'It's hard to expect more when society tells women, over and over, to expect less' (Drexler, 2013, np).

The importance of embodied infrastructure: role models and mentors

While women's experiences of careers advice reveal the influence of others' limited expectations on young women, the positive influence of the embodied infrastructure of role models and mentors was also significant for women both while at school and moving into the workplace (Dale et al, 2005; Moore et al, 2005). Here we are referring to the physical embodied support networks or infrastructures created by individuals and groups of women both formally and informally within schools, workplaces and communities. It is clear that women and girls are influenced by those around them, and are more able to imagine diverse futures for themselves when they can see role models whether that is in traditional or non-traditional jobs or being exposed to positive role models in education (Dale et al, 2005). Stepping outside expected gendered roles can bring disapproval, ridicule or isolation, and the process of changing gendered norms tends to be long and difficult. Young women are thus more likely to be attracted to occupations which they think are done 'by people like me' (Francis et al, 2005). For many women we spoke to, career choices were inspired by personal experience or by a key individual. Bess spoke about a key figure who influenced her decision to become a teacher while she was at school:

> 'I had an excellent primary school teacher and she was very, very encouraging and very affirming, and also expected the moon from every one of us, she expected a lot and she got a lot.' (Bess, early 60s, retired, mother, North Yorkshire)

Rachel also made clear to us that the active support and encouragement of others is often critical for women in feeling able to pursue their career goals:

> 'Quite often when you ask why women have gone into careers there's been somebody significant, they've either had a parent who's been in that area, they'd had a really good physics teacher...Very rarely do they just get there by accident. There's something, something that's actually, actually triggered it off.' (Rachel, early 40s, community sector manager, Humberside)

The significance of role models and mentors went much further than school for many of the women in our study and informed positive career choices and professional development. The benefits of formal embodied infrastructures of mentoring as a way of helping women overcome confidence issues is being increasingly recognised (Headlam-Wells, 2004; Dale et al, 2005; Women and Work Commission, 2006).

Women's structural positioning in the workforce – located in part-time and low-status jobs and more likely to be managing household labour – means they are often poorly placed to take advantage of informal mentoring relationships that occur within 'after work' and 'out of work' cultures (Ragins and Cotton, 1999, McGuire, 2002). Coupled with this there continue to be few women in the higher ranks of commercial and public professions from where mentors would be usually drawn, meaning that women often struggle to find an appropriate mentor, even when workplaces have formal mentoring schemes. Miranda's experiences were common among professional women in our study:

> 'The company I was working for had a mentoring scheme, but it was internal, not gender specific and there were hardly any women – so it was very unlikely you would be mentored by another woman.' (Miranda, late 20s, non-traditional sector, mother, East Yorkshire)

In fact, 'mentoring in professional contexts is being presented as a means of overcoming a range of inequalities and advancing the rights of groups which have, traditionally, experienced inequalities, such as ethnic minorities and women' (Holdsworth, 2006, 139). Paludi et al (2010, 80) argue that mentoring is particularly important in helping women to overcome the organisational cultures that privilege maleness and 'transform patriarchal practices by educating women on the ins and outs of the organization, how to navigate the old boys' network, and how to transmit this information to other women'. Time and again in our study women recounted how key figures helped them to find the confidence to apply for jobs, to seek promotion and to learn skills for negotiating organisational structures and working with colleagues.

Deborah, who conducted research in her own workplace, recognised the importance of mentoring, particularly for the role it can play in developing women's confidence in their own abilities:

> 'Usually, an older woman who had inspired them and guided them, and had really helped them. Particularly when they were thinking, "I can't do this," and they would say "Yes, of course you can, give it a go!"' (Deborah, early 60s, manager, education sector, mother, Humberside)

It is recognised that there is value in mentoring for both mentee and mentor alike:

> 'One of the reasons we wanted to have women-only mentoring was that the literature shows us that mentors get as much out of the process as mentees.' (Deborah, early 60s, manager, education sector, mother, Humberside)

Deborah is not alone in stressing the importance of this aspect of mentoring for women. Research also demonstrates that women in particular appreciate psychosocial aspects of mentoring and that women look for mentors to help them in areas such as self-confidence, motivation, personal development and counselling (Elliot et al, 2006; Headlam-Wells et al, 2006; Ragins and Cotton, 1999). This is particularly important as mentoring allows women to engage with people who can provide positive feedback, something that is shown to be significant in developing women's confidence (McCarty, 1986). Erica explained the crucial role a female mentor had played in her career development and, again shows how this mentoring relation was particularly important in developing confidence:

> 'I had a fantastic mentor to work with…she'd been working as a technical manager for, god, about 30-odd years, she was like a school mistress…but when you got beneath that, she was actually the most lovely lady and she knew her stuff inside out and I wouldn't have got to where I got to in that industry before having children if I hadn't have had this lady to, sort of, give me the confidence to do it.' (Erica, mid-30s, self-employed, mother, North Yorkshire)

Exploring the gendered nature of women's work

The EOC Report *Labourers of love?* (2007c) called for a challenge to society's perceptions around participation in feminised occupations and the tendency for such choices to be seen by women themselves and others to result from women's 'natural' propensity to care. We build on this here and now move on to explore the different influences that act to cause women's work to be seen to be intimately related to women's 'natural' qualities more than the skills they gain and the consequences of this for women's status and renumeration.

The concept of emotional labour (Hochschild, 1983) has been developed to describe the kinds of caring work women frequently undertake where management of their own emotions is fundamental to the good performance of the job. As Payne argues, '[e]motion workers are placed in a position of deference and subordination to the customer' (2009, 352). No wonder, then, that Morgan argues that '[p]aid emotional labour is gendered in that women tend to be found doing it more frequently than men and that, more profoundly, it is equated with commonsensical notions of femininity' (Morgan, 1996,105). Women who are trained from an early age within family and school environments to be demure, not to speak up for themselves, to put the needs of others first are ideally and 'naturally' suited to such tasks.

Such is women's association with emotional labour that some of the women in our research felt that they were expected to fulfil caring roles in their professional life, irrespective of whether they wanted, or felt qualified to do so. In a career that privileges research outputs when assessing status and promotion prospects, Alice felt strongly that the expectations students and colleagues had in terms of caring roles had serious implications for her career:

> 'Students tend to come to female members of staff more. You're seen as almost certain to spend much more time with students. Err, female [mothers], tend to spend more time doing administrative, um, work, and generally spend more time on their teaching and supervision, and the research goes out of the window.' (Alice, late 30s, manager, education sector, volunteer, mother, West Yorkshire)

While Alice felt that such roles were thrust upon her, almost against her will, she also recognised that she was likely to be more generous with the time she devoted to students, suggesting again how women come to be complicit in their own positioning, a sentiment echoed by Dawn:

> 'A fairly high percentage of my [female] colleagues…are more interested in the more caring/sharing aspects.' (Dawn, late 50s, civil service, mother, Humberside)

The close associations of women with caring and emotion are reflected, as we know in the high levels of gender segregation found in the workforce. Although many women actively chose to enter caring professions they also recognised that these are accorded low status but were limited by their own lack of confidence. Danielle had wanted to train in nursing or hairdressing, both also feminised areas of work, but had not pursued either career due to lack of self-belief, explaining this away by saying:

> 'Because I thought that catering was all I was capable of.' (Danielle, early 40s, manager, catering sector, North Yorkshire)

As we have seen in previous chapters, the strict gender segregation of the workforce is slowly being worn away and, although gendered social and cultural expectations influence the majority, there are women who are able to break the mould and enter masculinised professions.

There are, however, risks associated with doing so, and women in 'non-traditional' occupations reported to us experiences of working and barriers to career development which clearly resonate with other research. These included feelings of isolation, experiences of sexist comments and behaviour, feeling they have to constantly justify themselves and prove their worth, and a lack of female colleagues and role models to provide support networks around them (Dale et al, 2005). Women who make such choices are often met with familial or societal questioning, or even disapproval, as Fay notes here about attitudes to women who wanted to enter the construction industry:

> 'The other thing that they felt was there were…barriers with society as a whole, so the way that they would be looked on and that it wasn't right that they should be doing that, particularly families wouldn't want them to do it.' (Fay, early 50s, manager, education sector, mother, South Yorkshire)

Women in both traditional and non-traditional employment sectors reported experiencing gender discrimination at work, but for those who entered predominantly male professions the pressures they faced were greater because they were women. These problems have long been recognised. As Kanter pointed out in her important study into masculine work cultures during the 1970s, when women are in the minority in a workplace they will be subject to greater attention and scrutiny and as 'tokens' 'women were often measured by two yardsticks; how *as women* they carried out the sales or management role; and how *as managers* they lived up to images of womanhood' ([1977] 1993, 214). These gendered expectations make clear to women the special nature of their difference, that includes within it gender-based inequality. In a male-dominated profession, Miranda was targeted by her male colleagues as the object of sexualised remarks which she did not feel confident enough to object to:

> 'There were sexist jokes made at work – I was quite young then so I think that is why I tolerated it – now I'm older I think I would nip it in the bud a bit quicker – it was around the time of the Spice Girls so they used to call me Mel Double D.' (Miranda, late 20s, non-traditional sector, mother, East Yorkshire)

Such forms of everyday sexism are a recurring theme in our research, with other women telling us about nude calendars in work which they have not felt confident enough to ask to be taken down or about the continual 'banter' they are subjected to by male colleagues. These references to women's sexuality serve to undermine women's professional identity and, as a consequence, do violence to women's professional selves and their self-esteem.

For some women it seemed that one of the main barriers they faced was simply men's surprise at a woman being in the role. Lynne told us how, even though the men she worked with in the police force were verbally welcoming, her 'difference' was comment worthy and this meant that she felt her gender was subsequently always an aspect of how colleagues related to her:

> 'They looked at me as if to say, "Who are you?" And when I said to them, "I'm the DI" and they just looked at me as if to say, "Right, okay" and then they said, "Sorry, we've been referring to you as a male, sorry we didn't know it was a woman" and that was just typical…God, we haven't really changed that much, have we, from where we were?' (Lynne, late 30s, manager, civil service, East Yorkshire)

With just 26 per cent of police in England and Wales being women, the higher ranks continue to be male-dominated with just under 15 per cent of senior police officers being female (Dhani and Kaiza, 2011). Lynne goes on to tell us about how it felt to work in an all-male environment:

> 'And the other thing that really strikes me that's gender-related, is some of our senior management team, most of our senior management team are men, there's not many women, senior management team is chief inspector and above that…and when I worked at…the whole of the senior management team is male…you can feel the testosterone when you walk into the room.' (Lynne, late 30s, manager, civil service, East Yorkshire)

It is clear to us that the gender regimes we live within not only serve to guide men and women into appropriate careers but to ensure that, where women have the courage to follow careers that are less feminised, they feel that they have to be better than men, they have to deal with sexist and sexualising behaviour and they have to develop high levels of confidence to succeed in spite of this. It is clear that women who underestimate their skills and abilities and already feel that they are singled out as different are less likely to put themselves forward for promotion, something that Lynne was clear about in her research conducted in her own sector:

> 'Hardly any women go for promotion in comparison with men. It was this year…that seven women and 57 men went for promotion from constable to sergeant…so although we've increased women at constable level, we haven't increased…the percentages aren't equal really. However, when they do go for promotion assessments, 100 per cent of the women passed this year and only 54 per cent of the men.' (Lynne, late 30s, manager, civil service, East Yorkshire)

We could interpret these figures to mean that women are less likely to want promotion, and this may well be easy to understand given the extra burden they face within the reproductive sphere, but in fact the idea that women are satisfied to remain in positions of less authority and responsibility is both problematic and often wrong. Once again the voice in women's ear that whispers to them that they are not quite good enough is the significant factor:

> 'But about equally 80 per cent of men and women said that they wanted promotion. But when you ask them the question, "Do they think they've got the skills to be promoted?", a lot more men think that they've got the skills than women.' (Lynne, late 30s, manager, civil service, East Yorkshire)

The importance of self-confidence is echoed by women who had become successful in their chosen fields. They spontaneously told us, time and again, and in different ways, about the important part that confidence and self-belief had played in their success:

> 'I was always very strong willed…it also means that you are willing to go that bit further…and from my family as well [their attitude was], "You should do as much as you can."' (Christine, late 40s, self-employed, mother, North Yorkshire)

Gill, who runs her own farming business, was fairly dismissive of the idea that women may lack confidence and power as she claimed that this had not been her experience. She described herself as always having been in control of her destiny, known what she wanted and ambitious to achieve this:

> 'The gender thing? I don't know because I understand that some women really haven't had any power, but it's not happened to me. I've always…I've always done what I wanted…I've always been ambitious, I suppose, for what I wanted.' (Gill, early 60s, self-employed, agricultural sector, mother, North Yorkshire)

Norma's experiences are similar to Gill's above: self-confidence – which she self-depreciatingly describes as arrogance, a much less positive trait – has been key to her own perception of success:

> 'Definitely ambition, I have bags of energy, drive and positive mental attitude, I think that's it, not even the ambition so much, I mean I knew I wanted to be successful and I know I'm good at things, and it's probably quite an arrogant attitude but always been, probably every job I've done, looked at the person above me and thought I can do yours standing on my head and then you just set out to prove you can actually do it or do it better.' (Norma, mid-30s, private sector manager, engineer, Humberside)

The impact of motherhood on women's professional lives

We could not complete this chapter without considering the impact of motherhood on women's professional lives as we all know how closely interwoven mothering is with all aspects of women's being (whether they are mothers themselves or not). In previous chapters we have discussed the impact of motherhood on women's sense of self so here we develop our discussion around some of the ways motherhood links directly to women's working lives. While many women spoke to us about lacking the necessary self-belief to progress in their chosen careers such feelings were expressed particularly clearly by women who had spent time out of the labour market to raise children. Women in our study discussed their own loss of confidence and skills alongside the organisational and structural factors that meant that they felt others judged them differently when they had children. Mothers often feel devalued at work and many devalue themselves by taking part-time work or work that does not use all their skills. For some of the women in our study, returning to work was vital to their self-confidence and self-esteem:

> 'And you know, because they lose their own personality. You lose your individualism. You're a mum, you know?' (Jackie, early 40s, civil service, mother, North Yorkshire)

> 'I mean, the thing is you see, working since [daughter] was born has not been about the money because most of my money goes straight on childcare…it's not actually financially viable is work…It gives me a sense of identity. It gives me a sense of being useful. Not that being a full-time mother isn't. It's a very important job, but that's not something I can do solely.' (Becky, late 30s, part-time administrator, mother, East Yorkshire)

Kirsty neatly encapsulates her main motivations for returning to work in one sentence:

> 'It was being able to have a conversation with an adult, and I remember thinking I could go to the toilet on my own without having her [daughter] strapped to my leg.' (Kirsty, early 30s, catering sector, mother, North Yorkshire)

Many women opted for flexible working arrangements in an effort to reconcile home and work commitments. Christine, who used to be a teacher but now runs her own business, felt under-confident about returning to full-time employment after a maternity break and initially re-entered the workforce through a combination of voluntary and part-time work:

> 'It's much harder to…immediately start working, so I did voluntary work and some part-time teaching and, I mean, then you've got the huge problem of childcare, so effectively while I was doing the voluntary work and some of the teaching I worked for nothing [after paying for childcare].' (Christine, late 40s, self-employed, mother, North Yorkshire)

Flexible working manifests itself in various ways: interim work; temporary contracts; flexi-time arrangements for arriving and leaving work; three- or four-day weeks; or job sharing. Opting for flexible working was, though, felt to be significant in their experiences of lower self-worth and in the ways they felt that colleagues estimated women's abilities and commitment to their work. Many women also found that taking on part-time and flexible work often led to a decrease in responsibility and under-utilisation of skills. The EOC notes the high cost of this to both women and the economy in their 2005 report *Britain's hidden brain drain* (EOC, 2005a) that explores the causes and consequences of people in part-time jobs below their levels of education and experience, a position that is much more commonly experienced by women than men.

It is important to recognise that different forms of flexibility have different impacts upon equality of opportunity for workers. On the one hand, flexible working could open up opportunities to help highly skilled professional female employees resume and advance their career alongside family responsibilities. On the other hand, it may result in lower pay, status and job satisfaction. Women choose flexible working for varied reasons but the most common reason is the need to accommodate their childcare responsibilities and maintain a good work–life balance:

> 'If one of the kids is sick, I work at home or I can make up the hours. In the Easter holidays I'll probably change my days around according to when I can get some childcare. I'll take them to the office with me. It's all very, very flexible.' (Polly, early 40s, part time, community sector, mother, North Yorkshire)

Working from home does have some disadvantages, however. These can include the permeability of boundaries between domestic and paid work, social isolation and a lack of visibility and recognition for the work you do, as Gill, a self-employed home worker, explained:

> 'There was no demarcation then really between work and, and bringing up a family. It all happened all alongside each other. One of my daughters once said to me, "Mum, why don't you do any work? All my friends' mothers go to work and you don't do any"... Oh dear me!' (Gill, early 60s, self-employed, agricultural sector, mother, North Yorkshire)

Alice's experiences are not unusual, she returned to work full time when her first baby was a few months old and subsequently spent years trying to find an appropriate work–life balance through adjusting the number of working days and time at home. While Alice recognises that she was fortunate to have a flexible employer she also echoed the experience of many women working part time in that her work load was not always adjusted to meet her hours. This meant that Alice had the same experience of many women working part time, trying to fit the work into shorter hours, never feeling quite good enough, but not having the confidence to address these issues with her employer when they called on her days off to resolve work issues:

> 'I've gone up and down, and up and down, trying to get some kind of work–life balance and never achieving it, but they've gone with it, they've just said, "Okay." I mean, the difference is I suppose that, you know, you've still got the same job [laughs], you just try…you have to do it in a shorter time…It's hard trying to have a work conversation with a screaming baby jiggling up and down on your hip, and why the hell should I have to? I chose to reduce my salary so I could be with my child [on my days off].' (Alice, late 30s, manager, education sector, volunteer, mother, West Yorkshire)

Clear cultural messages about ideal characteristics for mothers set them in opposition to perceived ideal characteristics for workers (Correll et al, 2007) and lead to employers and colleagues perceiving women as less capable, committed and organised. In fact, many women who take time out to have children suggested that they are unaware of the range of skills and competencies involved in running a household and how these can translate into the workplace. Once again we see in the evidence provided by Elaine, who works in life skills coaching, how the skills which women develop are undervalued and denigrated:

> 'For instance, you know, the sort of juggling…children, school, home…husband's career…whatever…You are an organisational genius…because…you do have to sort of do all these things…it's just been in a different setting.' (Elaine, late 40s, civil service, mother, North Yorkshire)

Speaking about how realising she had valuable skills increased her self-esteem Charlotte said:

Charlotte: 'So when I went for the interview and I got it, I just couldn't believe it. I was doing this job, and it just felt so different, because everything else had been, you know, scrubber's jobs or menial jobs what anybody can do. And this just made me feel a bit more important. It wasn't, you know...'

Interviewer: 'It was making use of skills that you had?'

'**Charlotte:** 'That's what they said to me when I went for my interview. "You've had all these skills, all these life skills."' (Charlotte, early 40s, part time, community sector, mother, North Yorkshire)

That women experience lowering of confidence levels during the time which they take from work to raise children reflects the common assumption that child–rearing and housework are natural and require no particular skill. Such implicit messages serve to diminish women who return to work and may not feel powerful enough to challenge what they recognise to be changes in working conditions, responsibilities or reward. Heather returned to the same job after the birth of her child, but her wages fell in real terms as she has not had a pay rise since then. More significantly, Heather identified her own motherhood as the cause of feeling devalued at work:

'So I've taken a drop and I've maintained that drop. And I've always thought that was a price worth paying to be part time and to say "No" to lots of work which, in the past, I always had to say "Yes" to...A lot of my interesting projects went to colleagues which, at the time...it was really hard. Um, so yeah, I did feel, like, I got, sort of, much less interesting work.' (Heather, late 30s, self–employed, mother, North Yorkshire).

Fern experienced similar issues when she decided to work part time after having children:

'In a way it was a bit of a status thing but often I was missed out of meetings because of being part time and they had meetings when I wasn't there – I remember feeling annoyed that decisions that involved my future were being made without my being there just because of being part time.'

(Fern, mid–40s, manager, agricultural sector, mother, North Yorkshire)

Motherhood is a contradictory experience for many of the women in our study. Women can love their children while recognising that the cost for them in having children is much greater than for the child's father. Patriarchal gender regimes expect women to make sacrifices in terms of career and public life that can contribute to their under-confidence and low self-esteem.

The role of women's employment in building confidence

Women do, of course, work to earn money to support themselves and their families, but for many women working brings other rewards. It is worth considering, at the end of this discussion, the various ways that work outside the home can benefit women. In spite of women often being located in low–pay and low–status jobs women themselves often value the skills and attributes that these jobs require and so find them fulfilling and rewarding. Though we, of course, welcome people being happy and fulfilled in their work we do note that unless and until feminised care work is accorded higher status and value, women continue to be complicit in their own subjugation through their own valuation of caring roles in this way.

Hazel, who manages a children's centre, spoke about how she felt about the work that she does, emphasising that her job both 'made a difference' and involved a 'social conscience', both elements that many women felt are important in their work:

> 'I love my job, I'm passionate about my job. I don't think if you, I think that you need to be passionate about this way of working to make it succeed.' (Hazel, early 40s, manager, community sector, mother, North Yorkshire)

Jackie echoes similar sentiments about her work as a lone parent advisor:

> 'Just to see somebody move on through the cycle of change and, and you know, become themselves again…We all have the same ethos, really about, you know, life and our jobs and we all care passionately about our customers.' (Jackie, early 40s, civil servant, mother, North Yorkshire)

Paid employment and developing a career can also have a significant positive impact on women's mental wellbeing. The workplace and working role can provide people with an identity, a sense of belonging and social status allowing women to move beyond stereotypical roles in the home that they may find isolating and oppressive. For Danielle, her work has built her confidence and self-esteem:

> 'The safety, stability, the fact that I'm known. Finally I think I've achieved respect through all the places that I've worked and that's taken a lot of years to get there and do that...I just feel part of it and I'm comfortable. I can come in here on my day off and be happy, so, yes. I do enjoy my work, yes. I'm happier here than anywhere.' (Danielle, early 40s, manager, catering sector, North Yorkshire)

Tessa echoes similar thoughts:

> 'I cope with things better than when I'm at home because I've got something else to think about. I'm not...I don't dwell on things when I'm working [laughs] so, yes, it keeps me sane.' (Tessa, late 30s, part time, clerical, mother, North Yorkshire).

Conclusion

Women's working lives are diverse and the meaning of work for women is complex, no two women's stories are exactly the same. There are, however, numerous common threads of experience. The links between self-esteem and barriers to success in employment identified by women in this study are not surprising or new. Structural and symbolic (and indeed even physical) violence continue to permeate the world of employment as elsewhere. Women continue to face glass ceilings and sticky floors in their working lives and the numbers of women who are able to beat these barriers remain in the minority. Work cultures remain predominantly masculine and many of the jobs traditionally classed as feminine are neither well paid, high status nor valued by society. The 'value' of traditional 'women's work' is measured against labour market norms that are implicitly male. This situation means that the types of skills required in 'women's work' or displayed by women, are barely visible in a labour market constructed on skills based on male value systems (Grimshaw and Rubery, 2007). This situation needs to change if women are to gain parity with men.

Our research does reveal, however, the importance of work for reasons other than financial reward. Women's experiences in the workplace are not equitable with men's, but women in our study valued work for a wide range of reasons. Key among these were: providing an identity; status; and social networks; and increasing self-esteem. What constitutes success in terms of work may change and, for many women, is more than just a pay cheque. For many women in this study what they get out of work cannot be measured purely in terms of monetary reward or career progression. Women both suffer from lack of confidence in the workplace and gain key measures of self-esteem through engaging in paid work. In fact, as in many areas of women's lives, women are in contradictory positions where they feel they can 'never get it right', but they find it important to keep working at it. Because of this, current legislation that provides legal protection to women needs to be protected. Without this the continuing cultural shift that is slowly improving women's working lives will not continue and women will face increasing pressures to limit themselves to the home to allow men to succeed in the public sphere.

EIGHT

Conclusions: the embodied infrastructure of women's spaces, gender awareness, and the capacity for change

Throughout this book we have employed a gender analysis within a feminist standpoint epistemology (Stanley and Wise, 1990, 25) to explore both the ways in which processes of gendering are woven into the fabric of women's everyday lives and to understand some of the underlying factors which contribute to gender-based inequality in the UK. Our research is both located in and proceeds from a grounded analysis of the material experiences of women's lives as they explained these to us as situated knowers. From this starting point a key aim of this book has been to make critical links between continued gender-based inequalities, normative processes of gendering and the impacts of these processes for women through the lifecourse. We have focused in particular on women's experiences of mental wellbeing and self-esteem illustrated through the lens of pivotal gendered life experiences: women's formative years, education and training, motherhood, employment and career development. We have considered additionally the specific impacts of gender-based violence on women's life chances and opportunities.

We argue that there continues to be a strong connection between contemporary cultural constructions of femininity and negative experiences of mental wellbeing. Drawing on Bourdieu's (2001) concept of symbolic violence and Farmer's (2004) use of the idea of structural violence, we have demonstrated the ways in which gendering works along a broad continuum, to simultaneously enact both gentle and symbolic as well as visceral, literal violence on women's (and men's) lives. Making these links between gendering and symbolic as well as literal violence we can see how women's experiences of becoming and being a woman can be damaging to wellbeing. Locating our understandings in the frame of structural violence, played out both within and beyond the arenas we have explored in this book, we can see how the structural 'violence' of gendering can have significant impacts on women's opportunities and aspirations and become a driver of inequality. By bringing these elements together we can see how the violence of gendering forms a triad, a triangulation of powerful symbolic, structural and visceral forces at play.

Because this triad of violence enacted through processes of gendering is so deeply embedded within everyday gendered practices and experiences, and as such can be complex, amorphous and difficult to identify, these processes are often under-acknowledged in mainstream policy making. While certain policy arenas, such as family, reproductive and social welfare policies, are explicitly linked to gender (though often perceived to mean '*women*', or indeed conflated to '*womenandchildren*' to evoke Enloe (1990)), we would suggest that even policy that might be seen as gender-neutral is not. As Hearn and McKie state: 'not only is much policy and policy development constructed by and through assumptions about gender, but also much policy and policy development can be understood as policy on and about gender and gender relations…Gender constructs policy, as policy constructs gender' (2008, 75).

So we need to retain and value policy that we think is gendered, such as equalities policy and legislation, and we must remain ever vigilant that it is effectively progressed, updated and enforced. We must also, as Hearn and McKie (2008) similarly propose, examine policy that we think is gender-neutral (but which is not) through the lens of gender analysis. While this would go some way towards challenging structural gendering, it is not the only solution. In addition we should acknowledge that policy-led approaches alone are bound to be inadequate in and of themselves because they do not, and cannot, effectively address pernicious and persistent symbolic processes of gendering. Nevertheless, while the gendering of inequalities cannot be legislated away, policy forms a critical structural platform on which to build strategies to challenge and protect us from the worst manifestations of symbolic and visceral violence within our gender regime.

Although we emphasise the harms that negative processes of gendering can do, a critical argument of this book is that women are not passive victims of these processes. While the goal of gender equality has not been reached, what may be perceived as success in feminist terms is the way in which women are increasingly situated knowers, articulating sophisticated, nuanced and reflexive understandings of their gender identities and the socio-cultural frameworks they inhabit. Here we conclude by asking if this awareness itself could bridge the gap between persistent normative processes of gendering, material inequalities and the frameworks of equality policies.

Thus, rather than a more traditional conclusion that reiterates the key points emerging from each chapter, we provide something else, something more. Taking the over-arching point that women are situated knowers, we consider where we can see this gap being bridged: between persistent normative processes of gendering, the material inequalities of women's lives and the frameworks of equality policies and legislation. One critical site in which these connections are being made is in the arena of women's services and spaces. It is within these spaces, often at community level, that we are able to clearly see the ways that women are actively developing their gendered understandings and critically gendered engagements with both culture and polity to make differences to their own and other's lives. Here we argue that these spaces are themselves a form of embodied infrastructure, sites in which women themselves become a critical part of the infrastructure of support. Women's bodies and minds, working within physical spaces, become bridges, material supports for women accessing these services.

Thus the embodied infrastructures of women's organisations are important sites wherein women are, on the one hand, supported to address the effects of the structural, symbolic and visceral triad of violence. On the other hand, it is also in these spaces that women are actively recognising and challenging processes of gendering as forms of structural, symbolic and literal violence, enabling women to enhance their confidence, wellbeing and capacities for change as situated knowers. Thus, through exploring women's contributions to community and voluntary organisations we can see how women themselves possess a reflexive and sophisticated gender awareness as situated knowers, are able to reflect on their normative conditioning and are working to effect change.

Through the course of this chapter we provide a detailed analysis of this sector based on ethnographic and empirical research we have conducted over several years within and among women's services in the Yorkshire and Humber region. In the first part we focus on the contribution of women's spaces, as part of the community of public and voluntary sector organisations, in addressing the impacts of patriarchal gender regimes on women's sense of self and wellbeing. Through providing women-only safe spaces, non-threatening learning environments and with an emphasis on confidence building, assertion and capacity building, these arenas are meeting women's everyday needs, raising aspirations and providing the necessary support to enable women to achieve their ambitions.

In the second part of the chapter we acknowledge and explore the impacts of the triad of violence on women's services themselves, as they, too, are institutional victims of these processes. As such, we look at the challenges women's services face in the climate of financial crisis and ever-decreasing sources of funding. These challenges are being faced across the Third Sector, but are compounded by public (mis) conceptions, stereotyping and prejudices about women's centres and women-only spaces, and the lack of recognition they receive for their professional work: after all, are they not merely women doing 'natural' feminine care work?

Women's spaces: women transforming/transforming women

The women's voluntary and community sector in the UK has a long history, with recorded mass organising of women for political, economic and social purposes dating back to the 1800s (WRC, 2007, 28). The Suffragette movement of the early twentieth century is possibly the most renowned of the UK women's rights collectives, with their campaigning centred on women's (lack of the) right to vote. It is in the second wave feminist and Women's Movement of the 1970s and 1980s, however, that many women-only services and centres have their roots (WRC, 2007, 28). According to an extensive study conducted by the Women's Resource Centre (WRC) in 2006–7, there are over 30,000 organisations and groups in the UK that work specifically with women, to meet the needs of or to raise the profile of women.[1] Despite these large numbers, the work of the WRC in London notwithstanding, there is relatively little empirical research focusing on the work of these organisations, or the social and economic value of their contributions (WRC, 2006a).

In this chapter we go some way towards redressing that imbalance, focusing on the Yorkshire and Humber region in the North of England and complementing the research the WRC has produced with its focus in the South. We draw on the voices of service users and providers to explore women's differing experiences of, and motivations for, engaging with women's voluntary and community organisations and the impact of those services on women and the wider communities in the Yorkshire and Humber region.

A variety of both government funded and national charitable organisations such as Women's Aid, Well-Woman Centres, the Women's Institute, Home-start and Children's Centres[2] work across the region. In addition to these national bodies, however, independent women's voluntary and community organisations exist in a variety of forms in each sub-region of Yorkshire and Humberside. It is surprisingly difficult to gain accurate figures, but the Guidestar registry records approximately 80 registered charities within the Yorkshire and Humber region that work specifically with women (GuideStar UK, 2013). This is a significant underestimate of actual numbers: many more women's community and voluntary groups exist as not-for-profit organisations, informal networks and local groups. That many such groups are relatively informal makes it extremely difficult to calculate exactly how many exist, but we would estimate that numbers run into several hundred. These include organisations with specific aims or membership such as religious affiliations or refugee support networks in which women's services are a component of their work. It also includes women-only groups, women's refuges, women's centres and services that work with specific sectors of the community such as BME women.

In the context of this diversity of provision, we focus in this chapter on women-only services and do so for a number of reasons. First, the women who participated in our study frequently told us how important women-only services are to them. Second, recognising that women-only services are sometimes deemed contentious we wish to explore the wider benefits that these embodied infrastructures have for both women and men. Third, women-only services routinely operate without secure and stable financial support. That they are able to provide such crucial infrastructures not just for women but for the wider community, and without adequate funding is testament to the creativity, skill and hard work of both paid and unpaid service providers and volunteers. What is just as important, and in line with our feminist praxis, the evidence presented here demonstrates the positive impact of women-only services and provides a basis from which to press local and national government to take their role more seriously and provide greater investment and support for those who are doing this work. This chapter draws in particular on the experiences of women who work for, and/or have benefited from, women's organisations and networks across the region, for example, women's centres and networks in Hull, the South Yorkshire Women's Development Trust in Sheffield, and Rotherham Women's Network.[3]

The community and voluntary sector has been hit very hard during the recession and era of austerity beginning in the late 2000s. Many services, centres and projects have been lost, but others survive, largely thanks to a few dedicated volunteers. Between 2004 and 2007 one in five women's organisations in the UK were forced to close for financial reasons and 52 per cent have had to reduce their service provision due to funding reductions (WRC, 2011, 7). Moreover, as the WRC explains:

> While they encounter barriers to funding which are similar to other voluntary and community organisations, such as short-term funding, bureaucracy, the rise of competitive tendering and limited capacity for fundraising, women's organisations also face additional challenges including a lack of gender awareness in society; under-representation of women in public bodies and decision-making; and a lack of recognition of what women's organisations do and why they are needed. (WRC, 2011, 7)

One example of the rise and partial demise of a powerful women's network is that of Hull Women's Network (HWN). In 2004, women working with women's voluntary and community services in and around Hull established a strategic partnership of women-only services in the form of HWN. It had six partners: Hull Women's Centre incorporating the Women Arts and Media (WAM) project; 'Open Door' Bransholme Women's Centre, which was known particularly for its domestic and sexual violence support for women and children; 'Willow' North Hull Women's Centre, known for its training provision; 'Winner' Preston Road Women's Centre, a very active women's centre providing courses and support services; West Hull Women's Centre, a newly formed centre; and the SAFE Women's Training Company (Self-defence Action for Equality). In 2007, Hull Women's Aid also became a part of the Network and HWN sat on the steering committee of the Hull-Domestic Abuse Partnership (Hull-DAP).[4]

The broad aims of Hull Women's Network were for the member organisations to support each other both as a collective and as individual organisations to improve the lives of women across the region. HWN was successful in securing funding from a range of charitable trusts to develop joint projects for women in addition to supporting the work already carried out within its partner organisations. These projects included helping women into training, volunteering and employment, and projects focusing specifically on young women. HWN also secured significant financial support for an ambitious and long-term project involving the purchase of several properties across the city to provide at-risk women and their families with rental accommodation in a supported environment, and this project has since been taken forward by Preston Road Women's Centre.

In 2008 HWN disbanded largely due to resource issues in an increasingly difficult financial climate and pressures on each individual partner to focus on their own survival in the face of closures and staff cuts. Bransholme Women's Centre fell victim to the serious flooding that immersed much of the city of Hull in 2007. The building was destroyed and lack of funds meant that the centre was unable to reopen. The WAM and SAFE projects were closed when their time-limited funding cycle ended in 2007–8. West Hull Women's Centre closed due to lack of funds in 2008. North Hull Women's Centre (Willow) finally closed in 2013 due to financial difficulties largely in meeting core costs of building rental, although volunteers are looking at ways of maintaining some service on a limited basis housed in another location. Nevertheless, Preston Road Women's Centre (Winner) and Hull Women's Centre are still active, although all have lost a number of key paid staff. Hull Women's Centre is the longest running provision having been established in 1979. They have reduced services and rely more heavily on volunteers rather than paid workers, but they are still there, which in the straitened financial circumstances is in itself amazing and testament to women's strength and commitment to their communities.

Both authors have spent several years volunteering in women's centres in the city of Hull, community work which continues and which has provided the opportunity to gain first-hand experience of listening to, observing and participating in the day-to-day life of the centres. This has enabled us to garner a deep understanding and appreciation of the grassroots level from which these services operate. Here we take a closer look at some of the work of these centres and women's services, what those services mean for the lives of individual women, the role of individual women working in those centres and projects, the contribution these women see themselves making to the wider community and the everyday struggles they face in ensuring that the services they provide continues.

In focusing on women's centres and services in Hull, we are not claiming that what we found there is necessarily the same across the entire Yorkshire and Humber Region. As we have made clear from the outset in this volume, women cannot of course be treated as an undifferentiated, homogeneous category. Their experiences of the world are inevitably affected by intersections of complex and changing positionalities, including differences in terms of what point they are in their lifecourse, their socio-cultural background and ethnicity, whether they live in a rural or urban context, if they have children, and so on. Similarly, ethnic minority groups are not homogeneous, and, as Bhavnani (2006) has argued, making generalised statements and comparisons can be problematic, especially when the outcomes could influence legislative and policy changes. The Yorkshire and Humber Region is clearly made up of a range of diverse communities, each revealing specific needs and challenges for the women in those communities. It is also the case, of course, that provision of women's services across the region varies enormously, with some areas being better served than others. Here, however, as we have throughout this book, we focus more on what women have in common than what separates them. Employing the voices of individual women involved in women's services promotes the recognition that women experience and articulate their lives in different ways while allowing us to draw on common themes and experiences. It is worth reminding ourselves of the words of Stanley and Wise, as we set out in the introduction, who articulated that while:

> 'woman' is a socially and politically constructed category, the ontological basis of which lies in a set of experiences rooted in the material world...to say that women share 'experiences of oppression' is not to say that we share the *same* experiences. The social contexts within which different kinds of women live, work, struggle and make sense of their lives differ widely across the world and between different groupings of women. [Thus] the experience of 'women' is ontologically fractured and complex because we do not all share one single and unseamed material reality. (1990, 21–2)

So we need to recognise these ontological fractures and complexities of experience for women within the embodied infrastructure of services and spaces. We must, however, simultaneously acknowledge and understand the threads of commonality of experiences among and between women and women's spaces within the Yorkshire and Humber region.

In order to better understand the context within which women's services are working it is useful to remind ourselves of some key social indicators, as collated by the ONS (see Box 1.1). The Yorkshire and Humber Region is of course a large and diverse geographical area, with significant fluctuations in terms of wealth, class, educational attainment and so on. Nevertheless – and here we are focusing specifically on the negative – the region has marked areas of high unemployment and deprivation, which are often coupled with low aspirations. According to ONS (2012a) figures, more than a fifth (22 per cent) of households are workless, the second highest rate in the UK, and it has the second lowest level of disposable weekly income in England. The proportion of 16-year-olds in post compulsory education or training is the lowest in the England and one in three adults (34 per cent) aged 19–65 have no qualifications. It has one of the highest levels of alcohol consumption and smoking for men and women in the UK, lifestyle indicators that are often linked to lower levels of socio-economic class. The region as a whole has a slightly higher than average percentage of people not in good health coupled with a slightly lower than average life expectancy for both men and women. More specifically, Kingston upon Hull has the lowest life expectancy for both men and women in England (75 and 80 years respectively compared to national averages of 78 and 82) (Kay, 2009; ONS, 2012a). It is against this backdrop that the voluntary and community sector is working and statistics such as these underpin the importance that these embodied infrastructures of social, community and women's services have to play in the region.

Women-only services: meeting needs, raising aspirations

> The women's voluntary sector is extremely well-placed to provide public services, having built up a wealth of knowledge and expertise on a wide range of issues pertaining to women and domestic violence, sexual violence, forced marriages, immigration, housing, health, cultural constraints, drug and alcohol abuse, childcare and protection etc. Women's organisations have developed extremely effective ways of working with some of the most marginalised women and children (WRC, 2006b, 19).

In one of the few pieces of relatively recent and ongoing research on the women's sector in the UK, the Women's Resource Centre (see for example WRC, 2006a; 2007; 2013a) has identified five key features of women's organisations that define the services they offer, make them distinct and enable them to fill the gaps left by other mainstream publicly funded service providers. These features are: the provision of women-only spaces; a focus on empowerment and independence; service user involvement and high levels of peer support; an integrated needs-based service; and reaching the 'hard-to-reach' women (WRC, 2006a, 4; 2013a).

All of the women's centres we focused on in the course of this study share the features outlined above. In this final chapter we explore the value of what we conceptualise as the embodied infrastructures of women-only services in detail, before proceeding to discuss the ways that women's organisations fill the gaps left by other service providers. We also examine the importance of such provision in women's lives, particularly in terms of raising aspirations.

Women-only safe spaces

As was consistently reiterated and demonstrated by women who participated in this study, women-only spaces 'create a "safe space", both physically and emotionally. As a result, women feel supported, develop confidence, achieve greater independence and [enjoy] higher self-esteem. They are less marginalised and isolated and feel more able to express themselves' (WRC, 2013a, 1). Women working in women-only centres stressed that an underlying strength was that they are open to women in all situations and from all walks of life:

> 'Any person can come as long as they are female, it don't matter their marital status, whether they've got any income, anything, it doesn't matter.' (Deidre, early 40s, manager, community sector, volunteer, mother, Humberside)

While welcoming all women, such centres often exist in relatively deprived areas, providing outreach work to women who may otherwise be forgotten or missed by more mainstream services. They also attract women who hear about the services through friends, family and neighbours and may not have the confidence to seek help from or engage with formal services. Fiona, the co-coordinator of a women's centre until she was made redundant due to funding cuts, talked about the range of women with whom the centre worked:

> 'I'd say it's probably fair to say that the majority are from, you know, an area of…of recognised deprivation. A lot have left school with no formal qualifications…a lot have had their children early. But having said that, we've got women who have got university degrees and for one reason or another, you know, their life's taken on a change.' (Fiona, late 40s, manager, community sector, volunteer, mother, Humberside)

Abigail also works within women's organisations and describes women's centres as a 'stepping stone'; enabling women to regain self-confidence and re-establish their own identity. She feels that the inclusive atmosphere promoted by women's centres is one of their most positive aspects:

> 'We have all sorts of women...so we've had, you know, one woman who came in who had a law degree, however, she just really, really was lacking confidence because she'd been at home and had three children and really concentrated on putting her energies towards being mum and then when it comes to children going to school she felt like she'd lost who she was a little bit. So she came to us to, you know, just needed a little bit of hand-holding and reassurance... it's like they need the stepping stone of somebody saying "What you're doing is amazing and creative and you can do this!"' (Abigail, late 20s, manager, community sector, volunteer, Humberside)

Why women-only?

> 'There was a lot of controversy really about what women-only space was for, why we needed it, a lot of the senior managers, well a significant number of the senior management team at the [local authority] didn't respect it.' (Wendy, late 30s, manager, community sector, volunteer, Humberside)

Many people find the idea of women-only spaces contentious, but they remain important spaces that should be defended and preserved. As Sweetman states:

> The company of women represents an alternative form of social network which enables individual women to move away from dependency on the traditional social relations available to them via engagement with the family, marriage and the household. Collective association and sharing of experience challenges women's isolation, 'outs' women's sense of injustice, and raises hopes that gender relations can, and should, change (2013, 218).

Women's centres are run by women for women. They are inclusive of all women and exclusive to women, that is, they often have strict policies on the admission of men and teenaged boys for any purpose. One of the primary reasons for women-only spaces is to create a safe environment for women, where women feel comfortable, are able to express themselves with confidence, and in which their specifically tailored and holistic needs can be met. The WRC conducted an extensive study of women's services in 2007, and as part of their research they commissioned a random poll of 1000 women in the UK, of whom 97 per cent wanted the choice of women-only support services if they had been victim of a sexual assault and 78 per cent thought that it was important to have women-only professional services for personal support and counselling needs (WRC, 2007, 8). Pamela was the coordinator of a women's centre in Hull until she was made redundant due to funding cuts. She commented:

> 'We need a women's centre because it needs to be women-specific and it needs to be an environment where any woman can feel safe to come through the front door... not everybody has the confidence or the opportunity.' (Pamela, early 40s, manager, community sector, volunteer, Humberside)

Abigail's comments reveal further benefits of being a women-only service, creating a space within which women can share their experiences:

> 'Being part of a women-only project gives them the opportunity really, I think, to kind of talk of other things... for example, if they're having any difficulties at home in their personal life.' (Abigail, late 20s, manager, community sector, volunteer, Humberside)

Indeed, service providers are convinced of the need for provision of 'women-only' safe spaces despite sometimes being opposed by partner groups. Some groups of women experience intersectional discrimination on grounds of, for example, ethnicity, religion, sexuality, and can be further marginalised and isolated and this can make the provision of women-only spaces and services even more important (WRC, 2007, 9). For some culturally or faith-based women's groups, there may be additional imperatives to access services in women-only spaces. Here Kavshi talks about trying to run English classes for a group of Kurdish women at a centre for refugees which did not have an effective women-only space:

> 'When I first started, there was a large group of Kurdish women that used to come…and they stopped coming after the first couple of times. I got to know most of them in rather a short period of time and they stopped coming on the basis that my manager was walking around. Now the afternoon was women only, but he would stay in to just finish off some paperwork. But that wasn't acceptable, and yes it was a case of being chaperoned to and from the building. On one occasion, we had to ask a man to leave because it wasn't appropriate for him to be there in front of the other women, but he wanted to stay because of his partner. We explained that we couldn't do that, but she was in a safe environment, that the door would be locked behind him and, you know, no men would be allowed in apart from the manager and he wouldn't allow that so she had to leave and then they stopped coming altogether.' (Kavshi, late 20s, part time, community sector, student, Humberside)

A safe learning environment

Creating a sense of safety is not only about literally providing a safe, women-only, haven for those women who may be experiencing abuse or violence from men, though the latter is clearly important. Rather, it is about the need to provide a broader sense of security as a basis from which to meet women's other needs. Women's centres make a significant contribution to improving women's education as many of the women who access these services lack the confidence to enter formal educational establishments and may previously have had negative experiences of formal education. There are several key elements which contribute to making women's centres safe learning environments:

- Community-based: women can fit learning into other activities in their lives, such as dropping children off at school. Women can also stay in a local environment which is comfortable for them.
- Personal networks: many women have initial contact with this learning environment through attending with a friend or through a personal recommendation, meaning that there are friendly faces from the star

- Appropriate learning environments: women's centres aim to offer both accredited and non-accredited courses and to allow women to develop and progress at their own pace in an environment where they can feel safe to express themselves and explore their potential.

Octavia, whom we first met in Chapter Four, was introduced to her local women's centre by a relative who attended a range of activities there. Prior to this Octavia had been out of education and employment for many years, initially to raise her children, and subsequently due to health problems. She had also experienced domestic violence over a long period of time. This significantly contributed to problems with her mental health at one stage in her life. These experiences left her lacking in self-belief and, consequently, although she was keen to take up new opportunities such as education, she did not have the confidence to go to college or other formal environments. As with many women in her area, she was not comfortable travelling to parts of the city with which she was not familiar:

> 'I started off on the non-accredited courses and when I started going on computer courses and that, I still didn't have the confidence to go to proper college, what I call proper college, you know the college in town, and I still wanted to stay within the familiarity of the women's centre because I felt safe, I felt other people were in the same predicament as me, and I didn't feel confident to, you know, go further afield.' (Octavia, mid-40s, volunteer, mother, Humberside)

Octavia became involved with the women's centre for several years, during which time she built her confidence and gained new qualifications. She became a regular volunteer, and even secured part-time paid work supporting other women. She described how her involvement had changed her life for the better:

> 'For my health and my mental status it really did help me…I found that my getting out and I had something to focus on for myself and helping others then I wasn't taking as much medication and my whole health, I was physically better.' (Octavia, mid-40s, volunteer, mother, Humberside)

Focus on confidence building, empowerment and independence

Low levels of confidence were repeatedly raised by women as one of the major factors affecting their lives. As we have explored throughout this book, the underlying causes of this are complicated but are rooted in social and cultural expectations, processes of gendering and the consequences of these. Nasreen, coordinator of an Asian women's group, found that confidence was particularly significant for women accessing the group:

> 'I think the majority of them have no confidence…I'd say 90 per cent of women…I'm sure everyone has their dreams and ambitions, but they don't have the confidence and they don't know which way to go around it.' (Nasreen mid-20s, manager, community sector, mother, Humberside)

This common experience of low confidence for women was recognised as a fundamental aspect of service provision for each of the women's organisations with which we spoke. Explicit and implicit means were used to address low levels of self-confidence, ranging from confidence and assertiveness courses, social events and family fun days aimed at encouraging stronger social networks, to decorating women's centres so that they would appear friendly and welcoming.

Confidence-building courses are often a woman's first contact with a service provider. Specifically designed to be accessible and non-threatening, they are especially popular among women who have been out of employment and education for some time or at home for a period raising children. They are described in terms such as: 'a very short course with a minimal number of people so that they are not bombarded with too many new faces', 'there is no pressure', 'non-accredited so guided by the learners' pace', 'ice-breaking activities that are informal and fun', which demonstrate the importance of creating a non-threatening situation. It may have taken years for women to lose their self-confidence, so one important recognition is that rebuilding this is not a quick fix, it needs long-term and sustained effort. Carla describes how she builds regular confidence courses into her activities:

> 'Keep on doing confidence-building courses because they're very important, don't just think you've done it once and that's done and they're confident, because they're

not.' (Carla, mid-40s, manager, community sector, mother, North Yorkshire)

Many of the service providers started out as either service users or volunteers at the centre, which can lend itself to greater empathy for and understanding of issues of under-confidence and low self-esteem. Octavia started out by attending a weekly confidence-building course, eventually progressing to running this herself. She emphasised the need for non-judgemental and long-term engagements with women:

'I do stress that it had taken me three years to gain my confidence, so they know that…it's taken three years for myself, if it takes you three years, that's fine, that's what I try to put over.' (Octavia, mid-40s, volunteer, mother, Humberside)

Women's centres can be instrumental in allowing women to share their experiences and aspirations with people who have similar issues in their lives. Bridget is a single parent of three children after leaving her violent husband. She has been attending a women's centre for several years and completed a range of different courses, from confidence building to volunteer training and self-defence. Bridget fulfilled her long-term goal of going to university and started studying for a degree, something she would have not believed possible before coming to the women's centre. Here she describes the empowering impact of attending a women's centre:

'Oh, it has totally built my confidence up, it still needs building more, but it has really built my confidence up, it has totally made me a stronger person and to look up what I have actually been through to get this far…Within two weeks of being on the assertiveness course it was unbelievable, I got this bar job, a job behind the bar and it also gave me something to throw back at my ex as one thing he always said is "There is no way you are working behind a bar."…It makes you realise that there [are] many women out there who don't know that they have got so much talent and so much strength inside them, they think they are weak but they're not because of all the experiences they have been through and they [the women's centre] make you realise that…It was really seeing who you was and the compliments you got and the support you got was so good, and basically it was everyone talking about what they had been through and you knew you wasn't on your own...The biggest step was walking into university as I thought I would never be able to do that, walking in the first day I was absolutely petrified, totally petrified, I was totally petrified...but I stuck it out and kept saying to myself, "You can do it, you can do it!"' (Bridgett, early 40s, student, mother, Humberside)

For some groups expectations are changing, for example, the women we spoke to from ethnic minority backgrounds frequently noted that they aspire to quite different lives from their mothers or older female relatives. Gita, for example, originally from Bangladesh, married at 18, has an undergraduate degree and is currently thinking of progressing to postgraduate study. Gita accesses a women's centre working specifically with BME women which she says she appreciates particularly for its informality, a factor which encourages local women to make use of it. Gita's long-term aspirations reveal how she sees her role being outside the home:

'For myself, job-wise, I want a job and I want more to do with life really. I don't want to stay at home and just... like life around my husband, I want to offer more to the community, provide my services.' (Gita mid-20s, self-employed, Humberside)

Service user involvement and volunteer training

The women's centres we visited all aspired to have high levels of user involvement and governance and to promote a safe learning environment for all women through a variety of means. As Wendy explains, they offer:

'A safe space for women, services for women, opportunity for women to learn new skills and develop etc, etc, all those things, determined more specifically by what local women wanted, and the development phase of the project produced a development plan, detailing quite clearly what local women wanted.' (Wendy, late 30s, manager, community sector, volunteer, Humberside)

Many centres, for example, have users on the management committees so that local women are able to contribute to the running and direction of the centre, aiming to constantly reinforce and extend the embodied infrastructure of the service. As we discuss below, however, service user involvement extends beyond simple consultation. Women's centres provide genuinely user led services through the active participation and transformation of women from being simply service users to service providers both as volunteers and as professional staff. Volunteer programmes are often seen to be of vital importance when tackling social isolation and deprivation. Volunteering can provide a route back into training, employment and social inclusion and can thus assist in lifting women out of economic and social deprivation:

> 'We've got a very active volunteering programme, so women who are maybe bored at home with two kids under five can come in and do something and be with grown-ups for a little while, which is a life-line, really, in a lot of ways and get some experience and skills, do a few courses, to rediscover their own identity, do whatever they want to do.' (Wendy, late 30s, manager, community sector, volunteer, Humberside)

At one of the focus group sessions we asked women to tell us about why they chose to volunteer and what it meant to them. Some of the reasons they gave included wanting to give something back to the community/women's centre; having received support themselves they then wanted to help other women in similar positions; wanting to gain work experience; and because volunteering at the centre provides contact with other people. Rita has been attending a women's centre for several years, she volunteers on a regular basis and became a member of the management committee. She explained how having a disability sometimes affected her confidence levels and what she felt she could and could not do, which meant she often spent a lot of time in her house. We asked Rita why she volunteered:

> 'I think it's meeting people, I mean I live in a really quiet cul-de-sac, honestly if I didn't do any voluntary work I don't think I'd see anybody...think I'd just go crazy if I didn't have anything to do.' (Rita, early 40s, volunteer, Humberside)

The fact that women who work in women's organisations often began as service users themselves has several benefits. They offer strong, positive examples and role models for other service users, bringing a deep and personal understanding of the kinds of complex issues that many women have. Moreover, they are committed to the working methods of the women's centres and are living proof of the value of the services they provide. Quite often a key figure was mentioned as being a catalyst in women's lives, providing the embodied infrastructure needed at a particular time to guide and support them. This can be clearly seen below in the way that Deidre, who had experienced significant sexual violence and trauma in her earlier life, talked about an inspirational teacher she had at the women's centre who helped to turn her life around:

> 'She's fantastic…absolutely inspirational, I did a women's study course with her and she just opened all the wounds in it because it was about looking at…you know, you as a person and how these barriers had stopped you and everything…I'd wrote this massive essay thing and she said, "Do you want to do it?" and I actually showed it to me husband because he said, "Are you ready for this?" because I undid a lot of cupboards…and then…so then when I did this it was brilliant, you know, and we actually went and she read it and she said, "I'm so glad you've been able to trust me with that sort of information, you know"…and I said, "Yeah" I said, "Because you've just changed me life" and she did. She absolutely changed my life.' (Deidre, early 40s, manager, community sector, mother, Humberside)

Many of the women we spoke to articulated in various ways how important a stable role model or mentor can be at difficult times, as Carla illustrates here:

> 'The person who ran the women's group was somebody that I, sort of, looked up to because she, sort of, helped me, pushed me in directions, a role model, yes, definitely a role model, she pushed me into directions that I probably would never have got into not going to the women's group.' (Carla, mid-40s, manager, community sector, mother, North Yorkshire)

These sorts of positive and life changing experiences led to women feeling as if they wanted to give something back to women's organisations and their local communities. Below, Wendy is talking about a difficult phase in her life and how the support of a woman at the centre helped her through it and gave her the inspiration to support other women in similar ways:

> 'She was again absolutely the right person for me to be round at that time, because also of her experience of working with women…and her involvement with [organisation], so the whole…thing that was still going on while I was there, she was able to support me through that which was brilliant really…so that was quite a pivotal experience for me, and it led to me wanting to provide a similar kind of experience for women here at [women's centre].' (Wendy, late 30s, manager, community sector, volunteer, Humberside)

Daisy similarly found her involvement in a women's centre and with the women working there inspirational and this was pivotal in her positive life transition. Here she talks about how she came to the women's centre and the kind of impacts it has had on her life. In a clear illustration of the extension of these embodied insfrastructures, Daisy now serves as a positive role model to other women because from starting out on smaller courses she became the coordinator of a women's centre herself, until she was made redundant due to funding cuts. She continues to volunteer, however, and work with women at community levels:

> 'You know, we was between that bracket where I couldn't get anything 'cos we were not on benefits, but I can't do anything because I've got no valuable income of my own…I was very much isolated…a friend on the estate who I'd actually known for years gone by…she came round and she'd actually started at [women's centre] about three or four months previous, that's when she said, "Oh why don't you come along?", "Oh no," I said "I don't fancy nowt like that," and then she said about the reflexology class, I was thinking, "Oh yeah" [sarcastic], but…I came along to that and really that was it. It's always been a struggle, always, but I say, that's why I feel so much about coming here because it went from, I'd say, something daft like reflexology class, I then went on to start umm English…from that I started my GCSE English at [College] on a night…and I passed that. I mean I got a "B" in me English, which you know,

that just blew me away…Just think what I've wasted, what I could have done, you know, because I…I did cleaning, you did all the menial…you know, shop work, all what I'd class as menial jobs…where you're never going to get any better because you haven't got a chance to   That's why I love the job I'm in because I can relate so much to different aspects of women that come through the door and that is…it's having that empathy.' (Daisy, early 40s, manager, community sector, mother, Humberside)

Integrated, holistic and needs-based services

A fundamental feature of women's centres is their holistic nature. They attempt to see the whole woman and her needs as integrated and overlapping. Thus, they provide a range of facilities such as on-site childcare, social spaces, cafés, even gardens and allotments in addition to rooms specifically for training, counselling or sexual health advice/clinics. Moreover, women can access services and support over an extended period. The long-term and holistic nature of women's centres enables women to access services more freely and flexibly:

> 'The voluntary sector seems to be generally better at looking at women's lives in context…counselling and therapy can be a lot more holistic and long-term and much more suited to women's needs really.' (Sally, late 30s, manager, health sector, volunteer, West Yorkshire)

Thus, women's centres normally develop their service provision around the belief that they need to consider users as whole people, rather than simply dealing with one aspect of the women they see. The everyday demands placed on women means they are often 'time poor' (Moser, 1993; Clisby, 2005). Fear of, and lack of knowledge about, formal institutions often makes it difficult for women to access the information and services they need. Having many services under one roof means that women can access information readily and easily and in an environment where they feel safe and supported.

The UK Women's Resource Centre notes that, typically, women's organisations provide a plethora of services such as advocacy, counselling, advice and information, support, shelter, treatment, referrals, training and skills development, care and practical assistance (WRC, 2013a). This was confirmed by our research. Although provision levels vary greatly, there are core areas which centres focus on which influence the services they provide. These include education and training, providing accredited and non-accredited courses, self-defence, assertiveness training, health, fitness and relaxation classes, nutritional advice for women and children and creative arts. Women's centres also typically try to support women with confidence building and nurture independence, providing holistic and emotional support as well as, for example, help with writing formal letters, job applications and CVs. They also offer guidance and signposting to other services such as Relate, Victim Support and Citizens' Advice, benefits advice, sexual health and pregnancy services. An important aspect of the services is also the provision of more informal social events including day trips and informal social activities, user-run cafés and childcare facilities.

In what follows, we concentrate on two specific aspects of the above; the importance of 'first-rung' provision for women on the educational ladder and in providing a 'one-stop shop' for women.

First-rung provision

Service providers we spoke with were explicit about the importance of providing first-rung provision to women who had previously not had positive educational outcomes, as Fiona describes below:

> 'People for whatever reasons, maybe they had bad experiences, possibly they have no formal qualifications, so for them it is the first step into engaging with or back into learning.' (Fiona, late 40s, manager, community sector, volunteer, mother, Humberside)

First-rung provision is defined by its ability to respond to the needs of individuals and communities and can encompass a range of courses from self-confidence, self-esteem and assertiveness to information, advice and guidance and basic skills in maths, literacy and computing. Being based in local communities, women's centres are ideally placed to provide non-threatening, local learning environments for women seeking to re-engage with learning. Daisy makes this point clearly:

> 'When you've been out of the education loop for so many years, whether that's bringing your family up or working or not, you know, it could be illness or anything, to actually walk back into an educational establishment is very, very

difficult.' (Daisy, early 40s, manager, community sector, volunteer, mother, Humberside)

Although all the centres provided first-rung provision as a key part of their learning and development programmes, it is clear that some groups face additional educational needs. Women whose first language is not English feel that they stand little chance of obtaining employment. Many feel too embarrassed to look for employment for fear of rejection or being made to feel uncomfortable. As an outreach worker explained: 'One thing, one big thing is language barriers, if you can't speak English that will just put them off completely' (Ayisha, late teens, part time, community sector, Humberside).

Not being able to speak English becomes a triple burden for many BME women as it compounds their social isolation, marginalises them from the labour market and increases their economic dependency on male partners or family members. This can have disastrous effects on women's lives as is articulated in the quote below from Pamela who had worked as a service provider at a women's centre in West Yorkshire which was accessed by a high number of BME women:

> 'The main barriers economically were because a lot of them had no English at all, and they had perhaps ended up here with husbands or boyfriends or partners and then had to leave because of violence. So economically, some people were sort of fresh from their own country, and were totally left without anything in a foreign city.' (Pamela, early 40s, manager, community sector, volunteer, Humberside)

Women's centres as a 'one-stop shop'

First-rung provision, however, involves more than simply introducing women to the world of 'life-long' learning as the first step towards educational qualifications and employment. Rather, first-rung provision is only possible within a framework of a holistic and integrated service which recognises that women's lives are often very complex and that there are many factors that have an impact on the possibilities of women achieving their full potential:

> 'It's nice as well to be within an organisation that offers other support mechanisms, so you know a woman can come and be struggling with financial difficulties and then she

can see one of the outreach workers and I think it's really important for us as a project to be part of a bigger thing because I think when a woman comes to start a new hobby or you know begin an education, there's a whole host of other things that can be happening in her life.' (Abigail, late 20s, manager, community sector, volunteer, Humberside)

Being able to signpost women to other areas of service provision was seen to be an integral part of provision in all the women's centres and they all built up formal and informal links with other agencies to ensure this was possible. In all cases staff at women's centres had assisted people to find other provision, to make appointments and even accompanied women to the appointments, if necessary. This kind of care and attention was seen to be over and above other forms of service provision that women may receive, for example, at a college or through the NHS. As Abigail suggests:

'It's not that we necessarily have anything in place to help ourselves but we can signpost on and we're aware of all what there is so we know where they can get free contraception, pregnancy testing, and that's really important because certainly at a college you wouldn't get that level of support.' (Abigail, late 20s, manager, community sector, volunteer, Humberside)

At the time of the research, Wendy was the coordinator of a large, well established and successful women's centre. Below she is talking about the types of provision the centre offers. Her narrative illustrates aptly the importance of holistically geared service provision:

'We've got a number of support services, we've got the direct one-to-one support, a generic support service which is really fielding any issue that women bring with them as they walk through the door, either dealing with it, helping them to deal with it or making a referral to a more specialist service or agency, so it could be anything from debt, to housing, to problems with children, to anything that you can imagine, then we have a specialist domestic violence support service that comes from a person centred perspective in that the woman leads the service that she receives, so she may just want to come in and talk about what's happening to her, what her options are, she may come in wanting practical information, she may come seeking physical refuge, because if she's being chased down the street, it could be any one of the above really, so we provide a service that's tailored to her. It's absolutely confidential because we're a big building we've got loads going on, it's fairly anonymous, so she could be coming in to drop her kids off at the nursery or to access a course, or she could be coming in for domestic violence support. We've got a sexual health service, information and referral for any kind of sexual health issue, we do free, confidential pregnancy testing, Chlamydia testing, gonorrhoea testing on the premises, we train staff or volunteers to deliver that service. We have an active training programme, accredited and non-accredited courses. It's pretty much a one stop shop in a lot of ways, there aren't many needs we can't cater for, we don't offer specific legal advice, we refer on for that, very complicated housing issues we refer to specialist agencies, but pretty much women can get whatever they need from us, on their doorstep.' (Wendy, late 30s, manager, community sector, volunteer, Humberside)

Reaching 'hard to reach' women: the importance of long-term provision

Women's organisations are often established where mainstream services are inappropriate or non-existent such as in rural areas, in areas of socio-economic deprivation or for excluded communities such as some ethnic minority groups. In this way, they are often able to reach 'hard to reach' women who may not otherwise engage with public or third sector services (WRC, 2013a). Not only are women's services often well placed to meet the needs of isolated and marginalised women and their families, they can actually save women's lives. As the WRC state, the 'importance of women-only services is demonstrated by organisations providing VAWG services; these are often life-saving and have long-term impacts on the women and families they support' (WRC, 2013a, 1). What the WRC reports is borne out by the findings of this research. Women's lives are saved not only because of the work of women-only organisations in helping to raise awareness about, and prevent violence against women, providing physical shelter and a safe haven from abusive partners, but also because women's centres provide hope and inter-personal contact that can help save women from the sometimes life-threatening effects of poverty, isolation and despair. Offering that hope requires a sustained and on-going presence in the local communities where women live.

Samantha experiences periodic mental health issues and can at times find it difficult to cope with everyday life. She used to deal with this by shutting herself away in her house, where she felt isolated and suffered from depression. Samantha started attending a women's centre several years ago, beginning with confidence-building courses and has worked her way up from there. She has successfully completed several courses and volunteers on a regular basis for different organisations. Her long-term goal, with the support from the women's centre, is to return to university. She has this to say about the role of the women's centre in re-building her life:

> 'It started me off getting back into a proper life again, I spent several years just hiding away, then coming here I mixed with people, I've had something to get up for, I found a bit of a sense of purpose, and most of the groups have been lovely, really warm, caring people, the…session that I'm doing at the moment is perfect for me, and it's not so much the content of the group as just being in the room with people…it's really important to me to be able to come here and feel a little bit of belonging, because I feel quite isolated and I get very lonely…and without coming here the days would run into the night and it'd just be unbearable for me…it being an all women centre is imperative to me coming here, so there's a safe environment to come to.'
> (Samantha, late 30s, volunteer, Humberside)

Samantha is not alone. Many women who were accessing the women's centres had, for one reason or another, difficult lives. Those women told us how important it was for them to know that the service was there when they needed it: just knowing the centre was there for them assisted in creating some much needed security and stability. Bridget has been attending a women's centre for several years, initially she came to get support with domestic violence issues, she now attends courses and drops in when she feels she requires additional support:

> 'I can leave [the women's centre] for like seven months even and when I come back it is like I never left, they make you feel so welcome every time you walk through the door.'
> (Bridget, early 40s, student, mother, Humberside)

Similarly, service providers told us how important it was that they were able to provide long-term and on-going provision to support women throughout the lifecourse. Being embedded in local communities means that the service providers are also able to develop relationships with service users and other members of the local community:

> 'I could probably name 99 per cent of the women that come through the door. They'll see you walking around the estate and they'll say, 'Hello Daisy''. It's all that familiarity, it does break down that barrier…you're not just this face in an office, there is that relationship building and that enables, again women to open themselves up.' (Daisy, early 40s, manager, community sector, volunteer, mother, Humberside)

Filling gaps, transforming lives: the wider impacts of women's centres

Women begin attending centres for many different reasons. Often it is to effect change in their own lives, such as improving self-esteem or re-entering education. The impact of women's centres is clearly much broader than just on the individual lives of women service users, however. First, as described above, women's centres complement mainstream service provision by helping women find out about and access the range of services available to them *and* their families. Moreover, as women's centres are based in local communities they can often be well placed to respond to specific and changing local needs in ways that statutory sector organisations can find more difficult. Second, women's centres also plug some of the gaps in mainstream provision in health and in education and as such do not simply refer women on to other services, but often have women referred on or signposted to them from the statutory sector as it is recognised that they are frequently able to provide additional and/or long-term support. Third, working directly with women to improve their quality of life has a much wider impact on families and communities in terms of helping to raise aspirations and levels of educational attainment. One of the services which almost all women's centres provide is basic skills education. This was a draw for women who had previously not had very positive experiences of education. Those women were keen to improve their skills both for themselves, and in order to help their children. Molly's story of how she first began attending a woman's centre illustrates a route that is quite common:

> 'What it was, was that I was going through a bit of depression and that, and well I saw a counsellor at the doctors and she referred me to another counsellor but I didn't get no joy, but she recommended this place [women's centre].' (Molly late 40s, full-time mother, volunteer, Humberside)

Service providers were not only able to identify the 'gaps' they were filling in state funded provision, but also the economic contribution they made by keeping women (and through them their families) out of mainstream service provision:

> 'Picking up the pieces from the person who hasn't got the counselling and has decided that, that night they're going to self-harm or commit suicide. Add in those costs of the paramedics, ambulance, and casualty department. That's just an example of what the women's centre does. The benefits and advice, add that in, take that away from somebody then going to the benefits agency and taking four hours of one person's time, they would come here and get that.' (Pamela, early 40s, manager, community sector, volunteer, Humberside)

As the WRC found following their cost benefit analysis of the sector in 2011, women's services are excellent value for money in terms of social returns on investment. Conducted over a two-year period from 2009–11, their 'hidden value' study found that for every £1 invested in their services, women's organisations can generate over five years between £5 and £11 of social value to women, their children and the state (WRC, 2011, 8). This is a point we return to later in this chapter.

Engendering aspirations: women as role models for their children

In a region that scores highly on a range of indices of deprivation, as outlined at the beginning of this chapter, services offered through women's organisations are all the more critical and can help to raise aspirations for women and their families in ways that mainstream services may not be best placed to do. Women's centres are concerned with addressing issues related to social exclusion and deprivation through positive action and long-term, holistic, non-threatening, person-led support. This kind of support, as Wendy illustrates, can be instrumental in radically changing women's lives:

'A local woman, said to me,,,before she'd become involved with the women's centre she felt that she wanted to stay at home and look after her children until they were in their teens, and then after that she could see herself working on the till at [a frozen food store] and that now she knows that she can do whatever she wants to do, all the choices are open to her, and it's up to her to make those choices and that's what she's going to do, and that just completely opened her world by being exposed to different opportunities...I think we have a very clear role to play in addressing disadvantage in that way, because we do open doors, we provide practical help and assistance, but we also give women aspiration and that's something that's hard to quantify but enormously valuable.' (Wendy, late 30s, manager, community sector, volunteer, Humberside)

Similarly, service providers acknowledged the importance of aspiration and noted that women often engaged in education as they wanted their daughters to have more options available to them than they had had in their own lives. Women stated that both being a good role model and being able to help their children with school work were important motivators. They felt this was best achieved through educating themselves first:

'How I always looked at it myself is, educate the parent, you educate the child. You know, if I used to be sat there doing my homework with my children and it's, "Oh Mum. Oh, what're you doing?" You know...they see you learning and they want to learn.' (Daisy, early 40s, manager, community sector, volunteer, mother, Humberside)

Issues of education were especially relevant to women whose first language was not English. These women felt that lacking English language skills limited both their own life chances and their ability to take a more active role in their children's education and achievement, as Ayisha, an outreach worker, explains:

'Because they want to be involved with their children and it's a shame that they can't because of just one little thing, so if they can overcome it, they can be a part of their child's education in the future, which is really good, we all need a role model.' (Ayisha, late teens, part time, community sector, Humberside)

In sum, one of the most significant findings of this research was just how important women's centres are not just to the women who access their services but also to their children, their families and the local communities who benefit from the services provided to women. The wider impact of those services can be seen not only in the way that women's centres and organisations complement and fill the gaps in statutory service provision, but also in the way that the transformation of women's lives helps to engender in families and communities a sense of aspiration and achievement.

Barriers to service provision

Women's centres face a range of barriers in the provision of services. These barriers are both structural, such as accessing funding, and cultural, such as battling against a popular belief that, as there exists a perceived legal equality in the UK, gender inequalities are no longer an issue. Some people, especially some men, can also appear threatened by women-only spaces. The problems which women's services face are many and varied, and can be difficult to extricate into separate issues. Here, we focus on some of the main barriers that emerged through our study.

Public (mis)conceptions

Public understandings of the nature and role of women's services have a huge impact on both women's ability to access services and on providers' abilities to provide them. There are a number of stereotypes associated with women's centres which may be negative and problematic, and which are largely based on a lack of knowledge about such services. The key to dispelling negative stereotypes can be through greater understanding as Fiona notes:

'People say is it the men, but no it's not, it's the women themselves...they put us into categories; we're all lesbians, we're all battered by men, we hate men, we're all vegetarians…Well come and have a look…it's just…you find that the only criteria is you have to be a woman…The head of this Residents Association [wrote a letter] saying, "I never believed in women's centres before, now I think it's great." And it was just that one letter. Now [he] did more for our project and women's centres than if I'd have spent five years going round the estate…because they knew him, they trusted him.' (Fiona, late 40s, manager, community sector, volunteer, Humberside)

Other common assumptions are that women's centres only cater for women with particular kinds of problems, which can cause potential users to be nervous about getting involved:

'People have said, "Oh, the women's centre, that's for battered women isn't it?"' (Octavia, mid-40s, volunteer, mother, Humberside)

Service providers noted that women are far more likely to cease accessing a service if they come up against opposition from family, friends or the wider community. One Asian women's support service we spoke to overcame this issue by setting up a women's group at the local mosque. Removing this barrier enabled local women to freely access the service provided without causing difficulties at home.

'I think what we need to show is, we need to show to the men that we're not putting their wives against them but we're showing that you can compromise and you can do it on an equal level, so we're not enemies.' (Ayisha, late teens, part time, community sector, Humberside)

Lack of recognition

The women's sector provides services which enable women to enter education and employment, providing long-term economic benefits to individuals and local communities. What this and other research has consistently shown, however, is that those working with women in the voluntary sector often feel that the work they do is under-valued. In addition, there is a perception that little recognition is given to the gaps they fill or the economic burden they take away from the statutory services (WRC, 2004).

'I do feel social services have abused the women's centres over all because they give referrals, but they don't give us any contribution for the cost of doing, and basically we're doing their jobs for them...but we're also improving their statistics because they count for every lady that they put onto us they're still counting them in their budgets, but they keep the funding and we don't get it.' (Octavia, mid-40s, volunteer, mother, Humberside)

Although such services fill the gaps left by mainstream and statutory provision, they are often left without the resources in place to cope:

'The only thing that we find difficult sometimes is if a lot of the mental health service see a women's centre and they think, "Ooh, we can send them along to the women's centres."...and sometimes their needs...are much more you know, than anything that we can offer...And that's...that's... you know, that's not excluding them, that's just the...the reality of it.' (Fiona, late 40s, manager, community sector, volunteer, mother, Humberside)

In reference to the free counselling service that women's centres often provide and all the attendant costs associated with that, Fiona further notes:

'We've got a waiting list; she's currently doing two women as long as it takes. We've got a waiting list for that. We're providing that service free, we're providing the room, tea and coffee, the environment...All that saves already a GP practice or the health service paying for that person to have private counselling.' (Fiona, late 40s, manager, community sector, volunteer, mother, Humberside)

An independent study, based in London and commissioned by the WRC in 2006, found that all four of the women's organisations it looked at provided 'excellent' value for money in that the social and economic costs of delivery far exceeded the funding received. Furthermore: 'the women's organisations in the study made savings for the statutory sector by preventing domestic violence, reducing burdens on the health system, reducing women's re-offending, improving mental health and enabling parents to take custody of children previously "looked after" by social services' (WRC, 2006b, 18).

Without full economic costing of the benefits which women's services provide it can be difficult to measure the impact which they have on both individuals and local communities. The WRC's 'Social return on investment report' has gone the furthest to capture this data. The first of its kind in the UK, this economic analysis measured the impact of specialist domestic violence and other specialist women's services and found that the total social value created by investment in women's organisations ranged between £1,773,429 and £5,294,226 and for every £1 invested in women's services, the social value created for women, their families and the state ranged between £5 and £11 (WRC, 2011, 6–8). Further and continued studies are needed to quantify both the direct savings made by statutory services in terms of referrals to women's organisations and other indirect economic benefits that accrue as a result of their work, for example, in assisting women into education and employment. It is also important, however, to acknowledge that much of the work women's organisations do is essentially qualitative and therefore difficult to quantify in terms of simplistic monetary equivalents.

The observation below is from a service provider. She is referring to a focus group and interview session held at a women's centre during the course of this research. The quote captures perfectly how sometimes progress cannot be measured solely through statistics and outputs. Being involved with research can be challenging, specifically for those being interviewed about what are essentially both private and sensitive topics. The very fact that women felt able to discuss their lives with us is evidence in itself that the work these women's centres do has positive impacts on the lives of the women who access the service:

> 'There are two women in that particular group who months ago were at the stage where they weren't even coming through the front door of their own house, and with our help and support and sort of constant mentoring and chivvying along…they're now the people who can sit in a room and be interviewed.' (Pamela, early 40s, manager, community sector, volunteer, Humberside)

Funding and resource issues

Popular misconceptions about the work of women's organisations and the lack of recognition of the work and services they provide is directly linked to what women cited as the main barrier affecting an organisation's ability to provide consistent, high-level services; that is, the inability to find stable funding sources. In line with the findings of this study, the WRC (2006a) notes that women's organisations, along with the rest of the voluntary and community sector, experience particular funding problems including short-term, project oriented funding; a lack of funding for core costs, for example, staffing, utilities, maintenance of premises; limited capacity to effectively engage in constant and time-consuming fundraising; battling with bureaucracy and a climate of increased competition for smaller pots of money.

For most women's organisations, the lack of core funding to pay for premises and their upkeep, salaries for staff, and the cost of everyday running lies at the heart of their financial problems. As has been noted this has led to the significant loss of women's services across the Yorkshire and Humber region and the UK more generally in recent years. As charitable and not-for-profit organisations they do not usually receive any mainstream funding. Moreover, the majority of centres involved in this research provide services which are free at the point of access. Many service providers feel strongly about the continuing need for free provision as this benefits both families on low incomes and, because income distribution within families may be unequal; women may not have access to 'spending money' that they can use to buy services, training and support for themselves. Charging for services, therefore, may further exclude already marginalised people. Octavia explains here how the unequal distribution of power in families can lead to women being unable to access economic resources and so be unable to engage in self-development which incurs cost:

> 'Although she wants to educate herself she can't come into the category where to get her education free because her husband's got this job but he won't give her the money to do it.' (Octavia, mid-40s, volunteer, mother, Humberside)

The lack of both mainstream core funding and/or funding through revenues generated by service provision means that most women's organisations seek external funding through an on-going cycle of applications to other charitable and grant giving bodies. The funding that they are able to apply for is usually targeted to specific, short-term projects, rather than on everyday staffing and running costs, and unlike other not-for-profit and charitable foundations, their access to fundraising among the wider populace is limited by the general misconceptions about gender equality and the presumed restricted remit of women's centres.

Time and energy spent on funding bids was felt by many to be excessive and to divert their human resources from what they saw as their main purpose. The negative effects of cyclical 'panic funding' also absorbs organisational and emotional resources. Many women's centres we spoke to had regularly been weeks or days away from having to significantly reduce their services and opening hours or even close. Several have closed, and others have made all their paid staff redundant and manage a limited service with a team of volunteers, in some cases the very same staff who were made redundant, but who did not want to see the service close. An explicitly gendered issue is that these women now work for free as far as possible to ensure some level of service continues, but women's financial, emotional and labour capacity and time is not infinitely elastic.

Links can clearly be made here to the impacts of structural adjustment and cost recovery policies or 'austerity measures' as we have come to know them in the UK. The world over, when governments become heavily indebted and turn to the powerful international financial institution, the International Monetary Fund (IMF) for help to re-schedule their debts and extend further loans, the IMF imposes loan conditionalities known as Structural Adjustment Policies (SAPs) (Potter, 2000). These have been renamed several times over the years (to 'Poverty Reduction and Growth Strategies' for example) but the underlying principles remain the same (Hopper, 2012). Some of the common IMF conditions, underpinned by neo-liberal economics, are that the nation in question ensures debt repayment by rolling back the state, cutting government spending and privatising state industries and utilities (Momsen, 2010). We have seen this happen in the UK since the neo-liberal 1980s. In the mid-2000s the global financial crisis again led to a new round of similar austerity and structural adjustment across Europe and elsewhere. In recent years, we have seen the bite of austerity and the closure of state-funded services compounded by the reduction of charitable funding for third sector services. The impacts of these austerity measures are themselves gendered. As Fawcett has argued:

> The current austerity agenda and programme of deep spending cuts has left women facing a 'triple jeopardy' of cuts to jobs, benefits and vital services: Jobs – women make up around two-thirds of the public sector workforce, so cuts to this sector are hitting them harder. What's more, there is evidence that women are not sufficiently benefiting from government action to create jobs in the private sector. Benefits – caps and cuts to benefits and tax

credits such as housing benefit and carers allowance are hitting women disproportionately hard – around three-quarters of the money being cut is coming from women's pockets. Services – rolling back public services also affects women disproportionately as they tend to use things like childcare and social care services more frequently and more intensively than men. (Fawcett, 2013b, 1)

We would go further and argue that there is a fourth jeopardy at play. When social, health and educational services are cut women are not only disproportionately affected in the first place, but are the ones who tend to step into the gaps left, trying to stitch up the gaping holes in the safety net as best they can (Sparr, 1994; Momsen, 2010). The UK is no exception to this global commonality, and we have seen this happening within many women's organisations we looked at in this study. This is consistent with and an extension of a feminine ethic of care, the feminisation of care, the embodied infrastructure of women's support networks and women's roles in reproductive and community management work.

To return to the issue of funding, the underlying financial instability of women's organisations and the continual quest for new sources of funding poses particular problems. It makes it difficult for providers to plan strategically as they constantly try to shape their programmes to meet the aims and objectives of current funding. It also militates against efforts to provide a secure and stable environment for women. Dominant funding paradigms often take on board and operate in response to current social trends and 'buzz words' whether emanating from the government or from mainstream media and popular culture. The introduction of the contracts culture in the voluntary sector presents additional challenges for women's organisations as the emphasis moved to providing services that purchasers and funders identify and want to buy (Riordan, 1999, cited in Soteri, 2002). The problem posed by that approach is two-fold. Purchasers and funders may not always know about the specific needs of particular groups and individuals in particular social situations. They may also make categorical assumptions about the kinds of people who require certain kinds of services.

Service providers, for example, mentioned that the appropriation of certain language and labels was something they did not feel entirely comfortable with. Buying into these 'trends', however, often enabled them to secure future funding. The requirement to 'tick the boxes' of funding bids, for example, by detailing levels of socio-economic and educational deprivation experienced by the project beneficiaries (and indeed as the statistics we have provided in this chapter could be charged with doing), can then serve to perpetuate the very same stigmatising stereotypes women's centres work to break down, as one service provider commented:

> 'If the women saw this…It's like saying they're all on the bones of their ass…and they'd kick against it…because people don't like to be labelled with that deprived thing… And I think we're putting these in, funding bids, and this is all the…the barriers and the stigmas that we're trying to break down…but we're still putting them in because we have to get the money in to change that.' (Focus Group, women's service providers, Humberside)

This is not an isolated observation. Research carried out by The Women's National Commission also highlighted the dilemmas and contradictions faced by women's organisations between trying to pursue their own local objectives and compromising values that are forced upon them by the funding requirements of external bodies (Scott, 2001). Funding trends also mean that certain members of the community are prevented from accessing service provision. For example, there has been a recent focus on engaging 16–19 years olds in education and employment and, as Gabriel points out, this served to exclude older women:

> 'The [project] where I worked previously was aimed at 16 to 19s but there was so much provision for 16 to 19s. Whereas, we had so many women who came to us who were probably 19 to 24 who wanted to do things and even 24-plus, but there was nowhere they could get funded places to do things.' (Gabrielle, early 40s, part-time administrator, mother, Humberside)

The nature of that funding also required quantifiable objectives and outputs, with emphasis on accredited courses and progression upwards:

> 'The way learning is funded as well is a big barrier because you're expected to progress upwards, to get funding for courses…is very much hierarchical, so you'll do a level one and then you'll immediately go to a level two.' (Ella, late 30s, manager, community sector, volunteer, Humberside)

The accreditation of learning and the trend towards 'measurable outputs' is often seen as a barrier to service provision that aims to cater for *all* women; that is, it potentially excludes certain categories of women. For example, older women who do not need to be on structured learning pathways and those women who are experiencing difficulties and cannot commit themselves to regular learning. The importance of maintaining possibilities for non-accredited learning was a recurrent issue for many of the women who participated in this study, as the comment below illustrates:

> 'It's a shame nowadays that everything needs to be accredited, sometimes I just want to attend things for pleasure and fun or to meet people.' (Focus group, women accessing women's services, Humberside)

Cutting funding for non-accredited courses is also short-sighted as it often provides an essential stepping stone to accredited training. Moreover, women who have already had bad experiences of formal education and who do not feel ready to embark on accredited training may be set up to fail by being steered onto such a course due to lack of alternatives and then not managing to pass or complete the training. This could have deleterious consequences for their self-esteem and willingness to engage in future provision.

The constant chase for new sources of funding on projects initiated externally means that well-established and successful initiatives may have to be cancelled because of lack of funds. The unstable nature of many women-specific services often mirrors the lives of those women who most benefit from their service. Women need to feel confident that a service they come to trust is going to remain a permanent fixture in their lives as long as they need it:

> 'There's nothing worse than a service being available for the public and everybody's enjoying it and it's making an impact and then it gets taken away, and we're getting now where the community and the public are saying, 'Oh, another scheme which will be gone in a couple of months, couple of years" and they need consistency.' (Octavia, mid-40s, volunteer, mother, Humberside)

The emotional and experiential aspects of this dilemma are much harder to quantify and can easily be overlooked. Service providers who are struggling to secure future funding highlighted that the stress and pressure as well as the guilt and responsibility felt is at times overwhelming. Pamela was the coordinator of a thriving women's centre, but due to lack of funding the centre was forced to significantly reduce its services and make all paid staff redundant and, after trying to maintain some volunteer-led services, it finally closed. Here Pamela was talking about the fight to remain open and the impacts of having to close:

> 'Okay, so the funding is an absolute nightmare…the government and the statutory agencies don't see it as a right that a women's centre should be there…the money should be there…I try to remain optimistic, and we're working hard for it not to close…is there going to be this last minute pot of money?…I mean the absolute ludicrous thing is that this is not a sinking ship. How can they let it [close] when they see what we've done? It's always that knife-edge thing…I'll hang on to the last minute and if it closes I'll go, I'll be able to move on, I know that. But those people who were there, what do they do then? Where do they go?' (Pamela, early 40s, manager, community sector, volunteer, Humberside)

The reality of closing and changing services when vulnerable and disadvantaged women have come to rely on them can be detrimental to women's experience and their ability to continue moving forward, as Wendy reveals below:

> 'Yeah, well, you do harm, and you lose total credibility with the women in the community that you're there for. Because how do you then take away that lifeline?' (Wendy, late 30s, manager, community sector, volunteer, Humberside)

Moreover, taking the service away and causing more disruption in women's lives goes against the entire ethos of what women's organisations are working towards, placing service providers in difficult ethical positions. As mentioned earlier in this chapter, many women's response was to try and continue to run reduced provision on a voluntary basis. As Nasreen who works with BME women comments below:

> 'I would say even if I didn't get paid and there were some course here I'd happily just come in, volunteer and do it, but what we've seen the difference in the women it's amazing,

it's amazing what we've achieved.' (Nasreen, mid-20s, part-time manager, community sector, Humberside)

In summary, a lack of statutory funding directly limits the work of women's organisations to fill the gaps left by publicly funded mainstream service providers. However, the wider consequences of this underfunding is that women's organisations are frequently stretched and diverted from their core activities in the quest to find new sources of support, cannot engage in long-term planning, and are sometimes forced to alter their programmes according to the requirements of funding agencies rather than the needs of their users. As Riordan has stated, '[p]olitical rhetoric about women's equality fails to be matched by public investment in women's organisations' (Riordan, 1999, 32, cited in Soteri, 2002).

Conclusion: challenging the triad of violence through women's spaces and recognising the power of women as situated knowers

Drawing on our ethnographic empirical research in the Yorkshire and Humber region, this chapter has focused on the embodied infrastructure of women-only services as a vehicle through which we can see how women's gendered consciousness can act as a catalyst for social transformation. Here we have shown how women's organisations meet a wide variety of women's needs, fill gaps in mainstream service provision, and help women to transform their lives and the lives of others. Throughout the UK, and worldwide, we have an exciting and powerful resource, although much of the work that women's organisations do and the critical importance of these forms of embodied infrastructures is seriously undervalued, goes unrecognised and is sadly often in danger of being lost. That the work of women's centres is undervalued and under-resourced is tied to the more general lack of recognition given to women's work and contributions in society as a whole, a lack of recognition that is, ironically, further exacerbated by a popular perception that gender inequalities are now a thing of the past.

In order to ensure that women-only services are not overlooked in government strategies further research is needed that can continue to quantify the value of women's organisations and the work they do to complement statutory service provision. We already know that women's services are excellent value for money and give back more than is put into them (WRC, 2011), but we need to keep demonstrating this. The excellent value provided by women's services is in part, and not unproblematically, due to the additional unpaid labour of women who work in these sectors either above and beyond their contracted hours or for free. We need these statistics to provide evidence of the value of these sectors, although it is also important to acknowledge that it may not be possible to place an economic measure on much of the work that women's centres do. Moreover, such 'bean counting' can be counterproductive and exclusionary, forcing women's centres to address the requirements of funding bodies rather than meet the needs of the women whom they seek to serve.

There is a need for greater cooperation and knowledge-sharing between existing women's organisations and networks, particularly across and between ethnic, religious and community boundaries. Although women's needs vary considerably, there is nonetheless much that they share in common. Women's organisations need to form themselves into stronger strategic partnerships through which they are better placed to work with, and challenge, government policy and strategy. Indeed, it is only by greater collectivity – as demonstrated by notable examples such as the WRC in London, and the networks of women's services that have grown across the Yorkshire and Humber region – that women's organisations and women-only service providers can ensure that local and national government policy makers fully recognise and account for the contribution that women's organisations make both to the lives of individual women and to society as a whole.

Finally, we return to one of the core arguments and themes threaded through this book: that women are situated knowers. A key reason we have focused in some detail in this concluding chapter on the work and role of women's services is because it is within these spaces that we can see clearly the ways in which women squeeze themselves into the 'chinks in the world machine' (Lefanu, 1988). In doing so they actively make safe spaces for themselves to work together and consciously challenge many of the negative processes of gendering women experience within this framework or triad of symbolic, structural and visceral violence. At this point it seems appropriate to return to something Paul Farmer has said. Here Farmer is talking about the work of anthropologists – which relates to our work in the production of this research – but it can just as well also relate to the women with whom we have been working in women's services who have contributed to this study:

> Our job is to document, as meticulously and as honestly as we can, the complex workings of a vast machinery rooted in political economy that only a romantic would term fragile.

> What is fragile is rather our enterprise of creating a more truthful accounting and fighting amnesia. We will wait for the 'glitch in the matrix' so that more can see clearly just what the cost is...for those who still set their backs to the impossible task of living on next to nothing while others wallow in surfeit. (Farmer, 2004, 317)

Women's spaces are critical sites that can go some way towards exposing that 'glitch in the matrix', bridging the gap between the embedded yet often amorphous, symbolic, 'gentle' violence of gendering and the structural violence of state machinery and its' policy. They provide spaces in which women and children (and specifically *not* 'womeandchildren') can work towards recognising, healing and challenging the triad of violence: the structural, symbolic and physical wounds inflicted by the gender regimes in which they live. This links directly to one of the most significant things to emerge quite strongly through this study – the ways in which women of all ages and backgrounds were able to coherently articulate how processes of gendering have an impact on their sense of self, and on the material conditions of their lives. As we have demonstrated, given the opportunity to think and speak about their gendered lives, women are reflexive and situated knowers. This sophisticated gendered consciousness is significant and we believe that it could, with appropriate structural support, act both as a catalyst for positive transformation and as a form of embodied infrastructure that bridges the gap between policy and gendering in the future.

Notes

Chapter One: Gendering, inequalities, and the limits of policy

[1] David Cameron, Conservative Prime Minister at the time of writing, partially recognised, although possibly inadvertently, the importance of this work when he called for his 'Big Society' (BBC News Online, 2010). He saw this as a cheap way of plugging some of the welfare gaps that cuts to statutory services left, which were blamed on the economic recession following the banking scandal of the late 2010s. What he failed to wholly acknowledge was that people – for the most part women – have been performing this unpaid labour for centuries, if not millennia.

[2] Hull Women's Network established a working partnership with the Gender Studies Department at the University of Hull in order to collaborate on research into issues of gender discrimination for women in the job market. This collaboration resulted in the development of the Breakthrough Research Project proposal which was subsequently funded by the European Social Fund and the Learning and Skills Council.

[3] Based on a conversation with Sylvia Walby in 2011. This is not meant as a critique of her position, indeed we also refer to Walby's 'gender regimes' throughout this book.

[4] A 2012 UK survey by Kantar reveals that 47 per cent of women feel under-represented in politics, and only 30 per cent say that they take an interest in politics, compared to 47 per cent of men.

[5] The Gender Pay Gap refers to how much less women earn per hour than their male counterparts, calculated either as an average (mean), or based on majority (median) earnings, but excluding overtime and bonus payments. The ONS state that they prefer to calculate gender-based pay inequalities using median calculations (taking the majority earning rate) rather than mean (average earnings) (ONS, 2013a). One could argue that this way of calculating the statistics has the effect of narrowing the pay gap and can be criticised for two key reasons: it excludes all high earners, the majority of whom are male (and while the majority of low-paid workers are female, it is likely that this is more than counterbalanced by including the highest earners), and it also excludes overtime and bonus pay, from which again mostly men benefit, the combined effect of this could be to obscure men's higher earnings.

[6] The Coalition government has called for a review of the Equality Duty in a move that is likely to see this policy weakened. As Fawcett (2013c, 4) has argued: 'since the formation of the Coalition government in May, 2010, we have seen the articulation and now enactment, of a different approach to tackling equality. Rather than continuing to develop equality architecture, this has been weakened and reduced with far greater reliance placed on voluntary action as a means to deliver equality'.

Chapter Two: Gendering women's minds: identity, confidence and mental wellbeing

[1] In addition to Ussher's significant body of work in this field, see, for example, Nathanson, 1975; Pill and Stott, 1982; Cornwell, 1984; Graham, 1984; Hockey, 1993; Busfield, 1996, 2002; McCauley et al, 1998; Stewart and Robinson, 1998; Prior, 1999; Hunt, 2000; Chrisler and Ferguson, 2006; Tang et al, 2007; Kohen, 2000; Davar, 2001; Bendelow et al, 2002; O'Grady, 2005, to cite but a few.

[2] *Hegemonic masculinity* is a term coined by Connell to describe an 'ideal type' in society, 'the type of masculinity performed by popular heroes, fantasy figures' (Alsop et al, 2002, 140; see also Connell, 1987, 1992, 1995; Donaldson, 1993 or Kimmel, 1994). As Goffman (1963) stated, the ideal American man, and this would hold resonance in the UK context, is 'A young, married, white, urban, northern heterosexual, Protestant father of a college education, and a recent record in sports…Any male who fails to qualify in any one of these ways is likely to view himself…as unworthy, incomplete, and inferior' (cited in Alsop et al, 2002, 140).

Chapter Four: Gendering and engendering violence in women's everyday lives

[1] According to the Family Law Act 1996 Part IV, domestic violence is 'any violence or threat of violence that takes place in or outside the home between family and household members or partners in existing or previous relationships. It can include mental, emotional, financial, physical and sexual violence. It also includes harassment, for example persistent letters, or telephone calls, threats of violence and emotional, psychological, financial, or mental abuse' (Rights of Women, 2006, 2). Sexual violence is defined as '[a]ny violence, physical or psychological, carried out through sexual means or by targeting sexuality' (UN, 1998, 7–8). Sexual violence includes 'rape and attempted rape, and such acts as forcing a person to strip naked in public, forcing two victims to perform sexual acts on one another or harm one another in a sexual manner, mutilating a person's genitals or a woman's breasts, and sexual slavery' (Human Rights Watch, 2006, 1).

[2] The Everyday Sexism Project is an online forum for people to send in their personal experiences of everyday sexism. As the site states, 'The Everyday Sexism Project exists to catalogue instances of sexism experienced by women on a day to day basis. They might be serious or minor, outrageously offensive or so niggling and normalised that you don't even feel able to protest. Say as much or as little as you like, use your real name or a pseudonym – it's up to you. By sharing your story you're showing the world that sexism *does* exist, it *is* faced by women *every day* and it *is* a valid problem to discuss' (see http://everydaysexism.com/). Founder Laura Bates, who established the Project in 2012 said, 'When I started the Everyday Sexism Project…I never imagined that by now it would have attracted some 25,000 entries and be about to spread to 15 countries' (Bates in an interview with the *Guardian*, Martinson, 2013).

Chapter Five: Gendering education: the paradox of success versus status

[1] The Gender Equality Duty (GED) is a statutory duty which came into force in April 2007. All public authorities in England, Wales and Scotland must demonstrate that they are promoting equality for women and men and that they are eliminating sexual discrimination and harassment. The requirements of the duty place the responsibility for putting in place gender equality policies and practices on organisations. Organisations have to show that they are not directly or indirectly discriminating against employees or customers/service users because of their gender (EOC, 2007a). Recent criticisms by the Fawcett Society reveal concern over the potential weakening of gender equality policies in favour of more voluntary types of action (2013c).

[2] In 2009/2010 girls achieved grades A★ to C in 87 per cent of GCSEs they took compared to 81 per cent for boys. Similarly, at A level, 59 per cent of girls gained two A-level passes compared to 47 per cent of boys (DfE, 2012a).

[3] Part of the increase in women's participation in Higher Education is made up of women returning to education at a later stage in life, particularly following time to work or raise children.

[4] For example, during the period when the 11+ exam was used to divide children into different types of education, girls had to perform better than boys to gain entry to grammar schools, supposedly in order to counter for boys' 'later development' (Skelton, 1997, 306).

[5] Hermione Granger, the female hero in the Harry Potter Series is often quoted in this context as representative of this new kind of female hero. Her cleverness, superior ability with magic, problem-solving abilities and dedication are vital to the adventures of the three friends.

[6] Figures for the prevalence of sexting are hard to measure but a recent survey by The EU Kids Online Network suggests that in the UK 12 per cent of 11–16 year old internet users have received sexual messages, although only 4 per cent admit to having sent them (Haddon et al, 2012, 69). Cross et al (2009) found higher rates in their study, with a third of children saying that they have received a sex-related message and a quarter had received a sex-related image. Of these, 85 per cent were from people they knew.

Chapter Six: Gendering reproduction: women's experiences of motherhood and mental wellbeing

[1] Throughout this chapter we use the term 'motherhood' to mean the natural and/or social female parent of a child, and while we recognise that men can take prime responsibility for childcare, we are, here, focusing on the choices and constraints that women in particular face as mothers.

[2] The term 'childless' is problematic as it evokes the idea of 'lack' or 'loss'. For this reason a number of diverse groups prefer the term 'child free' which does not carry the same negative connotations (Basten, 2009).

[3] This is a group of Conservative MPs who hold seats in the 40 most marginal Conservative seats.

[4] The mean length of maternity leave taken by mothers in 2008 was 39 weeks, up from 36 weeks in 2006 and around three-quarters of women returned to work between 12 and 18 months after giving birth (DWP, 2011).

[5] OK! Did receive a lot of criticism for this cover, and subsequently issued an apology after many women took the opportunity, particularly through social media, to defend women's bodies however they look.

[6] THE NHS Information Centre Infant Feeding Survey is conducted every five years and the 2010 survey records that 81 per cent of babies are breastfed at birth in the UK, but that by three months the numbers of babies being exclusively breastfed drops to 17 per cent and falls to 12 per cent by four months old. The percentages of women doing any breastfeeding has risen in recent years and, at six weeks was 55 per cent and at six months was 34 per cent. Breastfeeding is also more common in certain groups, among mothers who were 'aged 30 or over, from minority ethnic groups, left education aged over 18, in managerial and professional occupations and living in the least deprived areas' (UNICEF, 2012, np).

[7] The poem is available at www.youtube.com/watch?v=KiS8q_fifa0

[8] We also feel that it is important to note the large numbers of women who are reclaiming public breastfeeding. Whether through 'lactivist' or other

consciously politicised actions or through more personal stands public breastfeeding is, increasingly, being fought for by ordinary women who know they have the support of the law.

[9] In British Social Attitude Surveys between 1984 and 2008 people were asked to what level they agreed with the statement 'A man's job is to earn money; a woman's job is to look after the home and family'. In 1984 43 per cent respondents agreed or strongly agreed with this statement but by 2008, this had fallen to 16 per cent (EHRC, 2011).

[10] Women spend an average of just over 3.5 hours per day on unpaid domestic and childcare tasks in addition to regular paid work, almost twice as much time as the average man spends on similar tasks (Gershuny et al, 2006).

[11] The Gender Pay Gap effectively means that women work for free across the EU for around two months of each year. The European Equal Pay Day, held each year, marks this event. The date changes according to the size of the gap and was held on 28 February in 2013.

Chapter Seven: Gendering women's labour: status, esteem and inequality in paid and unpaid work

[1] The 1997 general election doubled the number of women in parliament from 60 to 120 out 646 seats. The pace of change has slowed dramatically and in 2013 there were 147 female MPs from a total of 650 elected MPs.

Chapter Eight: Conclusions: the embodied infrastructure of women's spaces, gender awareness, and the capacity for change.

[1] Estimates of the true number of organisations are difficult to come by as not all organisations working with women are registered in the same way, or are properly formalised. The UK WRC suggests that there are an estimated 32,000 women's voluntary and community organisations in England and Wales (2006a).

[2] Women's Aid is a specialist service that works with, and on behalf of, women who have or who are experiencing domestic violence, they are a national charity with over 500 offices across the UK (www.womensaid.org.uk/). Well-Women Centres provide sexual health and family planning advice to women; they have female physicians only. The National Federation of Women's Institutes is the largest voluntary organisation for women in the UK with a total membership of approximately 210,000 women. The WI celebrates its centenary in 2015. In the Yorkshire and Humber region there

are over 430 individual Women's Institutes covering Humberside, North West, North East, South, West and East Yorkshire (www.womens-institute. co.uk/). Home-Start UK is a support organisation that carries out home visits to those families who are facing difficulties and may need additional assistance and support. They have over 310 offices across the UK and a sister organisation that works worldwide (www.home-start.org.uk/about_us/ what_we_do/support_services). Children's Centres provide community-based support for parents and children, including childcare provision, health clinics, courses and social activities to support new mothers and fathers and their children, targeted particularly at areas of relative deprivation. They are run with government funding through the Sure Start initiative, although they have been subject to severe financial cuts in recent years (www.education. gov.uk/childrenandyoungpeople/earlylearningandchildcare/a00191780/ core-purpose-of-sure-start-childrens-centres).

[3] South Yorkshire Women's Development Trust is an organisation run by women for women. It provides resources and funding for women's organisations across south Yorkshire. See www.sywdt.org/. Rotherham Women's Network was launched in March 2007 and aims to bring women across the community and social sectors together (see www.growproject.plus. com/project_rotherham_womens_network.htm).

[4] 'Hull Domestic Abuse Partnership Project' (Hull-DAP) was formed in 2005 as a multi-agency partnership to address domestic violence across the city. The Crime and Disorder Act (1998) places this obligation on a statutory footing, requiring some organisations to form partnerships to tackle crime and disorder, including domestic violence and abuse, and provides a legal power to share information. Hull Citysafe, the Crime and Disorder Reduction Partnership (CDRP), teamed up with key agencies in Hull as a multi-agency response to tackling domestic violence and abuse. The aims of the partnership are to 'reduce repeat victimisation by improving the safety of survivors and children in Hull through a coordinated and effective inter-agency response; holding abusers accountable from initial point of contact with police and throughout the criminal justice system; and working towards zero tolerance of domestic violence and abuse' (Hull-DAP, 2005, 3).

References

Ahmed, A, Smith, D, 2013, Somali woman wins appeal against sentence for claiming soldiers raped her, *Guardian* online, 3 March, www.guardian.co.uk/world/2013/mar/03/somali-woman-soldiers-raped?INTCMP=ILCNETTXT3487

Allen, J, 1996, *Sinuosities: Lesbian poetic politics*, Bloomington, IN: Indiana University Press

Alsop, R, Fitzsimons, A, Lennon, K, 2002, *Theorizing gender*, Cambridge: Polity Press

Andersen, M, 1993, *Thinking about women: Sociological perspectives on sex and gender*, New York: Macmillan

Anderson, K, Jack, DC, 1991, Learning to listen: Interview techniques and analysis, in SB Gluck, D Patai (eds) *Women's words: The feminist practice of oral history*, pp 11–26, New York: Routledge

Antai-Otong, D, 1997, Mental disorders, in KM Allen, JM Phillips (eds) *Women's health across the lifespan: A comprehensive perspective*, Philadelphia, PA: Lippincott-Raven Publishers

Appignanesi, L, 2008, *Mad, bad and sad: A history of women and the mind doctors from 1800 to the present*, London: Virago Press

Armstrong, J, 2006, Beyond 'juggling' and 'flexibility': Classed and gendered experiences of combining employment and motherhood, in *Sociological Research Online* 11, 2, www.socresonline.org.uk/11/2/armstrong.html

Arnot, M, 2007, Education feminism, gender equality and school reform in late twentieth century England, in R Teese, S Lamb, M Duru-Bellat, S Helme (eds) *International studies in educational inequality, theory and policy*, Netherlands: Springer

Arnot, M, David, M, Weiner, G, 1996, *Educational reforms and gender equality in schools*, England: Equal Opportunities Commission

Arnot, M, David, M, Weiner, G, 1999, *Closing the gender gap: Postwar education and social change*, Cambridge: Polity Press

Banyard, K, 2010, *The equality illusion: The truth about women and men today*, London: Faber and Faber

Barker, I, 2013, Teach girls to disrupt, subvert and challenge authority – don't always praise their attentiveness, *Times Educational Supplement*, 13 June, www.tes.co.uk/article.aspx?storycode=6338621

Barrett, M, McIntosh, M, 1990, The 'family wage': Some problems for socialists and feminists, in T Lovell (ed) *British feminist thought: A reader*, pp 134–50, Oxford: Blackwell

Bartkey, S, 1990, *Femininity and domination*, New York: Routledge

Basow, S, 2004, The hidden curriculum: Gender in the classroom, in M Paludi (ed) *The Praeger guide to the psychology of gender*, Westport: Praeger Publishers

Bassin, D, Honey, M, Kaplan, M, 1994, *Representations of motherhood*, Yale: Yale University Press

Basten, S, 2009, Voluntary childlessness and being childfree, *The future of human reproduction, Working Paper 5*, Oxford: University of Oxford, www.spi.ox.ac.uk/fileadmin/documents/PDF/Childlessness_-_Number_5.pdf

Batho, R, 2009, *The gender agenda final report*, Department for Children, Schools and Families, June, London: DfCSF

BBC News Online, 2002, *Housework 'worth' £700bn*, 24 April, http://news.bbc.co.uk/1/hi/uk/1948016.stm

BBC News Online, 2003, *Bad Maths Blights Public Holiday*, BBC News, 1 May, http://news.bbc.co.uk/1/hi/education/1967056.stm

BBC News Online, 2010, David Cameron launches Tories' 'big society' plan, BBC News, July 19, www.bbc.co.uk/news/uk-10680062

BBC News Online, 2013a, *Dubai rape case Norwegian woman 'free to go'*, 22 July, www.bbc.co.uk/news/world-middle-east-23404042

BBC News Online, 2013b, *Caroline Criado-Perez Twitter abuse leads to arrest*, BBC News, July 29, www.bbc.co.uk/news/uk-23485610

BBC Radio 4, 2013, *Woman's Hour*, programme aired 1 July, www.bbc.co.uk/programmes/b0367dzx

Beaman, R, Wheldall, K, Kemp, C, 2006, Differential teacher attention to boys and girls in the classroom, *Educational Review* 58, 3, 339–66

Bell, J, Stanley, N, 2005, *Tackling domestic violence at the local level: An evaluation of the Preston Road domestic violence project*, Hull: University of Hull

Bendelow, G, Carpenter, M, Vautier, C, Williams, S (eds), 2002, *Gender, health and healing: The public/private divide*, London: Routledge

Bender, D, Leone, B, 1989, *Human sexuality: 1989 Annual*, San Diego, CA: Greenhaven Press

Bennet, F, 2005, Gender and benefits, *Working Paper Series 30*, London: Equal Opportunities Commission

Bennet, S, 1996, Leading article, *Guardian*, 28 February

Bernheimer, C, Kahane, C (eds), 1985, *In Dora's case: Freud – hysteria – feminism*, London: Virago

Best, R, 1983, *We've all got scars: What boys and girls learn in elementary school*, Bloomington, IN: Indiana University Press

Bhavnani, R with Performance Through Inclusion, 2006, *Moving on up? Ethnic Minority women and work: Ahead of the game: The changing aspirations of young ethnic minority women*, London: Equal Opportunities Commission

Bianchi, S, Milkie, M, Sayer, L, Robinson, J, 2000, Is anyone doing the housework? Trends in the gender division of household labor, *Social Forces* 79, 1, 191–228

Billington, R, Hockey, J, Strawbridge, S, 1998, *Exploring self and society*, Basingstoke: Macmillan

Bittman, M, Wajcman, J, 2000, The rush hour: The character of leisure time and gender equity, *Social Forces* 79, 1, 165–89

Blackburn, R, 2009, Measuring occupational segregation and its dimensions of inequality and difference, *Cambridge Studies in Social Research* 12, Cambridge: SSRG Publications, www.sociology.cam. ac.uk/srg/workingpapers/CS12MeasuringSegregation.pdf

Blackburn, R, Jarman, J, 2006, Gendered occupations: Exploring the relationship between gender segregation and inequality, *International Sociology* 21, 2, 289–315

Blackburn, R, Browne, J, Brooks, B, Jarman, J, 2002, Explaining gender segregation, *British Journal of Sociology* 53, 4, 513–36

Blumberg, R, 2007, Gender bias in textbooks: A hidden obstacle on the road to gender equality in education, Background paper prepared for the *Education for All Global Monitoring Report 2008, Education for All by 2015: will we make it?*

Boulton, M, 1983, *On being a mother: A study of women with pre-school children*, London: Tavistock

Bourdieu, M, 2001, *Masculine domination*, Standford, CA: Stanford University Press

Bowcott, O, 2013, Rape conviction rate at an all-time high, in *Guardian*, 23 April, www.guardian.co.uk/society/2013/apr/23/rape-conviction-rate-high

Boyer, K, 2011, 'The way to break the taboo is to do the taboo thing': Breastfeeding in public and citizen-activism in the UK, *Health and Place* 17, 430–7

Bradley, H, 2013, *Gender* (2nd edn), Cambridge: Polity Press

Bradshaw, L, 2014, New lad or just like dad? Young masculinities and career choice in Hull, doctoral thesis, University of Hull

Brydon, S, 2009, Men at the heart of mothering: Finding mother in Finding Nemo, *Journal of Gender Studies* 18, 2, 131–46

Budig, M, Misra, J, Boeckmann, I, 2012, The motherhood penalty in cross-national perspective: The importance of work–family policies and cultural attitudes, *Social Politics* 19, 2, 163–93

Burke, J, 2013, Delhi gang rape: 17-year-old-accused to appear in juvenile court, *Guardian* online, 27 February, www.guardian.co.uk/world/2013/feb/27/delhi-gang-rape-accused-court

Busfield, J, 1989, Sexism and psychiatry, *Sociology* 23, 3, 343–64

Busfield, J, 1996, *Men, women and madness: Understanding gender and mental disorder*, Basingstoke: Macmillan

Busfield, J, 2002, The archaeology of psychiatric disorder: Gender and disorders of thought, emotion and behaviour, in G Bendelow, M Carpenter, C Vautier, S Williams (eds) *Gender, health and healing: The public/private divide*, London: Routledge

Butler, J, 1990, *Gender trouble: Feminism and the subversion of identity*, New York: Routledge

Cabinet Office, 2000, *Women's incomes over the lifetime*, London: Women's Unit, Cabinet Office

Caplan, PJ, 1995, *They say you're crazy: How the world's most powerful psychiatrists decide who's normal*, Reading, MA: Addison-Wesley

Carillo, R, 2000, Introduction: Planting the seeds of change, in C Spindel, E Levy, M Connor (eds) *With an end in sight: Strategies from the UNIFEM Trust Fund to Eliminate Violence Against Women*, New York: UNIFEM

Centre for Mental Health, 2010, *The economic and social costs of mental health problems in 2009/10*, London, www.centreformentalhealth.org.uk/pdfs/Economic_and_social_costs_2010.pdf

Centre for Women and Democracy, 2013, *Sex and power 2013: Who runs Britain?* http://fawcettsociety.org.uk/wp-content/uploads/2013/02/Sex-and-Power-2013-FINAL-REPORT.pdf

Charles, N, 2002, *Gender in modern Britain*, Oxford: Oxford University Press

Chesler, P, 1972, *Women and madness*, London: Allen Lane

Chrisler, J, Ferguson, S, 2006, Violence against women as a public health issue, *Annals of the New York Academy of Sciences* 1087, 1, 235–49

Clark, B, 1999, Introduction, in B Clark, M Higonnet (eds) *Girls boys books toys: Gender in children's literature*, Baltimore: John Hopkins University Press

Clark, B, Higonnet, M (eds), 1999, *Girls boys books toys: Gender in children's literature*, Baltimore: John Hopkins University Press

Clark, L, 2006, Boys are being failed by our schools, *Daily Mail*, 13 June, www.dailymail.co.uk/news/article-390319/Boys-failed-schools.html

Clisby, S, 2005, Mainstreaming or just more male-streaming? Experiences of popular participation in Bolivia, *Gender and Development* 13, 2, 23–35

Clisby, S, 2009, Summer sex: Youth, desire and the carnivalesque, in H Donnan, F Magowan (eds) *Trangressive sex: Subversion and control in erotic encounters*, Oxford: Berghan Books

Cohen, S, 1972, *Folk devils and moral panics*, London: Routledge

Collett, J, 2005, What kind of mother am I? Impression management and the social construction of motherhood, *Symbolic Interaction* 28, 3, 327–47

Connell, RW, 1987, *Gender and power*, Cambridge: Polity Press

Connell, RW, 1992, A very straight gay: Masculinity, homosexual experiences, and the dynamics of gender, *American Sociological Review* 57, 735–51

Connell, RW, 1995, *Masculinities*, Cambridge: Polity Press

Connell, RW, 2000, *The men and the boys*, Cambridge: Polity Press

Connell, RW, 2005, Change among the gatekeepers: Men, masculinities, and gender equality in the global arena, *Signs* 30, 1801–25

Connell, RW, 2009, *Gender in world perspective* (2nd edn), Cambridge: Polity Press

Connell, RW, Messerschmidt, J, 2005, Hegemonic masculinity: Rethinking the concept, *Gender and Society* 19, 829–59

Connolly, S, Gregory, M, 2008, Moving down: Women's part-time work and occupational change in Britain 1991–2001, *Economic Journal* 118, 52–76

Connelly, S, Gregory, M, 2009, The part-time pay penalty: Earnings trajectories of British women, *Oxford Economic Papers* 61, 76–97

Cornwell, J, 1984, *Hard earned lives: Accounts of health and illness from East London*, London: Tavistock

Correll, S, Bernard, S, Paik, I, 2007, Getting a job: Is there a motherhood penalty?, *American Journal of Sociology* 112, 5, 1297–339

Coward, R, 1992, The heaven and hell of mothering: Mothering and ambivalence in the mass media, in W Hollway, B Featherstone (eds) *Mothering and ambivalence*, Oxford: Taylor and Francis Psychology Press

Crittenden, A, 2001, *The price of motherhood: Why the most important job in the world is still the least valued*, New York: Metropolitan Books

Croghan, R, Miell, D, 2000, Naming abuse and constructing identities, in J Ussher (ed) *Women's health: Contemporary international perspectives*, Leicester: The British Psychological Society

Crompton, R, Brockmann, M, Lyonette, C, 2005, Attitudes, women's employment and the domestic division of labour: A cross-national analysis in two waves, *Work, Employment and Society* 19, 2, 213–33

Cross, E, Richardson, B, Douglas, T, Vonkaenel-Flatt, J, 2009, *Virtual violence: Protecting children from cyberbullying*, London: Beatbullying http://archive.beatbullying.org/pdfs/Virtual%20Violence%20-%20 Protecting%20Children%20from%20Cyberbullying.pdf

Dale, A, Jackson, N, Hill, N, 2005, Women in non traditional training and employment, *EOC Occupational Segregation Working Paper 26*, England: Equal Opportunities Commission

Davar, S (ed) 2001, *Mental health from a gender perspective*, London: SAGE

DCSF (Department for Children, Schools and Families), 2009, *Gender and education: Mythbusters. Addressing gender and achievement: myths and realities*, http://webarchive.nationalarchives.gov. uk/20130401151715/https://www.education.gov.uk/publications/ eOrderingDownload/00599-2009BKT-EN.pdf

de Beauvoir, S, 1949, *The second sex*, London: Vintage Classics, 1997

Dean, C, 1998, Failing boys: Public burden number one, *Times Educational Supplement*, 28 November, www.tes.co.uk/article. aspx?storycode=80917

Delamont, S, 1980, *Sex roles and the school*, London: Routledge, Abingdon: Routledge Library Editions, 2012

Dench, S, Aston, J, Evans, C, Meager, N, Williams, M, Willison, R, 2002, *Key indicators of women's position in Britain: Key findings*, London: London Institute for Employment Studies on Behalf of the Women and Equality Unit

DeVault, M, 1999, *Liberating method: Feminism and social research*, Philadelphia: Temple University Press

Dex, S, 2003, *Work and family in the twenty-first century*, York: Joseph Rowntree Foundation

Dex, S, Ward, K, 2007, Parental care and employment in early childhood: Analysis of the Millenium Cohort Study (MCS, Sweeps 1 and 2), *Working Paper Series 57*, London: Equal Opportunities Commission

DfE (Department for Education), 2012a, *Phonics screening check and national curriculum assessments at key stage 1 in England: 2012*, www. gov.uk/government/publications/phonics-screening-check-and-national-curriculum-assessments-at-key-stage-1-in-england-2012

DfE (Department for Education), 2012b, *National and local authority tables SFR03/2012*. www.gov.uk/government/publications/gcse-and-equivalent-attainment-by-pupil-characteristics-in-england-2010-to-2011

DfE (Department for Education), 2013, *GCSE and equivalent attainment by pupil characteristics in England, 2011/12, Statistical first release*, London: DfE, www.gov.uk/government/uploads/system/uploads/ attachment_data/file/219337/sfr04-2013.pdf

DfES (Department for Education and Skills), 2007, *Gender and education: The evidence on pupils in England*, http://boyseducation.blogspot. co.uk/2007/07/gender-and-education-evidence-on-pupils.html

DfID (Department for International Development), 2012, A theory of change for tackling violence against women and girls, *Violence against women and girls, CHASE Guidance notes series*, DfID practice paper, June, www.gov.uk/government/uploads/system/uploads/ attachment_data/file/67336/how-to-note-vawg-1.pdf

DH (Department of Health), 2004, Women's mental health strategy, *Policy and Guidance Series 32039* http://webarchive.nationalarchives.gov. uk/+/www.dh.gov.uk/en/Healthcare/Mentalhealth/DH_4002408

DH (Department of Health), 2010, *Health profile 2009: Yorkshire and the Humber*, www.healthprofiles.info

Dhani, A, Kaiza, P, 2011, *Police service strength: England and Wales*, 31 March, London: Home Office Statistical Bulletin

Diaz-Granados, N, Stewart, DE, 2007, Using a gender lens to monitor mental health, *International Journal of Public Health* 52, 197–8

Dobash, R, Dobash, R, 1992, *Women, violence and social control*, London: Routledge

Donaldson, M, 1993, What is hegemonic masculinity?, *Theory and Society* 22, 643–57

Douglas, S, Michaels, M, 2004, *The mommy myth: The idealization of motherhood and how it has undermined women*, New York: Simon and Schuster

Doyal, L, Elston, M, 1986, Women, health and medicine, in V Beechey, E Whitelegg (eds) *Women in Britain today*, Milton Keynes: Open University Press

Drexler, P, 2013, Women need more than confidence to succeed, they need ambition, *Forbes Woman*, 15 July, www.forbes.com/sites/ peggydrexler/2013/07/15/women-need-more-than-confidence-to- succeed-they-need-ambition/

Duncan, S, 2003, Mothers, care and employment: Values and theories, *CAVA Working Paper 1*, Leeds: CAVA (Care, Values and the Future of Welfare), University of Leeds, http://www.leeds.ac.uk/cava/research/ strand3a.htm

Duncan, S, Edwards, R, Reynolds, T, Alldred, P, 2003, Motherhood, paid work and partnering: Values and theories, *Work Employment Society* 17, 309–30

DWP (Department for Work and Pensions), 2011, *Publication of research report No. 777: Maternity and paternity rights and women returners survey 2009*/10, www.gov.uk/government/news/publication-of-research-report-no-777-maternity-and-paternity-rights-and-women-returners-survey-2009-10

Dykstra, P, Hagestad, G, 2007, Childlessness and parenthood in two centuries: Different roads different maps?, *Journal of Family Issues* 28, 1518–32

Earle, S, 2002, Factors affecting the initiation of breastfeeding: Implications for breastfeeding promotion, *Health Promotion International* 17, 3, 205–14

Edwards, R, Ribbens, J, 1998, Living on the edges: Public knowledge, private lives, personal experience, in J Ribbens, R Edwards (eds) *Feminist dilemmas in qualitative research: Public knowledge and private lives*, London: SAGE

EHRC (Equality and Human Rights Commission), 2011, *How fair is Britain? Equality, human rights and good relations in 2010: The first triennial review*, EHRC, www.equalityhumanrights.com/key-projects/how-fair-is-britain/

Ehrenreich, B, English, D, 1979, *For her own good: 150 years of the experts' advice to women*, London: Pluto Press

Elliott, C, Leck, J, Orser, B, Mossop, C, 2006, An exploration of gender and trust in mentoring relationships, *Journal of Diversity Management* 1, 1, 1–11

Elson, D, Pearson, R, 1981, 'Nimble fingers make cheap workers': An analysis of women's earnings in third world export manufacturing, *Feminist Review* 7, 87–109

Enloe, C, 1990, Womenandchildren: Making feminist sense of the Persian Gulf crisis, in *The Village Voice*, 25 September, 29–32, cited in A Phillips, 1998, *Feminism and politics*, Oxford: Oxford University Press

EOC (Equal Opportunities Commission), 2001, *Women and men in Britain. Sex stereotyping: From school to work*, London: EOC

EOC (Equal Opportunities Commission), 2005a, *Britain's hidden brain drain. Final report: The EOC's investigation into flexible and part-time working*, London: EOC

EOC (Equal Opportunities Commission), 2005b, *Response to women and Work Commission 'Closing the gender income gap'*, London: EOC

EOC (Equal Opportunities Commission), 2006, *Sex and power: Who runs Britain? 2006*, London: EOC

EOC (Equal Opportunities Commission), 2007a, *The gender agenda: The unfinished revolution*, London: EOC, http://webarchive.nationalarchives. gov.uk/20080108005727/http://equalityhumanrights.com/ Documents/Gender/General%20advice%20and%20information/ EOC%20Gender%20agenda.pdf

EOC (Equal Opportunities Commission), 2007b, *The gender equality duty and schools: Guidance for public authorities in England*, London: EOC

EOC (Equal Opportunities Commission), 2007c, *Labourers of love? The cost of undervaluing women's work*, London: EOC

Epstein, D, Elwood, J, Hey, V, Maw, J (eds), 1998a, *Failing boys? Issues in gender and achievement*, Buckingham: Open University Press

Epstein, D, Elwood, J, Hey, V, Maw, J, 1998b, Schoolboy frictions: Feminism and 'failing' boys, in D Epstein, J Elwood, V Hey, J Maw (eds) *Failing boys? Issues in gender and achievement*, Buckingham: Open University Press

European Commission, 2010, Report on equality between women and men 2010, http://ec.europa.eu/social/BlobServlet?docId=4613 and langId=en

Eurostat, 2012, *Fertility statistics*, http://epp.eurostat.ec.europa.eu/ statistics_explained/index.php/Fertility_statistics

Eurostat, 2013, *Persons employed part time* http://epp.eurostat.ec.europa. eu/tgm/refreshTableAction.do;jsessionid=9ea7d07e30e8b39c8ab00 a53497ab594fd2ae8ab4280.e34OaN8Pc3mMc40Lc3aMaNyTb38N e0?tab=table and plugin=1 and pcode=tps00159 and language=en

Everyday Sexism Project, 2013, *Homepage*, www.everydaysexism.com/

Fagan, C, Burchell, B, 2002, *Gender jobs and working conditions in the European Union*, Dublin: European Foundation for the Improvement of Living and Working Conditions

Fanslow, J, Robinson, E, 2004, Violence against women in New Zealand: Prevalence and health consequences, *Journal of the New Zealand Medical Association* 117, 1206, https://researchspace.auckland.ac.nz/bitstream/ handle/2292/4673/15570342.pdf?sequence=1

Farmer, P, 2004, An anthropology of structural violence, *Current Anthropology* 45, 3, 305–25

Fawcett, 2007, *Women and politics*, London: Fawcett

Fawcett, 2010, *Equal pay: Where next? Report from the 2010 equal pay conference*, London: Fawcett, www.equalityhumanrights.com/ uploaded_files/equalpay/equal_pay_report_-_final_1_.pdf

Fawcett, 2012, *If we're not at the table, we're not on the menu: Facts and stats on women and power*, London: Fawcett Society

Fawcett, 2013a, *The changing labour market: Delivering for women, delivering for growth*, London: Fawcett, http://fawcettsociety.org.uk/wp-content/uploads/2013/04/Fawcett-The-changing-labour-market.pdf

Fawcett, 2013b, *Cutting women out*, London: Fawcett, http://www.fawcettsociety.org.uk/cutting-women-out/

Fawcett, 2013c, *Red tape, red line: Five reasons why government should not 'drop its duty' to tackle women's inequality*, London: Fawcett, www.fawcettsociety.org.uk/wp-content/uploads/2013/07/Red-Tape-Red-Lines-five-reasons-why-government-should-not-drop-its-duty-to-tackle-womens-inequality.pdf

Fawcett, 2013d, *Pay gap widens as women's standing in the economy further undermined*, www.fawcettsociety.org.uk/gap-in-pay-between-women-and-men-widens-after-years-of-slow-steady-progress/

Fine, C, 2010, *Delusions of gender: The real science behind sex differences*, London: Icon Books

Foster, M, 1985, A curriculum for all? The relationship between racism, feminism and schooling: A personal view, in G Weiner (ed) *Just a bunch of girls*, Milton Keynes: Open University Press

Foucault, M, 1979, *Discipline and punish*, New York: Vintage Books

Francis, B, 2002, *Boys, girls and achievement: Addressing the classroom issues*, London: Routledge

Francis, B, 2006, Heroes or zeroes? The discursive positioning of 'underachieving boys' in English neo-liberal education policy, *Journal of Education Policy* 21, 2, 187–200

Francis, B, Osgood, J, Dalgety, J, Archer, L, 2005, Gender equality in work experience placements for young people, *EOC Occupational Segregations Working Paper Series 27*, London: Equal Opportunities Commission

Franken, M, Woodward, A, Cabó, A, Bagilhole, BM (eds), 2009, *Teaching intersectionality: Putting gender at the centre*, Utrecht: ATHENA.

Frick, K, 2002, *Women's issues then and now: A feminist overview of the past 2 centuries*, http://batstar.net/item/ulrichmi.htm

Fricker, M, 1994, Knowledge as construct: Theorizing the role of gender in knowledge, in K Lennon, M Whitford (eds) *Knowing the difference: Feminist perspectives in epistemology*, London: Routledge

Friedan, B, 1963, *The feminine mystique*, London: Penguin Classics ([1963] 2010)

Friedman, M, 2009, For whom is breast best? Thoughts on breastfeeding, feminism and ambivalence, *Journal of the Association for Research on Mothering* 11, 1, 26–35

Fuller, A, Beck, V, Unwin, L, 2005a, The gendered nature of apprenticeships: Employers and young people's perspectives, *Education and Training* 47, 4–5, 293–311

Fuller, A, Beck, V, Unwin, L, 2005b, Employers young people and gender segregation, England, *Working Paper Series 28*, London: Equal Opportunities Commission

Gatens, M, 1996, *Imaginary bodies: Ethics, power and corporeality*, Abingdon: Routledge

Gentile, K, 2011, What about the baby? The new cult of domesticity and media images of pregnancy, *Studies in Gender and Sexuality* 12, 38–58

Gershuny, J, Lader, D, Short, J, 2006, *The time use survey, 2005: How we spend our time*, Norwich: Office for National Statistics

Gillborn, D, 1990, Sexism and curricular 'choice', *Cambridge Journal of Education* 20, 2, 161–74

Gillespie, R, 1999, Voluntary childlessness in the United Kingdom, *Reproductive Health Matters* 7, 13, 43–53

Glover, D, Kaplan, C, 2000, *Genders*, London: Routledge

Gobbi, PE, 2011, A model of voluntary childlessness, *Discussion Paper 2011-1*, Belgium: Institut de Recherches Économiques et Sociales de l'Université catholique de Louvain, http://sites.uclouvain.be/econ/DP/IRES/2011001.pdf

Goffman, E, 1963, *Stigma: Notes on the management of spoiled identity*, New York: Simon and Shuster

Gooden, A, Gooden, M, 2001, Gender representation in notable children's picture books: 1995–1999, *Sex Roles* 45, 1/2, 89–103

Gordon, T, 1996, Citizenship, difference and marginality in schools, in P Murphy, C Gipps (eds) *Equity in the classroom: Towards effective pedagogy for girls and boys*, London: Falmer Press

Gottlieb, C, 2010, Reflections on judging mothering, *Baltimore Law Review* 39, 371–88, http://fixcas.com/news/2010/Gottlieb.pdf

Goudsmit, E, 1994, All in her mind! Stereotypic views and the psychologisation of women's illness, in S Wilkinson, C Kitzinger (eds) *Women and health: Feminist perspectives*, pp 7–12, London: Taylor and Francis

Gove, W, Tudor, J, 1973, Adult sex roles and mental illness, *American Journal of Sociology* 78, 812–35

Gow, R, Lydecker, J, Lamanna, J, Mazzeo, S, 2012, Representations of celebrities' weight and shape during pregnancy and postpartum: A content analysis of three entertainment magazine websites, *Body Image* 9, 172–5

Graham, H, 1984, *Women, health and the family*, Brighton: Wheatsheaf

Graham, S, Thrift, N, 2007, Out of order: Understanding repair and maintenance, *Theory, Culture and Society* 23, 1, 1–25

Gregg, P, 1998, The impact of unemployment and job loss and future earnings, Persistent poverty and lifetime inequality: The evidence. *CASE report 5*, Centre for Analysis of Social Exclusion, London: London School of Economics, and *Occasional Paper 10*, London: HM Treasury

Grimshaw, D, Rubery, J, 2007, Undervaluing women's work, *Working Paper Series 53*, England: Equal Opportunities Commission

GuideStar UK, 2013, http://ewww.guidestar.org.uk/Default.aspx

Haddad, T (ed) 1993, *Men and masculinities: A critical anthology*, Toronto: Canadian Scholars Press

Haddon, L, Livingstone, S, EU Kids Online Network, 2012, *EU kids online: National perspectives*, www.lse.ac.uk/media@lse/research/EUKidsOnline/EU%20Kids%20III/Reports/PerspectivesReport.pdf

Hakim, C, 1995, Five feminist myths about women's employment, *British Journal of Sociology* 46, 3, 429–55

Hallam, S, Creech, A, 2007, *A review of the literature relating to the parental aspirations of teenage mothers*, CfBT Education Trust, Institute of Education, London: University of London

Hammersley, M, 1995, *The politics of social research*, London: SAGE

Hansen, K, Joshi, H, Verropoulou, G, 2006, Childcare and mothers' employment: approaching the millennium, *National Institute Economic Review* 195, 84–102

Haraway, D, 1988, Situated knowledges: The science question in feminism and the privilege of partial perspective, in *Feminist Studies* 14, 3, 575–99

Harkness, S, Waldfogel, J, 1999, The family gap in pay: Evidence from seven industrialised countries, *CASE Paper 29*, Centre for Analysis of Social Exclusion, London: London School of Economics, http://sticerd.lse.ac.uk/dps/case/cp/CASEpaper30.pdf

Harkness, S, Machin, S, Waldfogel, J, 1997, Evaluating the pin money hypothesis: The relationship between women's labour market activity, family income and poverty in Britain, *Journal of Population Economics* 10, 137–58

Harrison, M, 2012, *Women under-represented in politics*, http://uk.kantar.com/public-opinion/politics/women-in-politics-poll-october-2012/

Hartman, M, 2004, *The household and the making of history: A subversive view of the western past*, Cambridge: Cambridge University Press

Hawkesworth, M, 1989, Knowers, knowing, known: Feminist theory and claims of truth, *Signs* 14, 3, 533–57

Headlam-Wells, J, 2004, E-mentoring for aspiring women managers, *Women in Management Review* 19, 4, 212–18

Headlam-Wells, J, Craig, J, Gosland, J, 2006, *Women's career progression: Barriers and solutions. The EMPATHY-EDGE E-mentoring project*, Hull: University of Hull Business School

Hearn, J, McKie, L, 2008, Gendered policy and policy on gender: The case of 'domestic violence', *Policy and Politics* 36, 1, 75–91

Heinämaa, S, 2003, *Toward a phenomenology of sexual difference: Husserl, Merleau-Ponty, Beauvoir*, Oxford: Rowman and Littlefield

Herbert, J, Stipek, D, 2005, The emergence of gender differences in children's perceptions of their academic competence, *Journal of Applied Developmental Psychology* 26, 276–95

HESA (Higher Education Statistics Agency), 2012, *Higher education student enrolments and qualifications obtained at higher education institutions in the United Kingdom for the academic year 2010/11*, www.hesa.ac.uk/index.php?option=com_content&task=view&id=2355&Itemid=161

HESA (Higher Education Statistics Agency), 2013, *Students and qualifiers at UK HE institutions*, www.hesa.ac.uk/content/view/1897/239/

Hester, M, Kelly, L, Radford, J, 1996, *Women, violence and male power: Feminist activism, research and practice*, Bristol: Open University Press

Higher Education Policy Institute, 2009, *Male and female participation and progression in higher education*, www.hepi.ac.uk/466-1409/Male-and-female-participation-and-progression-in-Higher-Education.html

Hill, A, 2009, Generation of boys 'being failed' by the school system, *Observer*, 3 May, www.theguardian.com/education/2009/may/03/boys-under-achievement-school-education

Hills, J, Brewer. M, Jenkins, S, Lister, R, Lupton, R, Machin, S, Mills, C, Modood, T, Rees, T and Riddell, S, 2010, *National Equality Panel, An Anatomy of Economic Inequality in the UK*, January 2010, © Crown copyright 2010

Hird, M, 2003, Vacant wombs: Feminist challenges to psychoanalytic theories of childless women, *Feminist Review* 75, 5–19

Hoare, J, 2007, Editorial, *Gender and Development* 15, 1, 1–10

Hochschild, A, 1983, *The managed heart: Commercialization of human feeling*, Berkeley, CA: University of California Press

Hochschild, A, 1990, *The second shift*, London: Piatkus

Hockey, J, 1993, Women and health, in D Richardson, V Robinson (eds) *Introducing women's studies*, London: Macmillan

Holdsworth, J, 2006, Qualitative Project Evaluation – Case Study Interviews, in J Headlam-Wells, J Craig, J Gosland (eds) *Women's career progression: Barriers and solutions. The EMPATHY-EDGE E-mentoring project*, Hull: University of Hull Business School

Holly, L, 1985, Ten year old girls talking, in G Weiner (ed) *Just a bunch of girls*, Milton Keynes: Open University Press

Holmshaw, J, Hillier, S, 2000, Gender and culture: A sociological perspective to mental health problems in women, in D Kohen (ed) *Women and Mental Health*, London: Routledge, 39–64

Home Office, 2012, Equality Act 2010, www.homeoffice.gov.uk/equalities/equality-act/

Home Office, 2013, *Ending violence against women and girls in the UK*, www.gov.uk/government/policies/ending-violence-against-women-and-girls-in-the-uk

Hopper, P, 2012, *Understanding development*, Cambridge: Polity Press

Houseknecht, S, 1982, Voluntary childlessness: Toward a theoretical integration, *Journal of Family Issues* 3, 459–71

Hull-DAP (Hull-Domestic Abuse Partnership), 2005, *Information sharing protocol*, Hull: internal document

Human Rights Watch, 2006, *Definitions of sexual violence, rape and sexual slavery*, http://hrw.org/reports/2003/sierraleone/sierleon0103-01.htm

Human Rights Watch, 2011, *'We'll show you you're a woman': Violence and discrimination against black lesbians and transgender men in South Africa*, USA: Human Rights Watch

Hunt, S, 2000, The subjective health of older women: Measuring outcomes in relation to prevention, *Quality of Life Research* 9, 709–19

Huppatz, K, 2009, Reworking Bourdieu's 'capital': Feminine and female capitals in the field of paid caring work, *Sociology* 43, 1, 45–66

Huppatz, K, Goodwin, S, 2013, Masculinsed jobs, feminised jobs and men's 'gender capital' experiences: Understanding occupational segregation in Australia, *Journal of Sociology* 49, 2–3, 291–309

Hutchinson, J, Rolfe, H, Moore, N, Bysshe, S, Bentley, K, 2011, *All things being equal? Equality and diversity in careers education, information, advice and guidance*, Derby: University of Derby, London: National Institute of Economic and Social Research, Manchester: Equality and Human Rights Commission

Hyder, T, MacVeigh, J, 2007, Gender-based violence against children in emergencies: Save the Children UK's response, *Gender and Development* 15, 1, 81–94

Ibson, L, 2007, Women on drink and drugs: Using women's accounts of their drug misusing careers to inform policy and practice in the delivery of Specialist Substance Misuse Services, doctoral thesis, Hull: University of Hull

Irigaray, L, 1977, *The sex which is not one*, translated by Catherine Porter, Ithica: Cornell University Press

Jarman, J, Blackburn, R, Racko, G, 2012, The dimensions of occupational gender segregation in industrial countries, *Sociology* 46, 6, 1003–19

Johnson, M, 2013, Migration infrastructures, surveillance and practices of care and control: Filipino Muslims in the Kingdom of Saudi Arabia, paper presented at the *Anthropology of the Gulf Arab States II: Ethnography and the Study of Gulf Migration*, MESA Annual Meeting, New Orleans, 7–11 October

Johnson, P, Kossykh Y, 2008, *Early years, life chances and equality: A literature review*, Research Report 7, Manchester: Equality and Human Rights Commission, www.equalityhumanrights.com/uploaded_files/research/7_earlyyears_lifechances.pdf

Johnston, D, Swanson, D, 2004, Moms hating moms: The internalization of mother war rhetoric, *Sex Roles* 51, 9–10, 497–509

Joint Council for Qualifications, 2012, *Examination results: A levels*, www.jcq.org.uk/national_results/alevels/

Jones, C, 1985, Sexual tyranny: Male violence in a mixed secondary school, in G Weiner (ed) *Just a bunch of girls*, Milton Keynes: Open University Press

Jones, L, Jones, L, 1989, Context, confidence and the able girl, *Educational Research* 31, 3, 189–94

Jones, M, Kitetu, C, Sunderland, J, 1997, Discourse roles, gender and language textbook dialogues: Who learns what from John and Sally?, *Gender and Education* 9, 4, 469–90

Jong, E, 1998, *What do women want? Bread, roses, sex, power*, New York: HarperCollins

Jordison, S, Kieran, D, 2003, *The idler book of crap towns: The 50 worst places to live in the UK*, London: Boxtree

Joseph, A, 2001, The media and women's mental health, in B Davar (ed) *Mental health from a gender perspective*, pp 370–89, London: SAGE

Joshi, H, 2002, Production, reproduction and education: Women, children and work in a British perspective, *Population and Development Review* 28, 3, 445–74

Joshi, H, Paci, P, Waldfogel, J, 1999, The wages of motherhood: Better or worse?, *Cambridge Journal of Economics* 23, 543–64

Joshi, H, Hawkes, D, Ward, K, 2004, *Unequal entry to motherhood and unequal starts in life: Evidence from the first survey of the UK millennium cohort*, Cambridge, MA: Kennedy School of Government, Harvard University

Kanter, R, 1977, *Men and women of the corporation*, New York: Basic Books, 1993

Kay, I, 2009, *Portrait of Yorkshire and the Humber: Regional trends 41*, London: Office for National Statistics

Kelle, H, 2000, Gender and territoriality in games played by nine- to twelve-year-old schoolchildren, *Journal of Contemporary Ethnography* 29, 164–97

Kelly, A, 1988, Gender difference in teacher–pupil interactions: A meta analytic review, *Research in Education* 39, 1–24

Kelly, L, 1988, *Surviving sexual violence*, Cambridge: Polity Press

Kelly, M, 2009, Women's voluntary childlessness: A radical rejection of motherhood, *Women's Studies Quarterly* 37, 3–4, 157–72

Kimmel, MS, 1994, Masculinity as homophobia: Fear, shame and silence in the construction of gender identity, in H Brod, M Kaufmann (eds) *Theorizing masculinities*, Thousand Oaks, CA: SAGE

Kirkup, G, 2011, Preparing women for dead-end jobs? Vocational education and training (VET) for information and communication technology (ICT), jobs, *International Journal of Gender, Science and Technology* 3, 3, 460–82

Kohen, D (ed) 2000, *Women and mental health*, London: Routledge

Kortenhaus, C, Demarest, J, 1993, Gender role stereotyping in children's literature: An update, *Sex Roles* 28, 3–4, 219–32

Kram, KE, 1985, *Mentoring at work: Developmental relationships in organizational life*, Glenview, IL: Scott Foresman

Lawler, S, 2005, Disgusted subjects: The making of middle-class identities, *Sociological Review* 53, 3, 429–44

Lawler, S, 2008, *Identity: Sociological perspectives*, Cambridge: Polity Press

Leach, F, Humphreys, S, 2007, Gender violence in schools: Taking the 'girls-as-victims' discourse forward, *Gender and Development* 15, 1, 51–65

Lees, S, 2000, Sexual assault and domestic violence: Implications for health workers, in J Ussher (ed) *Women's health: Contemporary international perspectives*, pp 143–53, Leicester: The British Psychological Society

Lefanu, S, 1988, *In the chinks of the world machine: Feminism and science fiction*, London: The Women's Press

Leigh Star, S, 1999, The ethnography of infrastructure, *American Behavioural Scientist* 43, 3, 377–91

Lenhart, L, 2009, Teens and sexting: How and why minor teens are sending sexually suggestive nude or nearly nude images via text messaging, *Pew internet and American life project*, www.pewinternet.org/Reports/2009/Teens-and-Sexting.aspx

Lennon, K, Whitford, M (eds), 1994a, *Knowing the difference: Feminist perspectives in epistemology*, London: Routledge

Lennon, K, Whitford, M, 1994b, Introduction, in K Lennon, M Whitford (eds) *Knowing the difference: Feminist perspectives in epistemology*, pp 1–14, London, Routledge

Leonard, T, 2011, The baby who is neither boy nor girl: As gender experiment provokes outrage, what about the child's future?, *Daily Mail*, MailOnline, 28 May, www.dailymail.co.uk/news/article-1391772/Storm-Stocker-As-gender-experiment-provokes-outrage-poor-childs-future.html

Letherby, G, 1999, Other than mother and mothers as others: The experience of motherhood and non-motherhood in relation to 'infertility' and 'involuntary childlessness, *Women's Studies International Forum* 22, 3, 359–72

Letherby, G, 2002, Challenging dominant discourses: Identity and change and the experience of 'infertility' and 'involuntary childlessness', *Journal of Gender Studies* 11, 3, 277–88

Letherby, G, 2003, *Feminist research in theory and practice*, Buckingham: Open University Press

Levine-Clark, M, 2004, *Beyond the reproductive body: The politics of women's health and work in early Victorian England*, Colombus, OH: Ohio State University Press

Lewis, J, Campbell, M, 2007, UK work/family balance policies and gender equality 1997–2005, *Social Politics: International Studies in Gender, State and Society* 14, 1, 4–30

Lloyd, T (Boys Development Project), 2011, *Boys underachievement in schools*, Ulster: Centre for Young Men's Studies

Lobhan, G, 1975, Sex roles in reading schemes, *Educational review* 27, 3, 202–10

Loftus, J, Andriot, A, 2012, 'That's what makes a woman': Infertility and coping with a failed life transition, *Sociological Spectrum* 32, 3, 226–43

Longhi, S, Platt, L, 2008, Pay gaps across equalities areas, *Equality and Human Rights Commission, Research Report 9* www.equalityhumanrights.com/uploaded_files/pay_gaps_accross_equalities_areas.pdf

McCann, CR, Seung-Kyung, Kcohen (eds), 2013, *Feminist theory reader: Local and global perspectives* (3rd edn), London: Routledge

McCarty, P, 1986, Effects of feedback on the self-confidence of men and women, *The Academy of Management Journal* 29, 4, 840–47

McCauley, J, Kern, D, Kolodner, K. Derogatis, L, Bass, E, 1998, Relation of low-severity violence to women's health, *Journal of General Internal Medicine* 13, 10, 687–91

Maccoby, E, Jacklin, C, 1978, *The psychology of sex differences*, Stanford, CA: Stanford University Press

McDowell, L, Pringle, R (eds), 1992, *Defining women: Social institutions and gender divisions*, Cambridge: Polity Press

McGuire, G, 2002, Gender, race, and the shadow structure: A study of informal networks and inequality in a work, *Gender and Society* 16, 303 22

McKinnon, C, 1979, *The sexual harassment of working women*, New Haven, CT: Yale University Press

MacLeavy, J, 2011, A 'new politics' of austerity, workfare and gender? The UK coalition government's welfare reform proposals, *Cambridge Journal of Regions, Economy and Society*, doi:10.1093/cjres/rsr023, 1–13, http://cjres.oxfordjournals.org/content/early/2011/09/16/cjres.rsr023.full.pdf+html

McMahon, P, Goodwin, M, Stringer, G, 2000, Sexual violence and reproductive health, *Maternal and Child Health Journal* 4, 2, 121–3

McNish, H, 2013, *Embarrassed*, www.youtube.com/watch?v=KiS8q_fifa0

McVeigh, T, 2013, Amazon acts to halt sales of 'Keep Calm and Rape' T-shirts, *Observer* online, 2 March, www.guardian.co.uk/technology/2013/mar/02/amazon-withdraws-rape-slogan-shirt

Madden, A, 2000, Challenging inequalities in the classroom: The role and contribution of the Equal Opportunities commission, in K Myers (ed) *Whatever happened to the equal opportunities in schools? Gender equality initiatives in education*, pp 27–60, Buckingham: Open University Press

Malatesta, V, 2007, Introduction: The need to address older women's mental health issues, *Journal of Women and Ageing* 19, 1–2, 1–12

Marshall, C, Rossman, G, 1995, *Designing qualitative research* (2nd edn), London: SAGE

Martin, J, 1996, A girl's pedagogy 'in relationship', in P Murphy, C Gipps (eds) *Equity in the classroom: Towards effective pedagogy for girls and boys*, London: Falmer Press

Martin, P, 1987, *Mad women in romantic writing*, Brighton: Harvester

Martino, W, Meyenn, B (eds), 2001, *What about the boys? Issues of masculinity in schools*, Buckingham, PA: Open University Press.

Martinson, J, 2013, The everyday sexism project: A year of shouting back, *Guardian* online, www.theguardian.com/lifeandstyle/the-womens-blog-with-jane-martinson/2013/apr/16/everyday-sexism-project-shouting-back

Mathur, K, 2004, *Countering gender violence: Initiatives towards collective action in Rajasthan*, New Delhi: SAGE

Maynard, M, 1994, Methods, practice and epistemology: The debates about feminism and research, in M Maynard, J Purvis (eds) *Researching Women's Lives from a Feminist Perspective*, London: Taylor and Francis

Maynard, M, Winn, J, 1997, Women, Violence and Male Power' in V. Robinson and D Richardson (eds) *Introducing women's studies* (2nd edn), pp 175–97, Basingstoke: Palgrave

Melzer, H, Gatward, R, Goodman, R, Ford, T, 2001, *Mental health of children and adolescents in Great Britain*, London: The Stationery Office

Mental Health Foundation, 2007, *The fundamental facts: The latest facts and figures on mental health*, www.mentalhealth.org.uk/publications/fundamental-facts/

Meyers, DT, 2002, *Gender in the mirror: Cultural imagery and women's agency*, New York: Oxford University Press

Miles, R, 1989, *The women's history of the world*, London: Paladin

Miller, L. Neathey, F, Pollard, E, Hill, D, 2004, Occupational segregation, gender gaps and skill gaps, *EOC Occupational Segregation Working Paper Series 15*, London: Equal Opportunities Commission

Mitchell, J, 1971, *Women's estate*, London: Pelican

Moi, T, 1991, Appropriating Bourdieu: feminist theory and Pierre Bourdieu's sociology of culture, *New Literary History* 22, 1017–49

Moi, T, 1999, *What is a woman?: And other essays*, Oxford: Oxford University Press

Momsen, J, 2010, *Gender and development*, London: Routledge

Moore, J, Green, E, Heggie, JJF, Myers, M, Swainston, KA, 2005, *Widening horizons: Improving the role of women in the workplace*, Teesside: University of Teesside

Morgan, DHJ, 1996, *Family connections: An introduction to family studies*, Cambridge: Polity Press

Moser, C, 1993, *Gender planning and development: Theory, practice and training*, London: Routledge

Moussavi, S, Chatterji, C, Verdes, E, Tandon, A, Patel, V, Bedirhan U, 2007, Depression, chronic diseases, and decrements in health: Results from the World Health Surveys, *The Lancet* 370, 9590, 851–58

Mulvey, L, 1975, Visual pleasure and narrative cinema, *Screen* 16, 3, 6–18

Murphy, P, 1996, Defining pedagogy, in P Murphy, C Gipps, *Equity in the classroom: Towards effective pedagogy for girls and boys*, London: Falmer Press

Myers, F, McCollam, A, Woodhouse, A, 2005, *National programme for improving mental health and wellbeing: Addressing mental health inequalities in Scotland - equal minds*, Edinburgh: Scottish Development Centre for Mental Health, www.scotland.gov.uk/Publications/2005/11/04145113/51135

Nathanson, C, 1975, Illness and the feminine role: A theoretical review, *Social Science and Medicine* 9, 57–62

Nayak, A, Kehily, MJ, 2008, *Gender, youth and culture: Young masculinities and femininities*, Basingstoke: Palgrave Macmillan

New Statesman, 2013, Cutting benefits for teenage mothers is a policy based on prejudice alone, *New Statesman*, 15 July, www.newstatesman.com/politics/2013/07/cutting-benefits-teenage-mothers-policy-based-prejudice-alone

NHS Choices, nd, *Pregnancy and baby*, www.nhs.uk/conditions/pregnancy-and-baby/pages/why-breastfeed.aspx

Nicholason, S, Kershaw, C, Walker, A (eds), 2007, *Crime in England and Wales 2006–7* (4th edn), London: Home Office

Nicoletti, C, Tanturri, M, 2005, Differences in delaying motherhood across European countries: Empirical evidence from the ECHP, *Institute for Social and Economic Research, Working Papers 2005–4*, Colchester: University of Essex

Nicolson, P, 1997, Motherhood and women's lives, in D Richardson, V Robinson (eds) *Introducing women's studies* (2nd edn), pp 375–99, Basingstoke: Palgrave

O'Brien Hallstein, DL, 2011, She gives birth, she's wearing a bikini: Mobilizing the postpregnant celebrity mom body to manage the post-second wave crisis in femininity, *Women's Studies in Communication* 34, 2, 111–38

O'Donnell, A, 2008, Gendered choices: Young women's perspectives on non-traditional training and careers in Northumberland, *Education and Training* 50, 6, 474–88

O'Grady, H, 2005, *Women's relationship with herself: Gender, Foucault and therapy*, New York: Routledge

Oakley, A, 1974, *The sociology of housework*, New York: Pantheon

Oakley, A, 1979, *Becoming a mother*, Oxford: Martin Robertson

OECD (Organisation for Economic Co-operation and Development), 2010, *Gender brief: Prepared by the OECD Social Policy Division*, March, www.oecd.org/social/family/44720649.pdf

OECD (Organisation for Economic Co-operation and Development), 2011, *Family database: Mean age of mothers at first childbirth*, Social Policy Division, Directorate of Employment, Labour and Social Affairs 1, www.oecd.org/social/family/database

ONS (Office for National Statistics), 2003, *Jobs about the house*, London: ONS

ONS (Office for National Statistics), 2006, *Focus on gender; work and family, Labour force survey, Spring 2005*, London: ONS

ONS (Office for National Statistics), 2007, *Labour force survey, April–June 2007*, London: ONS

ONS (Office for National Statistics), 2009, *Portrait of Yorkshire and the Humber. Regional trends 41: 2009 edition*, London: ONS

ONS (Office for National Statistics) 2010, *United Kingdom Health statistics, edition 4*, www.ons.gov.uk/ons/rel/ukhs/united-kingdom-health-statistics/2010/index.html

ONS (Office for National Statistics), 2011a, *Statistical bulletin births and deaths in England and Wales, 2010*, Newport: ONS

ONS (Office for National Statistics), 2011b, *Social trends 41: Labour market*, London: ONS

ONS (Office for National Statistics), 2011c, *Birth summary tables: England and Wales, 2011 (Final)*, www.ons.gov.uk/ons/rel/vsob1/birth-summary-tables--england-and-wales/2011--final-/index.html

ONS (Office for National Statistics), 2011d, *Mental health*, http://www.poverty.org.uk/62/index.shtml?3

ONS (Office for National Statistics), 2012a, *Regional profiles – social indicators – Yorkshire and the Humber*, February, www.ons.gov.uk/ons/rel/regional-trends/region-and-country-profiles/social-indicators/social-indicators---yorkshire-and-the-humber.html

ONS (Office for National Statistics), 2012b, *Statistical bulletin: Conceptions in England and Wales, 2010*, ONS, www.ons.gov.uk/ons/rel/vsob1/conception-statistics--england-and-wales/2010/2010-conceptions-statistical-bulletin.html

ONS (Office for National Statistics), 2013a, *Patterns of pay: Results from the annual survey of hours and earnings, 1997 to 2012*, www.ons.gov.uk/ons/dcp171766_300035.pdf

ONS (Office for National Statistics), 2013b, *Labour market statistics*, January, www.ons.gov.uk/ons/dcp171778_292911.pdf

ONS (Office for National Statistics), 2013c, *Focus on: Violent crime and sexual offences, 2011/12*, www.ons.gov.uk/ons/dcp171778_298904.pdf

Orenstein, P, 1994, *School girls: Young women, self-esteem, and the confidence gap*, New York: Anchor Books

Ortner, S, 1974, Is female to male as nature to culture?, in MZ Rosaldo, L Lamphere (eds) *Women, culture and society*, Stanford, CA: Stanford University Press

Pajares, F, 2003, Self-efficacy beliefs, motivation, and achievement in writing: A review of the literature, *Reading and Writing Quarterly: Overcoming Learning Difficulties* 19, 2, 139–58

Palmer, G, North, J, Kenway, P, 2003, *Monitoring poverty and social exclusion, 2003*, York: Joseph Rowntree Foundation

Paludi, M (ed) 2004, *The Praeger guide to the psychology of gender*, Westport, CT: Praeger Publishers

Paludi, M, Martin, J, Stern, T, DeFour, D, 2010, Promises and pitfalls of mentoring women in business and academia, in C Rayburn, F Denmark, M Reuder, A Austria (eds) *A handbook for women mentors: Transcending barriers of stereotype, race and ethnicity*, Santa Barbara, CA: ABC-CLIO

Parker, R, 1997, The production and purposes of maternal ambivalence, in W Hollway, B Featherstone (eds) *Mothering and ambivalence*, London: Routledge

Paton, G, 2012, Girls outperforming boys in 'masculine' subjects, *Telegraph*, www.telegraph.co.uk/education/educationnews/9376466/Girls-outperforming-boys-in-masculine-subjects.html

Paton, G, 2013, GCSE results 2013: Girls stretch to record lead over boys, *Telegraph*, www.telegraph.co.uk/education/educationnews/10260163/GCSE-results-2013-girls-stretch-to-record-lead-over-boys.html

Patton, MQ, 1990, *Qualitative research and evaluation methods* (2nd edn), Newbury Park, CA: SAGE

Payne, J, 2009, Emotional labour and skill: A reappraisal, *Gender, Work and Organization* 16, 3, 348–67

Peacock, J, Holland, D, 1993, The narrated self: Life stories in process, *Ethos* 21, 4, 367–83

Peacock, L, 2012, Women spend half as much time on housework today compared to 1960s, *Telegraph*, 5 December, www.telegraph.co.uk/women/womens-life/9721147/Women-spend-half-as-much-time-on-housework-today-compared-to-1960s.html

Perfect, D, 2012, Gender pay gaps, *Briefing Paper 6*, England: Equality and Human Rights Commission

Perry, E, Francis, B, 2010, *The social class gap for educational achievement: A review of the literature*, RSA Project, www.thersa.org/__data/assets/pdf_file/0019/367003/RSA-Social-Justice-paper.pdf

Pilcher, J, 2000, Domestic divisions of labour in the twentieth century: Change slow a-coming, *Work Employment and Society* 14, 771–80

Pill, R, Stott, N, 1982, Concepts of illness causation and responsibility: Some preliminary data from a sample of working class mothers, *Social Science and Medicine* 60, 43–52

Potter, GA, 2000, *Deeper than debt: Economic globalisation and the poor*, London: Latin America Bureau

Prieto-Carrón, M, Thompson, M, Macdonald, M, 2007, More killings! Women respond to femicides in Central America, *Gender and Development* 15, 1, 25–40

Prior, P, 1999, *Gender and mental health*, Basingstoke: Macmillan

Prior, P, 2002, The archaeology of psychiatric disorder, in G Bendelow, M Carpenter, C Vautier, S Williams (eds) *Gender, health and healing: The public/private divide*, London: Routledge

Prosser, M, 2005, Introduction, *A fair deal for women in the workplace: An interim statement*, Women and Work Commission, www.researchonline. org.uk/sds/search/download.do;jsessionid=618F43AD885AE84CF CBD2AF41E5380D8?ref=Y6083

Proudman, CR, 2013, War rape: The forgotten pandemic sweeping Syria, *Independent* online, 21 January, www.independent.co.uk/ voices/comment/war-rape-the-forgotten-pandemic-sweeping-syria-8460566.html

Radford, J, Russell, D (eds), 1992, *Femicide: The politics of woman killing*, Buckingham: Open University Press

Ragins, B, Cotton, J, 1999, Mentor functions and outcomes: A comparison of men and women in formal and informal mentoring relationships, *Journal of Applied Psychology* 52, 4, 529–50

Ratcliffe, R, 2013, The gender gap at universities: Where are all the men?, *Guardian*, www.guardian.co.uk/education/datablog/2013/ jan/29/how-many-men-and-women-are-studying-at-my-university

Rees, T, 1992, *Women and the labour market*, London: Routledge

Reinharz, M, 1992, *Feminist methods in social research*, New York: Oxford University Press

Remarkable Television, 2013, *Snog marry avoid*, BBC 3, 2008–13, www. bbc.co.uk/programmes/b01sblmd

Richardson, D, 2008, Conceptualizing gender, in D Richardson, V Robinson (eds) *Introducing gender and women's studies* (3rd edn), pp 3–19, Basingstoke: Palgrave Macmillan

Richardson, D, Robinson, V (eds), 2008 *Introducing gender and women's studies* (3rd edn), Basingstoke: Palgrave Macmillan

Rights of Women, 2006, *Domestic violence injunction handbook* (2nd edn), London: Rights of Women

Ringrose, J, 2007, Successful girls? Complicating post-feminist, neoliberal discourses of educational achievement and gender equality, *Gender and Education* 19, 4, 471–89

Ringrose, J, Epstein, D, 2008, Gender and schooling: Contemporary issues in gender equality and educational achievement, in D Richardson, V Robinson (eds) *Introducing gender and women's studies* (3rd edn), Basingstoke: Palgrave Macmillan

Ringrose, J, Gill, R, Livingstone, S, and Harvey, L, 2012, A qualitative study of children, young people and 'sexting': A report prepared for the NSPCC, London: NSPCC

Riordan, S, 1999, *Women's organisations in the UK voluntary sector*, London: Centre for Institutional Studies, University of East London

Rodgers, D, O'Neill, B, 2012, Infrastructural violence: Introduction to the special issue, *Ethnography* 13, 4, 401–12

Rowbotham, S, 1973, *Woman's consciousness, man's world*, London: Penguin.

Russo, M, 1995, *The female grotesque: Risk, excess and modernity*, New York: Routledge

Sandberg, S, 2013, *Lean in: Women, work and the will to lead*, New York: Random House

Savaricus, N, 2013, Greece's neo-fascists are on the rise...and now they're going into schools: How Golden Dawn is nurturing the next generation, *Independent* online, 2 February, www.independent.co.uk/news/world/europe/greeces-neofascists-are-on-the-rise-and-now-theyre-going-into-schools-how-golden-dawn-is-nurturing-the-next-generation-8477997.html

Schober, P, 2007, Inequality or total workload? How domestic work matters to childbearing among British dual-earner couples, paper presented at the BHPS (British Household Panel Survey) Conference, Essex University

Scott, M, 2001, *Resourcing women: An E-forum/think tank on the resourcing needs of women's organisations*, London: The Women's National Commission

Seager, J, 2006, *The atlas of women in the world*, London: Earthscan

Shilling, C, 1993, *The body and social theory*, London: SAGE

Showalter, E, 1987, *The female malady: Women, madness and English culture 1830–1980*, London: Virago Press

Simone, AM, 2004, People as infrastructure: Intersecting fragments in Johannesburgh, *Public Culture* 16, 3, 407–29

Skeggs, B, 1997, *Formations of class and gender*, London: SAGE

Skeggs, B, 2004, Context and background: Pierre Bourdieu's analysis of class, gender and sexuality, *The Sociological Review* 52, 2, 19–33

Skelton, C, 1993, Women and education, in V Robinson, D Richardson (eds) *Introducing women's studies*, Basingstoke: Palgrave

Skelton, C, 1997, Women and education, in V Robinson, D Richardson (eds) *Introducing women's studies* (2nd edn), Basingstoke: Palgrave

Skelton, C, Francis, B (eds), 2003, *Boys and girls in the primary classroom*, Maidenhead: Open University Press

Skelton, C, Francis, B, Valkanova, Y, 2007, Breaking down the stereotypes: Gender and achievement in schools, *EOC Working Paper Series 59*, London: Equal Opportunities Commission

Sleeter, C, Grant, C, 2010, Race, class, gender and disability in current textbooks, in E Provenzo, A Shaver, M Bello (eds) *The textbook as discourse: Sociocultural dimensions of American schoolbooks*, London: Routledge

Smeaton, D, 2006, Work return rates after childbirth in the UK – Trends, determinants and implications. A comparison of cohorts born in 1958 and 1970, *Work, Employment and Society* 20, 1, 5–25

Smeaton, D, Hudson, M, Radu, D, Vowden, K, 2010, *The EHRC triennial review: Developing the employment evidence base*, Manchester: Equality and Human Rights Commission

Smith, A, 2006, Feminised curriculum 'has thrown boy out with bathwater', *Guardian* online, 13 June, www.theguardian.com/education/2006/jun/13/schools.uk3

Smith D, 1979, A sociology for women, in J Sherman, E Black (eds) *The prism of sex: Essays in the sociology of knowledge*, pp 135–87, Madison, WI: University of Wisconsin Press

Smith, K, Osborne, S, Lau, I, Britton, A, 2012, *Homicides, firearm offences and intimate violence: Supplementary volume 2 to crime in England and Wales 2012/11*, London: Home Office Statistical Bulletins, www.homeoffice.gov.uk/publications/science-research-statistics/research-statistics/crime-research/hosb0212/hosb0212?view=binary

Smyth, L, 2008, Gendered spaces and intimate citizenship: The case of breastfeeding, *European Journal of Women's Studies* 15, 83–99

Soni-Raleigh, V, 1996, Suicide patterns and trends in people of Indian sub-continent and Caribbean origin in England and Wales, *Ethnicity and Health* 1, 1, 55–63

Soteri, A, 2002, *Funding in London's women's organisations: A first report*, London: Centre for Institutional Studies, University of East London

Southall Black Sisters, 2011, *Safe and sane: A model of intervention on domestic violence and mental health, suicide and self-harm amongst black and minority ethnic women*, London: Southall Black Sisters

Sparr, P (ed) 1994, *Mortgaging women's lives: Feminist critiques of structural adjustment*, London: Zed Books

Standing, H, 2007, Gender, myth and fable: The perils of mainstreaming in sector bureaucracies, in A Cornwall, E Harrison, A Whitehead (eds) *Feminisms, contradictions, contestations and challenges in development*, London: Zed

Stanley, L (ed) 1990, *Feminist praxis: Research, theory and epistemology in feminist sociology*, London: Routledge

Stanley, L, Wise, S, 1990, Method, methodology and epistemology in feminist research processes, in L Stanley (ed) *Feminist praxis: Research, theory and epistemology in feminist sociology*, London: Routledge

Stanley, L, Wise, S, 1993, *Breaking out again*, London: Routledge

Stanworth, M, 1983, *Gender and schooling: A study of sexual divisions in the classroom*, London: Hutchinson, in association with the Explorations in Feminism Collective

Stanworth, M, 1997, Just three quiet girls, in C Ungerson, M Kember (eds) *Women and social policy*, Basingstoke: MacMillan Press

Stearns, CI, 1999, Breastfeeding and the good maternal body, *Gender and Society* 13, 308–25

Stein, J, 1997, *Empowerment and women's health*, London: Zed Books

Stern, V, 2010, *The Stern review*, London: Home Office, http://webarchive.nationalarchives.gov.uk/20110608160754/http://www.equalities.gov.uk/PDF/Stern_Review_acc_FINAL.pdf

Stewart, D, Robinson, GE, 1998, A review of domestic violence and women's mental health, *Archives of Women's Mental Health* 1, 83–9

Stewart-Knox, B, Gardiner, K, Wright, M, 2003, What is the problem with breast-feeding? A qualitative analysis of infant feeding perceptions, *Journal of Human Nutrition and Dietetics* 16, 4, 265–73

Sweetman, C, 2013, Introduction: Feminist solidarity and collective action, *Gender and Development* 21, 2, 217–29

Tang, T, Oatley, K, Toner, B, 2007, Impact of life events and difficulties on the mental health of Chinese immigrant women, *Journal of Immigrant and Minority Health* 9, 4, 281–90

Tavarni, C, Losh, S, 2003, Motivation, self confidence, and expectations as predictors of the academic performances among our high school students, *Child Study Journal* 33, 3, 141–51

Taylor, F, 2003, Content analysis and gender stereotypes in children's books, *Teaching Sociology* 31, 3, 300–11

Taylor, M, Quinn, B, 2013, Man held after banknote campaigner receives rape threats on Twitter, *Guardian*, 28 July, www.guardian.co.uk/uk-news/2013/jul/28/man-arrested-rape-threats-twitter

The Women's Room, 2013, *The women's room homepage*, http://thewomensroom.org.uk/index.php

Thompson, C, 1996, Caring consumers: Gendered consumption meanings and the juggling lifestyle, *Journal of Consumer Research* 22, 388–407

Thompson, J, 2013, Manslaughter charge over Dawn Warburton's death in Hull's Westbourne Avenue, *Hull Daily Mail*, www.hulldailymail.co.uk/Manslaughter-charge-Dawn-Warburton-s-death-Hull-s/story-20395778-detail/story.html

Tomasulo, G, McNamara, J, 2007, The relationship of abuse to women's health status and health habits, *Journal of Family Violence* 22, 4, 231–35

True, J, 2012, *The political economy of violence against women*, New York: Oxford University Press

TUC (Trade Unions Congress), 2010, The gender impact of the cuts: A TUC cuts briefing, November, www.tuc.org.uk/sites/default/files/extras/genderimpactofthecuts.pdf

Turner-Bowker, D, 1996, Gender stereotyped descriptors in children's picture books: Does 'Curious Jane' exist in the literature?, *Sex Roles* 35, 7–8, 461–88

Tyler, D, 2008, *Working Mothers: The Essential Guide*, Peterborough: Need2Know

Tyler, I, 2008, Chav mum chav scum, *Feminist Media Studies* 8, 1, 17–34

UCAS, 2011, *End of cycle report 2010/2011*, Cheltenham: UCAS, www.ucas.com/sites/default/files/end-of-cycle-report-2011.pdf

UCAS, 2012, *End of cycle report 2011/2012*, Cheltenham: UCAS www.ucas.com/sites/default/files/ucas-end-of-cycle-report-2012.pdf

UN (United Nations), 1995, *International conference on population and development: Summary of the programme of action*, United Nations Department of Public Information, www.unfpa.org/public/home/sitemap/icpd/International-Conference-on-Population-and-Development/ICPD-Summary

UN (United Nations), 1998, *Contemporary forms of slavery: Systematic rape, sexual slavery and slavery-like practices during armed conflict*, New York: United Nations

UN Women (2014) Facts and Figures on VAW, www.unifem.org/gender_issues/violence_against_women/facts_figures.html

UNICEF, 2012, *New infant feeding survey shows more UK babies are being breastfed for longer: Summary report*, www.unicef.org.uk/Documents/Baby_Friendly/Statements/IFS_Survey_Summary_211112.pdf

UNICEF Innocenti Research Centre, 2005, *1990–2005 celebrating the Innocenti Declaration on the Protection, Promotion and Support of Breastfeeding: Past achievements, present challenges and the way forward for infant and young child feeding*, UNICEF, www.unicef-irc.org/publications/pdf/celebrating_2nded.pdf

UNIFEM, 2003, *Not a minute more: Ending violence against women*, New York: UNIFEM

Ussher, J, 1991, *Women's madness: Misogyny or mental illness?*, Amherst, MA: University of Massachusetts Press

Ussher, J (ed) 1997, *Body talk: The material and discursive regulation of sexuality, madness and reproduction*, London: Routledge

Ussher, J, 1999, Feminist approaches to qualitative health research, in M Murray (ed) *Qualitative Health Psychology*, London: SAGE

Ussher, J, 2000a, Women's madness: A material-discursive-intrapsychic approach, in D Fee (ed) *Psychology and the postmodern: Mental illness as discourse and experience*, London: SAGE

Ussher, J, 2000b, Women and mental illness, in L Sherr, J St Lawrence (eds) *Women, health and the mind*, London: John Wiley

Ussher, J (ed) 2000c, *Women's health: Contemporary international perspectives*, Leicester: BPS Books

Ussher, J, 2011, *The madness of women: Myth and experience*, London: Routledge

Veevers, J, 1973, Voluntary childlessness: A neglected area of family study, *The Family Coordinator* 22, 2, 199–205

Veevers, J, 1980, *Childless by choice*, Toronto: Butterworths

Walby, S, 1986, *Patriarchy at work*, Cambridge: Polity Press

Walby, S, 1990, *Theorizing patriarchy*, Oxford: Blackwell

Walby, S, 1994, Is citizenship gendered?, *Sociology* 28, 2, 379–95

Walby, S, 1997, *Gender transformations*, London: Routledge

Walby, S, 2004, *The costs of domestic violence*, London: Women and Equality Unit

Walby, S, 2007, Gender (in)equality and the future of work, *Working Paper Series 55*, England: Equal Opportunities Commission

Walby, S, 2009, *Globalization and inequalities: Complexity and contested modernities*, London: SAGE

Walby, S, 2011, *The future of feminism*, London: Polity Press

Walby, S, Allen, J, 2004, *Domestic violence, sexual assault and stalking: Findings from the British Crime Survey*, Home Office Research Study 276, London: Home Office

Walkerdine, V, 1989, *Counting girls out*, London: Virago

Walter, N, 2010, *Living dolls: The return of sexism*, London: Hachette Digital

Warren, T, Rowlingson, K, Whyley, C, 2001, Female finances: Gender wage gaps and gender assets gaps, *Work, Employment and Society* 15, 3, 465–88

Weaver-Hightower, M, 2003, The 'boy turn' in research on gender and education, *Review of Educational Research* 73, 4, 471–98

Weiner, G, 1985, Introduction, in G Weiner (ed) *Just a bunch of girls*, Milton Keynes: Open University Press

Weiner, G, 1986, Feminist education and equal opportunities: Unity or discord?, *British Journal of Sociology of Education* 7, 3, 265–74

Wenchao, J, Muriel, A, Sibieta, L, 2010, *Subject and course choices at ages 14 and 16 amongst young people in England: Insights from behavioural economics*, Institute for Fiscal Studies: Department for Education Research Report DFE-RR160, www.gov.uk/government/uploads/system/uploads/attachment_data/file/182677/DFE-RR160.pdf

WHA (World Health Assembly), 2007, *Integrating gender analysis and actions into the work of WHO: Draft strategy*, Agenda item 12.12, Sixtieth World Health Assembly, Eleventh Plenary Meeting, WHA60.25/A60/VR/11, 23 May, http://apps.who.int/gb/ebwha/pdf_files/WHA60/A60_R25-en.pdf

Wharton, A, 2005, *The sociology of gender: An introduction to theory and research*, Oxford: Blackwell

Whitbeck, C, 1989, A different reality: Feminist ontology, in A Garry, M Pearsall (eds) *Women, knowledge, and reality: Explorations in feminist philosophy*, London: Unwin Hyman

Whitehead, S, 2002, *Men and masculinities*, Cambridge: Polity Press

Whitehead, S, Barrett, F (eds), 2001, *The masculinities reader*, Cambridge: Polity Press

WHO (World Health Organisation), 2002, *Gender and mental health*, www.who.int/gender/other_health/en/genderMH.pdf?ua=1

WHO (World Health Organisation), 2012, *Gender and women's mental health*, www.who.int/mental_health/prevention/genderwomen/en/

Wilkinson, S, Kitzinger, C (eds), 1994, *Women and health: Feminist perspectives*, London: Taylor and Francis

Wilks-Heeg, S, Blick, A, and Crone, S, 2012, *How democratic is the UK? The 2012 audit*, Liverpool: Democratic audit?, http://democracy-uk-2012.democraticauditarchive.com/how-democratic-is-the-uk-the-2012-audit

Wittig, M, 1981, One is not born a woman, in C McCann, K Seung-Kyung (eds), 2013, *Feminist theory reader: Local and global perspectives* (3rd edn), pp 246–51, London: Routledge

Wolf, N, 2002, *The beauty myth: How images of beauty are used against women* (2nd edn), New York: Perennial

Women and Equality Unit, 2004, *Equality, opportunity and choice: Tackling occupational segregation*, London: Department of Trade and Industry

Women and Work Commission, 2005, *A fair deal for women in the workplace*, Women and Work Commission, www.researchonline.org.uk/sds/search/download.do;jsessionid=618F43AD885AE84CFCBD2AF41E5380D8?ref=Y6083

Women and Work Commission, 2006, *Shaping a fairer future*, London: Women and Equality Unit, Department for Trade and Industry

Women and Work Commission, 2007, *The gender pay gap*, London: Women and Equality Unit, Department for Trade and Industry

Women in Mind, 1986, *Finding our own solutions*, London: Mind

Women's Aid, 2013, *Statistics about domestic violence*, www.womensaid. org.uk/domestic_violence_topic.asp?section=0001000100220041 and sectionTitle=Domestic+violence+%28general%29

Working Mother Research Institute, 2011, *What moms choose: The working mother report*, www.workingmother.com/research-institute/ what-moms-choose-working-mother-report

World Bank, 2004, *Mental health and the global development agenda: What role for the World Bank? Proceedings of a November 2003 seminar on an overview of World Bank interventions in mental health*, http://siteresources.worldbank.org/INTPH/ Resources/376086-1256847692707/6526326-1287681563483/ RachelMentalHealth.pdf

WRC (Women's Resource Centre), 2004, *Shadow report to CEDAW in response to the United Kingdom Government's 5th periodic report*, London: Women's Resource Centre

WRC (Women's Resource Centre), 2006a, *Why women? The women's voluntary and community sector: Changing lives, changing communities, changing society*, London: Women's Resource Centre

WRC (Women's Resource Centre), 2006b, *Response to HM Treasury's third sector review (Comprehensive Spending Review and Report of the women's sector consultation event)*, 3 October, London: Women's Resource Centre

WRC (Women's Resource Centre), 2007, *Why women? The value and benefits of by women, for women services*, London: Women's Resource Centre

WRC (Women's Resource Centre), 2011, *Hidden value: Demonstrating the extraordinary impact of women's voluntary and community organisations*, London: The Women's Resource Centre

WRC (Women's Resource Centre), 2013a, *Women-only services*, London: Women's Resource Centre, http://thewomensresourcecentre.org.uk/ resources/defending-women-only-services-2/

WRC (Women's Resource Centre), 2013b, *The source: The Women's Resource Centre newsletter*, London: WRC, Spring.

Yeandle, S, Bennet, C, Buckner, L, Escott, K, Grant, L, Price, C, Shipton, L, Stilee, B, Tang, N, 2006, *Gender and employment in local labour markets (2006)*, Sheffield: GELLM Project, Sheffield Hallam University.

YouGov Ltd, 2010, *End violence against women poll results*, www. endviolenceagainstwomen.org.uk/preventing-violence-against- women

Young, IM, 1990, *Throwing like a girl and other essays in feminist philosophy and social theory*, Bloomington, IN: Indiana University Press.

Youth Work Now, 2007, *Advice and guidance: Young women say career advice is biased*, September, www.ypnmagazine.co.uk/news/index. cfm?fuseaction

Ziegler, A, Heller, KA, 2000, Conditions for self-confidence among boys and girls achieving highly in chemistry, *Journal of Secondary Gifted Education* 11, 3, 144–51

Index

Printed in Great
Britain
by Amazon